HANDBOOK OF PUBLIC LIBRARY SYSTEM

HANDBOOK OF PUBLIC LIBRARY SYSTEM

By
Dr. Ajaykumar Raval *Ph.D.*
Librarian
B.K. Mercantile Bank Law College
Palanpur
(India)

DPH

DISCOVERY PUBLISHING HOUSE PVT. LTD.
NEW DELHI-110 002

Published by:
Tilak Wasan
DISCOVERY PUBLISHING HOUSE PVT. LTD.
4383/4B, Ansari Road, Darya Ganj
New Delhi-110 002 (India)
Phone : +91-11-23279245, 43596064-65
Fax : +91-11-23253475
E-mail : discoverypublishinghouse@gmail.com
sales@discoverypublishinggroup.com
parul.wasan@gmail.com
web : www.discoverypublishinggroup.com

First Edition: **2013**

ISBN: 978-93-5056-385-4

Handbook of Public Library System

Printed at:
Dynamic Printers
Delhi

Contents

Preface

A public library is a library that is accessible by the public and is generally funded from public sources and operated by civil servants. There are five fundamental characteristics shared by public libraries. The first is that they are supported by taxes; they are governed by a board to serve the public interest; they are open to all and every community member can access the collection; they are entirely voluntary in that no one is ever forced to use the services provided; and public libraries provide basic services without charge.

Public libraries exist in many countries across the world and are often considered an essential part of having an educated and literate population. Public libraries are distinct from research libraries, school libraries, and other special libraries in that their mandate is to serve the general public's information needs.

In India: It is clear then that the public library scenario is not uniform in India. It is difficult to collect authorized statistics on public libraries in the country, as they are under the responsibility of a variety of agencies who, for various reasons, never disclose such information on a national scale. This forces us to guess about the state of a vast number of public libraries, though it is not hard to imagine the difficulties they face in facilitating information and library support to the mass of over a billion population, spread over 32 lakh square kilometres, with a spectrum of literacy, intelligence, money, cultural and caste values. And just as States differ in size, population, literacy rate, status of books produced in the particular regional language, and economic growth, so does the public library system also differ from State- to-State. Also there are administrative problems such as the fact that rural libraries in some States form a part of the public library system and in some other States they came under the jurisdiction of the Adult Education Department or Public Relations Department. Wide-spread illiteracy is the greatest handicap for developing library services, both in certain urban and rural areas set in the traditional pattern.

Public Libraries also provide free services such as preschool story times to encourage early literacy, quiet study and work areas for students and professionals, or book clubs to encourage appreciation of literature in adults. Public libraries typically allow users to take books and other materials off the premises temporarily; they also have non-circulating reference collections and provide computer and Internet access to patrons.

—Author

1

Public Library: Origin and Growth

INTRODUCTION

A public library is a library that is accessible by the public and is generally funded from public sources and operated by civil servants. There are five fundamental characteristics shared by public libraries. The first is that they are supported by taxes; they are governed by a board to serve the public interest; they are open to all and every community member can access the collection; they are entirely voluntary in that no one is ever forced to use the services provided; and public libraries provide basic services without charge. Public libraries exist in many countries across the world and are often considered an essential part of having an educated and literate population.

Public libraries are distinct from research libraries, school libraries, and other special libraries in that their mandate is to serve the general public's information needs. Public libraries also provide free services such as preschool story times to encourage early literacy, quiet study and work areas for students and professionals, or book clubs to encourage appreciation of literature in adults. Public libraries typically allow users to take books and other materials off the premises temporarily; they also have non-circulating reference collections and provide computer and Internet access to patrons.

SERVICES OFFERED

In addition to print books and periodicals, most public libraries today have a wide array of other media including audiobooks, e-books, CDs, cassettes, videotapes, DVDs, and video games, as well as facilities to access the Internet and inter-library loans. Readers' advisory is a fundamental public library service that involves suggesting fiction and nonfiction titles. Public libraries may also provide other services, such as community meeting rooms, storytelling sessions for infants, toddlers, preschool children, or after-school programmes, all with an intention of developing early literacy skills and a love of books.

In person and on-line programmes for reader development, language learning, homework help, free lectures and cultural performances, and other community service programmes are common offerings. One of the most popular programmes offered in public libraries are summer reading programmes for children, families, and adults. In rural areas, the local public library may have, in addition to its main branch, a mobile library service, consisting of one or more buses furnished as a small public library, serving the countryside according to a regular schedule. Public libraries also provide materials for children, often housed in a special section. Child-oriented websites with on-line educational games and programmes specifically designed for younger library users are becoming increasingly popular. Services may be provided for other groups, such as large print or Braille materials, Books on tape, young adult literature and other materials for teenagers, or materials in other than the national language.

California and Nevada now offer a new service called Link+. This new programme links county libraries across the two states, allowing patrons access to books their library may not have in their collection. Librarians at most public libraries provide reference and research help to the general public, usually at a reference desk but can often be done by telephone interview. As online discussion and social networking allow for remote access, reference is becoming available virtually through the use of the Internet and e-mail. Depending on the size of the library, there may be more than one desk; at some smaller libraries all transactions may occur at one desk, while large urban public libraries may employ subject-specialist librarians with the ability to staff multiple reference or information desks to answer queries about particular topics at any time during regular operating hours.

Often the children's section in a public library has its own reference desk. Public libraries are also increasingly making use of web 2.0 services, including the use of online social networks by libraries. Public libraries in some countries pay authors when their books are borrowed from libraries. These are known as Public Lending Right programme.

DIGITAL DIVIDE

As more commercial and governmental services are being provided online, public libraries increasingly provide Internet access for users who otherwise would not be able to connect to these services. Part of the public library mission has become attempting to help bridge the digital divide. A study conducted in 2006 found that "72.5 per cent of library branches report that they are the only provider of free public computer and Internet access in their communities". A 2008 study found that "100 per cent of rural, high poverty outlets provide public Internet access, a significant increase from 85.7 per cent last year".

The American Library Association (ALA), addresses this role of libraries as part of "access to information" and "equity of access"; part of the profession's ethical commitment that "no one should be denied information because he or she cannot afford the cost of a book or periodical, have access to the internet or information in any of its various formats." In addition to access, many public libraries offer training and support to computer users. Once access has been achieved, there still remains a large gap in people's online abilities and skills. For many communities, the public library is the only agency offering free computer classes and information technology learning. As of 2008, 73.4 per cent of public libraries offered information technology training of some form, including information literacy skills and homework assignment help.

A significant service provided by public libraries is assisting people with e-government access and use of federal, state and local government information, forms and services. Internationally, public libraries offer information and communication technology (ICT) services, giving "access to information and knowledge" the "highest priority." While different countries and areas of the world have their own requirements, general services offered include free connection to the Internet, training in using the Internet, and relevant content in appropriate languages. In addition to typical public library financing, non-governmental organizations (NGOs) and business fund services that assist public libraries in combating the digital divide.

ORIGINS AS A SOCIAL INSTITUTION

The culmination of centuries of advances in the printing press, moveable type, paper, ink, publishing, and distribution, combined with an ever growing middle class, increased commercial activity and consumption, new radical ideas, massive population growth and higher literacy rates forged the public library into the form that it is today. Public libraries are not a new idea; Romans made scrolls in dry rooms available to patrons of the baths, and tried with some success to establish libraries within the empire. Naturally, only those few that could afford an education would be able to use the library, where those less than rich or without control of money; women, children and slaves could not.

In the middle of the 19th century, the push for truly public libraries, paid for by taxes and run by the state gained force after numerous depressions, droughts, wars and revolutions in Europe, felt mostly by the working class.

Matthew Battles states that:

"It was in these years of class conflict and economic terror that the public library movement swept through Britain, as the nation's progressive elite recognized that the light of cultural and intellectual energy was lacking in the lives of commoners."

Libraries had often been started with a donation, an endowment or were bequeathed to various, parishes, churches, schools or towns, and these social and institutional libraries formed the base of many academic and public library collections of today. Andrew Carnegie had the biggest influence in financing libraries in the United States of America, from the east to west coast. From just 1900 to 1917, almost 1,700 libraries were constructed by Carnegie's foundation, insisting that local communities first guarantee tax support of each library built.

The establishment of circulating libraries by booksellers and publishers provided a means of gaining profit and creating social centers within the community. The circulating libraries not only provided a place to sell books, but also a place to lend books for a price. These circulating libraries provided a variety of materials including the increasingly popular novels. Although the circulating libraries filled an important role in society, members of the middle and upper classes often looked down upon these libraries that regularly sold material from their collections and provided materials that were less sophisticated. Circulating libraries also charged a subscription fee, however the fees were set to entice their patrons, providing subscriptions on a yearly, quarterly or monthly basis, without expecting the subscribers to purchase a share in the circulating library. Circulating libraries were not exclusively lending institutions and often provided a place for other forms of commercial activity, which may or may not be related to print.

This was necessary because the circulating libraries did not generate enough funds through subscription fees collected from its borrowers. As a commerce venture, it was important to consider the contributing factors such as other goods or services available to the subscribers. Many claims have been made for the title of "first public library" for various libraries in various countries, with at least some of the confusion arising from differing interpretations of what should be considered a true "public library". Difficulties in establishing what policies were in effect at different times in the history of particular libraries also add to the confusion.

The first libraries open to the public were the collections of Greek and Latin scrolls which were available in the dry sections of the many buildings that made up the huge Roman baths of the Roman empire. However, they were not lending libraries. The "halls of science" run by different Islamic sects in many cities of North Africa and the Middle East in the 9th century were open to the public. Some of them had written lending policies, but they were very restrictive. Most patrons were expected to consult the books on site. The later European university libraries were not open to the general public, but accessible by scholars.

HISTORY

A public library is a library funded by public money, such as taxpayer money. The purpose of a public library is to provide books, Internet access and many other resources to the public for free. Even DVDs and movies are available for free rentals. Public libraries are not new, in fact the first organization that was considered to be a public library was created in the late 1500s.

* The first public library was created in England. At that time, the only people who were able to use libraries were individuals who joined a cathedral or were enrolled in college. This public library was called Francis Trigge Chained Library. This public library actually still exists and is famous for its long standing history of giving the people free access to all library resources. Although this library was the first, it stood nearly alone in its existence until the mid 1800s. That was the time period in which public libraries began to become popular.
* In England, Parliament decided to make a committee dedicated to considering the creation of multiple

public libraries. The committee was supposed to decide if a public library was something that would benefit the public. The committee reported back that public libraries would be beneficial, since so many people were poor. The recommendation was to open multiple public libraries throughout the country. This decision led to the Public Libraries Act of 1850. The act allowed all cities to collect taxes for public library support, providing that the population of the city had at least 10,000 people.

* This was quickly followed by the Public School Law, created in 1870. The point of this law was to raise the literacy rate of the public, since it was very low at the time. The only people who really knew how to read were rich people and scholars. Obviously, this literacy need increased the need for public libraries. By the 1870s, over 50 cities had created public libraries of their own. Only 30 years later, the number of public libraries hit 300. This was the time when public libraries began opening everywhere, and the United States began funding them as well. A public library was funded by public money, but it was also common for the people to help out these public libraries grow and flourish. Womens' clubs and the wealthy donated books to these public libraries to improve their selections.

Today, there are hundreds of thousands of public libraries in the world. The larger the city, the more public libraries will be found there. Unfortunately, despite the great need and desire for public libraries, funding for them are cut consistently by the state legislature. Large amounts of money to fund public libraries are made by private donors who have the wealth and desire to see a public library being used.

17th Century

In the early years of the 17th century, many famous collegiate and town libraries were founded throughout the country. Francis Trigge Chained Library of St. Wulfram's Church, Grantham, Lincolnshire was founded in 1598 by the rector of nearby Welbourne. Norwich City Library was established in 1608, and Chetham's Library in Manchester, which claims to be the oldest public library in the English-speaking world, opened in 1653.

Other early town libraries of the UK include those of:

* Ipswich (1612),
* Bristol (founded in 1613 and opened in 1615), and
* Leicester (1632).

Shrewsbury School also opened its library to townsfolk. In Bristol, an early library that allowed access to the public was that of the Kalendars or Kalendaries, a brotherhood of clergy and laity who were attached to the Church of All-Hallowen or All Saints. Records show that in 1464, provision was made for a library to be erected in the house of the Kalendars, and reference is made to a deed of that date by which it was "appointed that all who wish to enter for the sake of instruction shall have 'free access and recess' at certain times".

Early 18th Century

At the turn of the 18th century, libraries were becoming increasingly public and were more frequently lending libraries. The 18th century saw the switch from closed parochial libraries to lending libraries. Before this time, public libraries were parochial in nature and libraries frequently chained their books to desks. Libraries also were not uniformly open to the public. In 1790, The Public Library Act would not be passed for another sixty-seven years. Even though the British Museum existed at this time and contained over 50,000 books, the national library was not open to the public, or even to a majority of the population.

Access to the Museum depended on passes, of which there was sometimes a waiting period of three to four weeks. Moreover, the library was not open to browsing. Once a pass to the library had been issued, the reader was taken on a tour of the library. Many readers complained that the tour was much too short. At the turn of the century, there were virtually no public libraries in the sense in which we now understand the term *i.e.* libraries provided from public funds and freely accessible to all. Only one important library in Great Britain, namely Chetham's Library in Manchester, was fully and freely accessible to the public.

However, there had come into being a whole network of library provision on a private or institutional basis. Subscription libraries, both private and commercial, provided the middle and middle to upper class with a variety of books for moderate fees. The increase in secular literature at this time encouraged the spread of lending libraries, especially the commercial subscription libraries. Commercial subscription libraries began when booksellers began renting out extra copies of books in the mid-18th century. Steven Fischer estimates that in 1790, there were 'about six hundred rental and lending libraries, with a clientele of some fifty thousand.

The mid to late 18th century saw a virtual epidemic of feminine reading as novels became more and more popular. Novels, while frowned upon in society, were extremely popular. In England there were many who lamented at the 'villanous profane and obscene books' and the opposition to the circulating library, on moral grounds, persisted well into the 19th century. Still, many establishments must have circulated many times the number of novels as of any other genre. In 1797, Thomas Wilson wrote in The Use of Circulating Libraries: "Consider, that for a successful circulating library, the collection must contain 70% fiction". However, the overall percentage of novels mainly depended on the proprietor of the circulating library. While some circulating libraries were almost completely novels, others had less than 10% of their overall collection in the form of novels.

The national average at the turn of the century hovered around novels comprising about 20% of the total collection. Novels varied from other types of books in many ways. They were read primarily for enjoyment instead of for study. They did not provide academic knowledge or spiritual guidance; thus they were read quickly and far fewer times than other books. These were the perfect books for commercial subscription libraries to lend. Since books were read for pure enjoyment rather than for scholarly work, books needed to become both cheaper and smaller. Small duodecimo editions of books were preferred to the large folio editions. Folio editions were read at a desk, while the small duodecimo editions could be easily read like the paperbacks of today. Much like paperbacks of today, many of the novels in circulating libraries were unbound.

At this period of time, many people chose to bind their books in leather. Many circulating libraries skipped this process. Circulating libraries were not in the business of preserving books; their owners wanted to lend books as many times as they possibly could. Circulating libraries had ushered in a completely new way of reading. Reading was no longer simply an academic pursuit or an attempt to gain spiritual guidance. Reading became a social activity. Many circulating libraries were attached to the shops of milliners or drapers. They served as much for social gossip and the meeting of friends as coffee shops do today. Another factor in the growth of subscription libraries was the increasing cost of books.

In the last two decades of the century, especially, prices were practically doubled, so that a quarto work cost a guinea, an octavo 10 shillings or 12 shillings, and a duodecimo cost 4 shillings per volume. Price apart, moreover, books were difficult to procure outside London, since local booksellers could not afford to carry large stocks. Commercial libraries, since they were usually associated with booksellers, and also since they had a greater number of patrons, were able to accumulate greater numbers of books. The United Public Library was said to have a collection of some 52,000 volumes--twice as many as any private subscription library in the country at that period. These libraries, since they functioned as a business, also lent books to non-subscribers on a per-book system.

Private Subscription Libraries

Private subscription libraries functioned in much the same manner as commercial subscription libraries, though they varied in many important ways. One of the most popular versions of the private subscription library was a gentleman's only library. The gentlemen's subscription libraries, sometimes known as proprietary libraries, were nearly all organized on a common pattern. Membership was restricted to the proprietors or shareholders, and ranged from a dozen or two to between four and five hundred.

The entrance fee, *i.e.* the purchase price of a share, was in early days usually a guinea, but rose sharply as the century advanced, often reaching four or five guineas during the French wars; the annual subscription, during the same period, rose from about six shillings to ten shillings or more. The bookstock was, by modern standards, small and was accommodated, at the outset, in makeshift premises--very often over a bookshop, with the bookseller acting as librarian and receiving an honourarium for his pains. The Liverpool Subscription library was a gentlemen only library. In 1798, it was renamed the Athenaeum when it was rebuilt with a newsroom and coffeehouse.

It had an entrance fee of one guinea and annual subscription of five shillings. While no records survive of the commercial library lendings, we have the Bristol Library's continuous record of borrowings from 1773 to 1857. An analysis of the registers for the first twelve years provides some fascinating glimpses of middle-class reading habits in a mercantile community at this period. The largest and most popular sections of the library were History, Antiquities, and Geography, with 283 titles and 6,121 borrowings, and Belles Lettres, with 238 titles and 3,313 borrowings. Far below came Theology and Ecclesiastical History, Natural History and Chemistry, Philosophy, Jurisprudence, Miscellanies, Mathematics, etc., and Medicine and Anatomy, all with fewer than 100 titles.

The most popular single work was John Hawkesworth's Account of Voyages in the Southern Hemisphere which was borrowed on 201 occasions. The records also show that in 1796, membership had risen by 1/3 to 198 subscribers and the titles increased five-fold to 4987. This mirrors the increase in reading interests. A patron list from the Bath Municipal Library shows that from 1793 to 1799, the library held a stable 30% of their patrons as female. It was also uncommon for these libraries to have buildings designated solely as the library building during the 1790s, though in the 19th century, many libraries would begin building elaborate permanent residences. Bristol, Birmingham, and Liverpool were the few libraries with their own building.

The accommodations varied from the shelf for a few dozen volumes in the country stationer's or draper's shop, to the expansion to a back room, to the spacious elegant areas of Hookham's or those at the resorts like Scarborough, and four in a row at Margate. Private subscription libraries held a greater amount of control over both membership and the types of books in the library. There was almost a complete elimination of cheap fiction in the private societies. Subscription libraries prided themselves on respectability.

The highest percentage of subscribers were often landed proprietors, gentry, and old professions. Towards the end of the 18th century and in the first decades of the nineteenth the need for books and general education made itself felt among social classes created by the beginnings of the Industrial Revolution. The late 18th century saw a rise in subscription libraries intended for the use of tradesmen. In 1797, there was established at Kendal what was known as the Economical Library, "designed principally for the use and instruction of the working classes".

There was also the Artizans' library established at Birmingham in 1799. The entrance fee was 3 shillings. The subscription was 1 shilling 6 pence per quarter. This was a library of general literature. Novels, at first excluded, were afterwards admitted on condition that they did not account for more than one-tenth of the annual income.

Rate-supported Libraries

Although by the mid-19th century, England could claim 274 subscription libraries and Scotland, 266, the foundation of the modern public library system in the U.K. is the Public Libraries Act 1850. Prior to this, the municipalities of Warrington and Salford established libraries in their museums, under the terms of the Museums Act of 1845. Warrington Municipal Library opened in 1848. Salford Museum and Art Gallery first opened in November 1850 as "The Royal Museum and Public Library", as the first unconditionally free public library in England. The library in Campfield, Manchester was the first library to operate a free lending library without subscription in 1852.

Norwich lays claims to being the first municipality to adopt the Public Libraries Act 1850 but theirs was the eleventh library to open, in 1857, being the eleventh in the country after:

* Winchester,
* Manchester,
* Liverpool,
* Bolton,
* Kidderminster,
* Cambridge,
* Birkenhead and
* Sheffield.

The Scottish-American philanthropist and businessman, Andrew Carnegie, helped to increase the number of public libraries from the late 19th century. County libraries are a later development which were made possible by the establishment of County Councils in 1888. They normally have a large central library in a major town with smaller branch libraries in other towns and a mobile library service covering rural areas.

NORTH AMERICA

Canada

In 1779 Frederick Haldimand, the Governor of Québec City, founded the first subscription library in Canada. Until then, Canada's libraries were mostly religious institutions, and the general public was not admitted. However, even though "Haldimand's library, like other subscription libraries, appealed primarily to an urban elite", it was the nation's first step towards the public library as it is known today. Haldimand's library later merged with the Literary and Historical Society of Quebec, which displays the original

Québec Library collection within its library. This and similar association/social libraries were examples of early prototypes of public libraries.

They were public in that membership was allowed regardless of class or religion, and many in Canada eventually evolved into free public libraries. Subsequently legislative collections were established in 1791 in Upper and in 1792 in Lower Canada; and in 1796 the first public library was founded in Montreal. In 1800, libraries were established in King's College, Nova Scotia, and at Niagara, where the first public library in Upper Canada operated for twenty years, in spite of losses during the War of 1812. In Saint John, New Brunswick in 1883, following the efforts of Colonel James Domville in procuring a collection of materials to replace the many private collections lost in the Great Fire of Saint John, New Brunswick the first free, tax-supported public library was established. Guelph, Ontario and Toronto, Ontario opened public libraries that same year as well. Due to Canada's size and diversity, the development of the modern Canadian public library was more of a slow evolution than a quick transition as each of the provinces' specific conditions had first to be addressed.

The public library therefore took on many forms in Canada's earlier years; the three most prevalent of these forms were school-district libraries, Mechanics Institutes, and association/social libraries. In 1850, school-district libraries were initiated in Canada. Public servant Joseph Howe started one in Nova Scotia, and politician Egerton Ryerson started one in Ontario. New Brunswick and Prince Edward Island followed suit in 1858 and 1877, respectively. The hope was that both children and adults could benefit from the local school authorities, where financial assistance was provided from colonial legislatures, but the departments of education proved to be too centralizing for locals and this practiced was phased out. Mechanics Institutes also contained libraries that the working class could access inexpensively. The first Canadian library of its kind was established in 1828 in Montréal, Québec. Other communities took up this idea as well – notably those in Halifax, Nova Scotia, Hamilton, Ontario, Toronto, Ontario and Victoria, British Columbia. Like the school-district libraries, these institutes eventually ceased or were replaced by public libraries.

The public library that opened in Toronto, Ontario, was mostly due to a campaign by city alderman John Hallam. James Bain became the first chief librarian, and built a comprehensive collection of Canadian literature and history. The Toronto Public Library was one of the first libraries to choose free status, and it was the largest of them all. Its development flourished after 1900 when Carnegie grants began to aid in building construction and the expansion of collections and services. During this time, open access and children's departments were introduced, and standard cataloguing and classification systems were adopted. Many of the original branches, funded by a Carnegie grant, still stand and continue to be operated by the Toronto Public Library. Other provinces were affected by Carnegie as well and followed Ontario's lead in legislating tax support for library services. British Columbia acted in 1891, Manitoba in 1899, Saskatchewan in 1906, and in Alberta, the first legislation officially passed by the legislative assembly was the Library Act.

The act was passed March 15, 1907. The next provinces to follow were New Brunswick in 1929, Newfoundland in 1935, Prince Edward Island in 1936, Nova Scotia in 1937, Québec in1959, and then the Northwest Territories in 1966. As they stand today, public libraries in Canada are "governed by provincial statues and are primarily financed by municipal tax revenues and other local income, with provincial grants supplementing local funding. [They are also] the responsibility of a local or regional library board with authority to appoint or dismiss employees, control library property, establish policies, and budget for library operations."

Though the services offered vary from local branch to local branch, public libraries in Canada are not only places to read and borrow books; they are also hubs of community services, such as early reading programmes, computer access, and tutoring and literacy help for children and adults. Throughout the years, Canadian libraries have been subject to the political and economic influence of the nation. During World War II, public libraries experienced development setbacks, but expansion resumed in 1945. Then, in the 1960s, Canadian public libraries felt the benefits of the era's emphasis on education – service expanded, buildings were remodeled or constructed from scratch, and Centennial Grants were provided in order to improve the system.

This period of growth ended in due to the inflationary period in the 1970s and the two recessions during the 1980s. However, in the late 1990s this trend reversed and the National Core Library Statistics Programme reported in 1999 that public libraries served 28.5 million municipal residents – a total of 93% of the Canadian population. Nevertheless, in 2011 the tides turned for public libraries in Canada once again, specifically in Toronto. The city is now undergoing a heated debate regarding Mayor Rob Ford's proposed budget cuts for the Toronto Public Library, which is currently one of the most efficient public library systems in all of North America.

Mexico

In 1646, Don Juan de Palafox y Mendoza, bishop of Puebla and Viceroy of New Spain, expelled the Jesuits from New Spain, and with the confiscated books founded the Biblioteca Palafoxiana—the first public library in New Spain. It was in Puebla and open to all readers. The Biblioteca Palafoxiana exists today and is listed on the UNESCO Memory of the World Programme.

United States

As the United States developed from the 18th century to today, growing more populous and wealthier, factors such as a push for education and desire to share knowledge led to broad public support for free libraries. In addition, money donations by private philanthropists provided the seed capital to get many libraries started. In some instances, collectors donated vast book collections. William James Sidis in *The Tribes and the States* claimed the public library, as such, was an American invention. But exactly what constitutes a "free public library" is subject to dispute, and the term "invention" doesn't seem applicable to the many facets of an institution such as a library.

Throughout history, knowledge in different forms has been shared in different ways. Writing was recorded on papyrus and stored in scrolls and kept in vast libraries such as the Library of Alexandria in Egypt. In ancient Greece, knowledge was passed by one person reading aloud to a group of scribes from a text; this resulted in sometimes different and error-prone versions of the same text. Monks in the Middle Ages copied manuscripts by hand. After the invention of the printing press by Johann Gutenberg, books became prevalent, and different institutions such as universities and governments and churches found ways to keep and share them. There are disputes about which was the first public library in the nation. Early American cities such as Boston and Philadelphia and New York had the first organized collections of books, but which library was truly "public" is subject to dispute. Sidis claims the first public library was Boston's in 1636, although the official Boston Public Library was organized later in 1852.

In 1698, Charleston's St. Philip's Church Parsonage had a parish library. In 1731, Benjamin Franklin and his friends, sometimes called "the Junto", operated the Library Company of Philadelphia partly as a means to settle arguments and partly as a means to advance themselves through sharing information. Franklin's subscription library allowed members to buy "shares" and combined funds were used to buy more books; in return, members could borrow books and use the library. Today, the Library Company continues to exist as a nonprofit, independent research library.

A town in Massachusetts wanted to name itself Franklin in honour of the famous Pennsylvanian, and in return, Benjamin Franklin donated books for use by local residents; while Franklin had been asked to donate a church bell instead, he declined on the basis that "sense" was preferable to "sound". One source considers the Franklin library in Massachusetts to be the first public library in the United States. Another source claims the library in Darby, Pennsylvania which opened in 1743 is the "oldest continuously operating free public library" in the United States. But other libraries claim to be the first public library, including the Scoville library in Salisbury, Connecticut, which was established in 1803. The library in the New Hampshire town of Peterborough claims to be the first publicly-funded library; it opened in 1833. And a library in Massachusetts in the town of Arlington claims to have had the first free children's library; it opened in 1835.

Finances

In the trend from private to public libraries, big city libraries had the largest book collections and the most funding. The forerunner of the New York Public Library in Manhattan was a library established by the Earl of Ballamont around 1700. A newspaper described the call for the "first public librarian" demanding that "he must not be too young, for this would render him liable to be despised by the youth" and "he must be of an even temper" with "great diligence" and "sufficient learning" and "have a genius peculiarly adapted to the calling." In 1849, the library was officially established, and consolidated in 1901.

Today, it is considered to be one of the most important public libraries in the nation. New York governor and book lover Samuel J. Tilden bequeathed millions to build the New York Public Library. He believed Americans should have access to books and a free education if desired. In 2005, the library offered the "NYPL Digital Gallery" which made a collection of 275,000 images viewable over the web; while most of the contents are in the public domain, some images are still subject to copyright rules.

In 1902, one account suggested "the village library is growing more and more an indispensable adjunct to American village life." Around the turn from the 19th to the 20th century, Scottish-American businessman Andrew Carnegie donated over $60 million, which was a vast fortune in 20th century dollars, to build over 2,811 free public library buildings in the United States. They were often known as Carnegie libraries. Carnegie envisioned that libraries would "bring books and information to all people." Libraries have been started with wills from other benefactors; for example, the Bacon Free Library in South Natick, Massachusetts was founded in 1881 after a benefactor left $15,000 in a will; it has operated as a public library since then. Once the idea of the public library as an agency worthy of taxation was broadly established during the nineteenth and early twentieth centuries, librarians through actions of the American Library Association and its division devoted to public libraries, the Public Library Association, sought ways to identify standards and guidelines to ensure quality service.

In 2009, with the economic downturn, many public libraries have budget shortfalls. The library in Darby, Pennsylvania found expenses were greater than revenues from local property taxes, state funds, and investment income; it was on the risk of closing, according to a newspaper report. Many public libraries face budgetary problems; the report noted that "tax dollars that support them are dwindling as property tax revenue declines along with home values and sales taxes fall as consumers spend less. As local funding drops, libraries are turning to their endowments and draining the investments." Many libraries have foundations behind them to support them financially, and rely on the help of well-heeled donors as well as local corporations for funds.

Services

Most public libraries today are supported by tax monies from local and state governments, and some have foundations to support them with additional capital. Libraries lend books and materials freely, but charge fines if materials are returned late or damaged. Libraries often keep many historical documents relevant to their particular town, and serve as a resource for historians in some instances; for example, the Queens Public Library kept letters written by unrecognized Tiffany lamp designer Clara Driscoll, and the letters remained in the library until a curator discovered them. In 2009, big city libraries have multiple branches and offer numerous services. For example, the Boston Public Library has 26 neighbourhood branches and offers free Internet service; it has two restaurants and an online store which features reproductions of photographs and artwork; and it promotes itself with a website. It answers more than one million reference questions annually.

The library uses wireless technology software networks to offer more services and keep costs under control. The Boston library offers digitized content, video, a wider range of formats and, as a result, "research documents now have broader accessibility within the community and around the world," and help communities by offering public access computers, mobile Wi-fi access, and free job search tools. Libraries promote cultural awareness; in Newark, New Jersey, the public library celebrated black history with exhibits and programmes. Libraries also partner with schools and community organizations to promote literacy and learning. One account suggested libraries were essential to "economic competitiveness" as well as "neighbourhood vitality" and help some people find jobs. Some library buildings are notable for their particular architectural styles; in the town of Beaver Dam, Wisconsin, architects designed the Williams Free Library in the style of Richardsonian Romanesque.

EUROPE

France

The National Library of France is one of the oldest libraries in the world still in service today as it traces its origin to the royal library founded at the Louvre by King Charles V in 1368, but at the time it was conceived as the private library of the French kings and it opened to the public only in 1692, during the reign of Louis XIV. Claude Sallier, the philologist and churchman, had an idea that was advanced for its era—to make culture accessible to all. From 1737 to 1750 he made books available to the town of Saulieu, forming France's first public library. The pioneer of modern public libraries in France was Eugène Morel, a writer and one of the librarians at the Bibliothèque nationale. He put forward his ideas in the 1910 book La Librairie publique.

Italy

The Malatestiana Library also known as the Malatesta Novello Library, is a public library dating from 1452 in Cesena, Emilia-Romagna. It was the first European civic library, *i.e.* belonging to the Commune and open to everybody. It was commissioned by the Lord of Cesena, Malatesta Novello. The works were directed by Matteo Nuti of Fano and lasted from 1447 to 1452.

Poland

The Zaluski Library was built in Warsaw 1747– 1795 by Józef Andrzej Zaluski and his brother, Andrzej Stanis³aw Zaluski, both Roman Catholic bishops. The library was open to the public and indeed was the first Polish public library, the biggest in Poland and one of the earliest public libraries in Europe. In 1794, the library was looted on orders from Catherine II of Russia. Much of the material was returned in the period of 1842-1920, but once again the library was decimated during World War II during the period following the Warsaw Uprising. The Zaluski Library was succeeded by the creation of the National Library of Poland in 1928.

Australia

Library services in Australia developed along different paths in the different States. In 1809 the Reverend Samuel Marsden advertised in England for donations to help found a 'Lending Library for the general benefit of the inhabitants of New South Wales'. The library would cover 'Divinity and Morals, History, Voyages and Travels, Agriculture in all its branches, Mineralogy and Practical Mechanics'. No Public Library came to fruition from this although some of the books brought to the colony after this call survive in the library of Moore Theological College.

The place of Public Libraries was filled by Mechanics' Institutes, schools of arts, athenaeums and literary institutes. Some of these provided free library services to visitors. However lending rights were available only to members who were required to pay a subscription. In 1856, the Victorian colonial government opened the Melbourne Public Library. This was however purely a reference library. In September 1869, the New South Wales (NSW) government opened as the Free Public Library, Sydney by purchasing a bankrupt subscription library. In 1896, the Brisbane Public Library was established. The Library's collection, purchased by the Queensland Government from the private collection of Mr. Justice Harding. In 1932, the Carnegie Corporation of New York, funded a survey into Australian libraries. It found 'wretched little institutes' which were 'cemeteries of old and forgotten books'.

There was also criticism of the limited public access, poor staff training, unsatisfactory collections, lack of non-fiction, absence of catalogues and poor levels of service for children. Lending libraries in Sydney and Prahran were praised as examples of services which were doing well, but these were seen as exceptions. In NSW, The Free Library Movement was established in response to the Munn-Pitt Report. This collection of concerned citizens, progress associations, returned servicemen and trade unions advocated a system of public libraries to serve the needs of all people. The birth of the movement took place at a public meeting in the Chatswood-Willoughby School of Arts, Sydney, in 1935. George Brain, President of the Middle Harbour Progress Association, ran the meeting.

George Brain initiated the resolution which brought the Free Library Movement into existence in NSW as well as the election of provisional office bearers, including himself as Honourary Secretary. This movement was stalled by the onset of World War II in 1939. In 1943, the Queensland Parliament passed the Libraries Act, establishing the Library Board of Queensland to manage the operations of the Public Library of Queensland, and coordinate and improve library facilities throughout the State of Queensland. In November 1943, at the official opening of the new Public Library of New South Wales building, William McKell, the New South Wales Premier, announced that the Library Act would be fully proclaimed from 1 January 1944. After the war, and with George Brain now in NSW parliament as a principle advocate for the Free Library Movement, the passing of Library Acts in NSW and the other states at the end of the war marked the beginning of modern public libraries in Australia.

Even after the war, the development of free lending libraries in Australia had been agonizingly slow: it was not until the 1960s that local governments began to establish public libraries in suburban areas. Currently there are 1402 Australian public libraries plus 78 mobile libraries. Australians generate more than 110 million library visits per year. There are more than 9.9 million library members more than 41.5 million items to use and borrow, plus more than 11,600 computers for public use. It costs $882.3 million to run Australian public libraries. They return at least $2.6 billion-worth of community benefits. All this costs Australians $830 million - just over 10c a day each with a benchmark for best practice funding being 20c per day.

The 2007 Americans for Libraries Council (ALC) report on library valuation stated, 'A benefit-to-cost ratio of 3:1 or better is common among the library valuation studies ALC reviewed. Because this type of economic analysis is commonly used across industries and businesses, it puts libraries into an evaluative framework that permits comparisons with other types of organizations. When this occurs, public libraries consistently outpace other sectors, such as transportation, health, and education, on the efficient use of tax dollars'.

FUNDING PROBLEMS

Most public libraries rely heavily on local government funding. Some proactive librarians have devised alliances with patron and civic groups to supplement their financial situations. Library "friends" groups, activist boards, and well organized book sales supplement government funding. With the cost of running local government increasing at a rate far above inflation, libraries are compelled to look beyond the tax base of the communities they serve. In the United States, among other countries, libraries in financially strapped communities compete financially with other public institutions, such as police, firefighters, and schools.

Many communities are closing down or reducing the capability of their library systems, at the same time balancing their budgets. Jackson County, Oregon, closed its entire 15-branch public library system for six months in 2007, reopening with a private-public 'partnership' and a reduced schedule. This example of a funding problem followed the failure to pass of a bond measure and cessation of federal funding for counties with dwindling timber revenue, in a state with no sales tax. In December 2004, Salinas, California almost became the first city in the United States to completely close down its entire library system. A tax increase passed by the voters in November 2005 allowed the libraries to open, but hours remain limited.

The American Library Association says media reports it has compiled in 2004 showed some $162 million in funding cuts to libraries nationwide. Survey data suggests the public values free public libraries. A Public Agenda survey in 2006 reported 84 per cent of the public said maintaining free library services should be a top priority for their local library. Public libraries received higher ratings for effectiveness than other local services such as parks and police. But the survey also found the public was mostly unaware of financial difficulties facing their libraries. Recently, many US cities, including Philadelphia, New York, Trenton and San Diego, have been facing the issue of making job cuts and service reductions in order to save money.

Most of these cities have decided to cut library funding by closing down several branches and cutting hours and staff members in the branches that will remain open. Philadelphia, however, has decided to keep their 54 branches open. In order to save money during this financial crisis, Mayor Michael Nutter has proposed to cut funding for recreational parks and decrease the budget for police and fire services. Nutter has announced that the Philadelphia public library branches will not be affected by the budget cuts at this time. In various cost-benefit studies libraries continue to provide an exceptional return on the dollar. A 2008 survey discusses comprehensively the prospects for increased funding in the United States, saying in conclusion "There is sufficient, but latent, support for increased library funding among the voting population." Public libraries, long supported by various government entities, have seen a decline in monetary support for several decades, due to various influences.

The American Library Association states that 41% of states saw a decline in state budgets for public library funding in 2009 Cases in point are the libraries in Salinas, California, Rochester, New York, and Buffalo, New York, but there are many other long-standing public libraries now having to find new sources of income to keep them operating.

* In California, the passage of Proposition 13 in 1978 removed the property tax as a source of funding for libraries, school programmes, and other public services. This action provided tax relief for homeowners on one hand, but forced severe budget cuts to the services they enjoyed.
* The cost of creating, maintaining, and upgrading electronic hardware, networks, and resources has put a strain on many library budgets.
* The cost of printed matter such as books and magazines has risen over time, while funding has remained static or declined.

DEVELOPMENT OF PUBLIC LIBRARIES IN INDIA

Public libraries arose worldwide along with growth in education, literacy, and publications. Every country has its own public library history with influential leaders. Monarchs, wealthy people, and philanthropists have all made a contribution to society in the form of public library development. India is no exception. Libraries were established in ancient India mainly by the patronage extended by emperors, major capitalists, and scholars. Indian emperors and kings were supported scholars and scholarship. There is evidence of well-developed libraries even in the sixth century A.D. The famous Nalanda University in Bihar had its own magnificent library with a massive collection of manuscripts covering the universe of knowledge. Admission to library was restricted to scholars.

Other ancient universities, such as Taxila and Vikramashila, also had valuable libraries. Muslim influence in India during the 13th century A.D. marked the dawn of another era of learning and scholarship. The Mughal period gave a further stimulus to the growth of libraries. Mughal rulers attached considerable importance to libraries and appointed scholars as librarians. The Mughal emperors were patrons of art and literature. In the period of Emperor Babur, Humayun, and Akbar many new libraries were established and existing ones further developed. Mughal libraries featured magnificent buildings, rare manuscripts, and scholar librarians.

The names of Maharaja Sawai Man Singh of Jaipur and Maharaja Ranjit Singh of Punjab will be remembered with appreciation in the history of library services in India. The Maharaja of Tanjuar started the famous Saraswati Mahal Library in 17th century A.D. It remains a unique institution in its nature of collection and services Libraries established by the kings and capitalists functioned like private institutions and the admission was limited. Service to the general public had to wait for the British. Unfortunately, the arrival of the British and resulting political disorder also brought chaos to the Indian way of life.

This was a severe blow to the cultural heritage of India, which had arisen from the Indus valley civilization. When libraries began developing in India during the early nineteenth century, they were a western product. In 1808, the Government of Bombay proposed to register libraries, which were to be given copies of books published from the "funds for the encouragement of literature". The "Sinha Committee", this was the beginning of the first phase of public library development in India. During the first half of the 19th century, the three presidency towns of Bombay, Calcutta, and Madras had public libraries. These libraries were mostly financed by Europeans residing in these towns. Of these, the establishment of the public library at Calcutta in 1835 was the most significant. This was the library which later developed into the National Library of India. Almost simultaneous, subscription libraries were started in many Indian cities.

These were, of course, not public libraries in the true sense of the term, and did not provide free books for all. Founded in imitation of their western counterparts, the use of these libraries was confined to small, affluent portion of society. The first three decades of the 20th century can be looked on as the golden age of the Indian library system. On January 31, 1902, the Imperial Library Act was passed and Lord Curzon transformed the Calcutta Public Library into the Imperial Library in 1906. Developments in Baroda were also notable.

The development of public libraries in Baroda was unique. Baroda developed a network of public libraries to serve the entire Princely State. Maharaja Sayaji Rao Gaekwad III of Baroda who traveled all over the world was deeply impressed by the role played by public libraries in the promotion of education in the United States and thought of extending such benefits to his own subjects. In 1910 he invited an American expert, William Alson Borden to organize the public library system for his state. The public library movement that flourished in Baroda was a glorious one. But that was not a general trend of that period because in no other part of India, a parallel development occurred.

Yet another development during the period was the organisation of a host of conferences such as:

* The first conference of library workers and persons interested in the library movement was held at Beswada, Andhra in 1914.
* The first All India Library Conference of Librarians was held in 1918 at Lahore.
* The first All India Library Conference was held at Calcutta in 1933.
* The first All India Public Library Conference was held at Madras in 1934.

With the existence of democratic governments in several provinces beginning in 1937, another phase of the library movement began. Between 1937 and 1942, a number of village libraries and travelling libraries sprang up in Assam, Bihar, Punjab, and Travancore. It was estimated that there were about 13,000 village libraries in India in 1942. Another remarkable development was the appointment of the 'Library Development Committee' by the Government of Bombay, with A.A.A. Fyzee as its chairman. The Committee ambitiously recommended a comprehensive library system to be implemented in three successive stages. Because of financial constraints, the government could only implement part of the recommendations.

After Independence

After independence, the growth of libraries in general has been remarkable, although not as remarkable as that of academic and special libraries. At the time of independence, India was facing a host of challenges. Those in the rural population, 88 per cent of the total, were nearly all illiterate. Transportation was poor and mass media merely nominal. Nevertheless, the public library scene in India improved considerably during the post independence period, though it is still lacking on several fronts. Verma and Agrawal argue that to compare our public libraries with those of the developed nations on equal footing, we have to go a long way. The 1951 census, the first conducted after independence, found 2,843 local governments in the urban and rural areas in India, of which 320 were rural district boards.

Only about one third of local governments maintained public libraries, about 950. In addition, there were about 1,500 subscription libraries. So-called public libraries were primarily reading rooms with a few hundred books for reading on the premises. The Delhi public library deserves special mention. It was founded in 1951 as the first UNESCO Public Library Pilot Project under the joint auspices of UNESCO and Government of India.

The purpose of the library was to adapt "modern techniques to Indian conditions" and to serve as a model public library for Asia. The establishment of Delhi Public Library, the involvement of union government in the public library movement, and the enactment of public library legislation in some states are the main factors which contributed to the improvement of public libraries after independence. Although the government of India allotted funds for public library development in its five-year plans, this funding was not connected to effective planning.

Advisory Committee for Libraries

The Government of India appointed a committee in 1957 to report on the status of public library development in the country. It is also called the Sinha Committee, after its chair, the late Dr. A.P. Sinha, who was at that time Director of Public Instruction in Bihar.

The Sinha Committee's charge included:

* Determining present reading needs, how they are met, and what part existing library systems play in meeting the needs;
* Determining reading tastes, what agencies provide suitable literature, and how reading taste can be improved;
* Recommending future library structure in India;
* Recommending areas of cooperation between libraries and education systems;
* Considering the training of librarians and the conditions of their service;
* Recommending the administrative and financial measures necessary to support public libraries in India.

The committee submitted its report to Dr. K.L. Shrimali, who was Minister for Education, on the 12th of November, 1958. The Committee described the situation as dismal and called libraries in most cases, "a stagnant pool of books," because new books were not added regularly. The committee at the same time observed that wherever large collections did exist, they were not fully used because of rigid rules. Library users were not trusted and were required to deposit large sums of money as a kind of insurance, which lower income people could not afford.

As of March 1954 there were 32,000 libraries in India, with a little more than 7,100,000 books and a total circulation of about 37,700,000. The report observed that genuine public library service was rarity, and that public library service throughout the country was unsatisfactory. The committee recommended creating state library networks based on uniform library legislation.

The chief recommendations of the report were:

* Library service should be made free to every citizen of India;
* The hierarchy of public library service in the country should begin with National Library, and proceed to State Central Library, District Library, Block Library, and Panchayat Library;
* An independent Director of Social Education and Libraries should be set up in every state, with a fulltime senior class-1 officer of the rank of Deputy Director of Education to plan, organize, and administer library services;
* An All India Library Advisory Council should be constituted as a central agency to review and assess the work done at the state level;
* Library Associations should actively assist the development of libraries in the country;
* University libraries should cooperate with public library systems by allowing selected public readers to use their collection;
* State governments should accept responsibility for public library services in their states;
* Librarians and social education workers should cooperate to promote literacy;
* A library cess of six paisa for each rupee of property tax should be levied with the permission of local bodies.
* The Government of India should match the amount collected in the states. State governments should also give matching grants to local bodies over the succeeding 25 years, their contribution should be raised to three times the cess collected.

* State and national governments should enact comprehensive state library laws incorporating the right of every citizen to have free access to libraries. The Government of India should provide necessary financial assistance to the state governments for this purpose.

RAJA RAM MOHAN ROY LIBRARY FOUNDATION

Another positive step taken by the Central Government was the establishment of the Raja Ram Mohan Roy Library Foundation (RRRLF) at Calcutta on May 22, 1972, as a part of the bicentenary celebrations of the birth of Raja Ram Mohan Roy, a social reformer of the early 19th century. Its objectives are library development in general and rural library development in particular. It provides financial assistance to public libraries in the form of matching grants. It assists State Central Libraries and District Central Libraries, which has helped many states and Union Territories develop rural public library services.

Main Objectives of RRRLF

The main objectives of RRRLF are:

* Promotion of the library movement in India;
* The adoption of a national library policy by the central and state governments;
* Development of a National Library System by integrating the services of National Libraries, State Central Libraries, District Libraries, and other types of libraries through an interlibrary lending system;
* Propagation and adoption of library legislation in the country;
* Provision of financial and technical assistance to libraries;
* Provision of financial assistance to voluntary organizations and library associations for the promotion of library development;
* Periodic publication of reports on library development;

* To act as a clearing house for ideas and information on library development in India and abroad;
* To advise the Government of India library development;
* Promotion of research in problems of library development

The primary objective of RRRLF is the promotion of the library movement. The rest are subsidiary objectives. RRRLF is the first government-sponsored body specifically created for this purpose.

The foundation also has a programme of assistance to libraries for workshops, conferences, and exhibits. The foundation has taken the major initiative for the formulation of a national policy on library and information systems by the Government of India.

The current programmes of assistance are:

* Collection building;
* Rural libraries and mobile library service for rural areas;
* Seminars, workshops, conferences, training courses, and exhibits;
* Facilities and equipment for storage and display of materials;
* Public library buildings;
* Television and VCR equipment for educational purposes;
* Assistance to voluntary organisations providing public library services;
* Assistance to children's libraries or children's sections of general public libraries

During the last three decades, the foundation has assisted more than 500 libraries, including many in rural areas

NATIONAL POLICY ON LIBRARY AND INFORMATION SYSTEM (NAPLIS)

In 1985, a committee was set up under the chairmanship of Prof. D.P. Chattopadhyay to formulate a National Policy on Library and Information System (NAPLIS). The Committee submitted its report in May 1986. Following that, another committee looked at implications of the report and created an action plan for its implementation. The Empowerment Committee submitted its report in April 1988 and an Implementation Cell was formed to implement its recommendations within a period of six months. Yet another Working Group, under the Joint Secretary to the Government of India in the Department of Culture, was constituted to examine its recommendations for implementation. The Working Group submitted its report in July 1993 and suggested implementing only 29 of 60 recommendations made by the NAPLIS.

The following are some of the recommendations of NAPLIS related to public libraries:

* Proposals for maintenance and development of public libraries should preferably come from State Legislative Enactment. The Central Government may revise the Model Public Library Bill. Funds for library development should come from each state, either from general revenue or from local taxation. Central Government agencies may provide funds under Plan Expenditure.
* Efforts should emphasize rural public libraries. A village or a cluster of villages with an adequate population should have a community library/rural community centre, which will also serve as an information centre. Resources from various agencies engaged in the public health, adult education, State and central government, etc., should be used to build up and maintain this centre.
* The central government increase its assistance to state governments in the development of public libraries. The RRRLF, as the national agency for coordinating and assisting the development of public libraries, should be suitably strengthened in order to do this.
* Standards and guidelines for library service should be created.

* There should be a system of national libraries consisting of National Library, Calcutta as the National Library of India, National Depository libraries in Delhi, Bombay, Madras, National Subject Libraries, and others. These national libraries should form part of one integrated system.
* A National Commission on Libraries and Information System or National Commission on Informatics and Documentation may be constituted by an Act of Parliament to serve under the Ministry of Human Resource Development. The Commission will have representation from appropriate central and state agencies and could provide guidance and coordinate library development programmes in all sectors. This body will have the primary responsibility for the implementation of NAPLIS programmes.
* National Depository libraries; Connemara Public library, Chennai; Central Library, Bombay; and Delhi Public Library, Delhi should concentrate on development of collections and preservation of Indian culture produced in the languages of their regions, supplementing and complementing the efforts of the Indian National Library.
* The Indian National Bibliography should have a comprehensive coverage of the national output of documents and should be updated regularly. This responsibility should be vested in the National Library.
* Government should create a national awareness of the need to preserve the nation's cultural heritage. National libraries should be responsible, with preservation facilities created there. Links between libraries, archives, and museums should be established for the purpose of national preservation.
* The Ministry of Rural Development has a plan for one community centre in every Panchayat Centre.

The Department of Culture and the Ministry of Rural Development have agreed to provide library services at each of these Rural Community Centres.

* An important link should be established between community centre library and primary schools. If the schools do not have libraries of their own, the community centre library should provide children with adequate services.
* A community centre library should have an important role in adult education programmes.
* A district library should provide facilities and recreation for the disabled and low-income people, *e.g.*, literature in Braille.
* Libraries should be built in areas of tribal concentration and in minority communities to help in developing and sustaining their distinctive cultures.
* Libraries should be equipped with relevant resources, such as publications covering Open University and vocational educational courses, for their role in support of distance education.
* All public libraries within a state should form a part of a network extending from village library through community centre library, district library, and state network, and should be linked to the national information grid.

1951-1956

* The first five-year plan for educational development included a proposal for "Improvement of Library Service." This proposal envisioned a network of libraries throughout the country, coordinated by National Central Library at New Delhi
* During the first five-year plan, nine state governments, *i.e.* Assam, Madhya Pradesh, West Bengal, Punjab, PEPSU, Rajasthan, Savarashtra, Bhopal, and Vindhya Pradesh, decided to set up State Central Libraries.

1956-1961

* At this time, the government allocated funds to set up a national network of libraries in its 320 districts. As a result, most states established State Central Libraries and District Libraries as the main distributing centres

1961-1966

* During this period, the system of central government assistance to the states was changed, and funding for libraries was kept to a minimum. It was up to the individual states to take initiative and develop their public libraries. The programme to assist state governments in establishing state central libraries, district central libraries, and block development libraries was abandoned.
* The decision was a major setback to the development of public libraries. During this period four national libraries were established at Delhi, Calcutta, Bombay, and Madras. A Working Group on libraries was appointed by the Planning Commission in 1964 to take a stock of library development.

The working group submitted its report on 7th September 1965 with following recommendations:

* The central and state governments should share responsibility for providing adequate public library service. New government agencies in the central government under the Minister of Education, a directorate of libraries and a state library advisory council in each state should be set up to execute the programmes effectively.
* State central libraries should be established in four states: Madhya Pradesh, Mysore, Nagaland, and Orissa.
* States which do not possess adequate functional buildings for their state central libraries should be provided with library buildings.

* The state central library must have a children's section.
* There should be 335 District Libraries for the 327 districts in the country, *i.e.*, in large and populous districts, two district libraries may be provided.
* New buildings should be constructed for the existing 100 district libraries.
* Block libraries are the chief feeding centre for the rural reading public, and therefore, 2,500 new block libraries, covering 75% of blocks in the country should be constructed.
* A sum of 10 million rupees shall be provided for distribution of grant in aid to such libraries of urban and rural areas which depend on subscription and donations.
* Three public libraries on model of Delhi Public Library should be set up
* The Institute of Library Science established by the Ministry of Education at Delhi University in 1958-59, and then closed in 1962, should be reopened. Such institutes should be established at the state levels also to train graduate and undergraduate librarians to meet future requirements.
* A sum of Rs.10,000 shall be allocated as financial assistance to all national level and state level library associations to create library consciousness in the country by organizing seminars, conducting surveys, and producing library literature.
* A programme of book production should be undertaken.
* A draft of the Library Act should be produced

1969-1974

This plan proposed a substantial sum for the social education programme. A much lower sum was allocated. Of this, only a very small amount was available for the development of libraries in the country.

1974-1979

This plan included measures to strengthen the buildings, collections, and staff of the central and state libraries, as well as strengthening the district, block, and village libraries. During this period, attempts were made to develop a district-level library system, so that district library could act as a leader for the smaller libraries in the district. The adult education programme was the hallmark of this plan. The programme was to be supported by a network of libraries at the village and block levels and various community centres. Thus steps were taken to strengthen not only the village and block libraries, but also the central, state libraries and the district libraries

1980-85

This plan emphasized establishing a network of rural public libraries to sustain literacy and disseminate information to rural areas. It discussed the necessity of integrating school and college libraries with the system of public libraries. During this period, 26 states or union territories out of 31 had established state central libraries and 291 district libraries.

1985-90

During this period, the Commission's objective was to address the needs of 90 million people in the Adult Education Programme. The network of libraries was to play a role in the development of literature for neo-literates. Library systems were to be strengthened, with specific attention given to improvement of facilities at national level institutions. An important development was the 1986 adoption of National Literacy Mission, which emphasised the education of women and the establishment of rural libraries. In addition, the RRRLF set up an Integrated Research Cell-cum-Computer Unit for promoting research in librarianship and database of public libraries in the country There were two annual plans for the years 1990-91 and 1991-92.

1992-97

During this period it was proposed to reorganize the Central Reference Library into the National Bibliographical and Documentation Centre, which would also have a computer centre. The Delhi Public Library set up two new libraries in its service area. RRRLF created programmes to help state central libraries purchase reprographic equipment, to help libraries process rare books, and to give special assistance to networks of public libraries that were at least 100 years old.

1997-2002

During the 9th five year plan, the National Library, Kolkatta, undertook several major initiatives to upgrade and modernize its collection building programme, reader services, and conservation of library material. The major activities completed during the period were automation of the circulation system in the lending section, setting up of a local area network, improved reader services, and more efficient collection management. The conservation activities in the library got a major advance with the purchase of modern equipment to preserve rare books and other materials. The Central Reference Library, Kolkatta computerised various functions during the Ninth Plan.

As a result, the publication of the Indian National Bibliography is now up to date, with records available online. Funds were provided to the Delhi Public Library and Central Secretariat Library, Delhi, for acquisition of new material in different languages and media as well as for modernizing their infrastructure. The benefits of these efforts can be seen in improved reader services, networking, and resource sharing.

The Central Secretariat Library organized a number of computer training programmes for resource sharing, standardization of cataloguing formats, and co-operative acquisition. Funds for modernizing and computerization were also provided from central grants to the Connemara Library, Chennai, Thanjavur Maharaja Serovji Sarasvati Mahal Library,

Thanjavur and the State Central Library, Mumbai. Besides these, the RRRLF provided assistance to public libraries across the country for collections and storage, construction, and seminars and workshops.

Tenth Five-year Plan (Action Plan)

The Planning Commission proposed further modernization of central and public libraries during the Tenth Plan. A national bibliographic database would be developed to encourage resource sharing, networking, and to improve reader services. The Commission resolved to strengthen public library infrastructure through the RRRLF. The Tenth Plan focused on upgrading existing libraries, including private collections, and widening the programme for bibliographic control and documentation. To make readers services more comprehensive and effective, the National Library is expected to act as the ultimate referral centre for various subjects. To keep pace with the latest developments in information technology in public libraries, the upgrading and networking of central and state libraries was also planned

PRESENT STATUS

The current status of the public library system in India is hard to ascertain and describe, because a consolidated picture is not available. There are twenty-eight states and seven union territories in India. All have their own public library systems, structure, and pattern of financial assistance. Twelve of the states have enacted library legislation and the rest are providing public library service without legislation.

Among the states enumerated, the provision of the respective Acts are more or less fully operative in the states listed under 1-5. In the rest of the states, although an Act has been passed, full operation is still pending. In the Acts of Andhra Pradesh, Haryana, Karnataka, and Tamil Nadu, provision for levying library cess has been made among other sources of finance, whereas there is no provision for collecting library cess in other states.

The states that have enacted library legislation are:

S.No.	State	Name	Year
1.	Tamil Nadu	Tamil Nadu (formerly Madras) Public Libraries Act.	1948
2.	Andhra Pradesh	Andhra Pradesh Public Libraries Act	1960
3.	Karnataka	Karnataka Public Library Act	1965
4.	Maharashtra	Maharashtra Public Libraries Act	1967
5.	West Bengal	West Bengal Public Libraries Act	1979
6.	Manipur	Manipur Public Libraries Act	1988
7.	Kerala	Kerala Public Libraries Act	1989
8.	Haryana	Haryana Public Libraries Act	1989
9.	Mizoram	Mizoram Public Libraries Act	1993
10.	Goa	Goa Public Libraries Act	1993
11.	Gujarat	Gujarat Public Libraries Act	2002
12	Orissa	Orissa Public Library Act	2002

CONCLUSION

Public libraries have always been the door to learning for a great majority of the populations that they serve. They are knowledge centres and contribute to lifelong learning. For India, there are bumps in the road that leads to the goal of having an institution to serve the masses, which is even more imperative in the present information society, in a nation where 40 per cent of the population is living below the poverty line. A massive investment in public libraries is needed to make them true information resource centres for the layman.

2

Public Library and Society

THE ROLE OF LIBRARIES IN MODERN SOCIETY

First, the general development of the information society is pushing to re-evaluation of all the institutions which work with information, data, and knowledge - indirectly also with culture. In this connection the roles of education and media have been discussed already quite largely also in the European Union. But libraries - as well as other memory institutions like archives and museums - have not been considered. Still, there is a clear need in the information society to maintain an institution which is concentrating in collecting and organizing information and offering general access to it. Until now, this work has been underestimated, but I argue the situation will change! Libraries are especially important now when the whole idea of education is stressing more and more independent learning and acting. All citizens must be able to find and use information. It is the key raw material - but it is a zero resource, if there are no access points to it and if documents are in chaotic order.

Here we can see libraries enter the stage:

* The unique function of libraries is to acquire, organize, offer for use and preserve publicly available material irrespective of the form in which

Paper on libraries by the Commission
npleted.

position must be taken in account in the
directive process, the balance must be
- this was politically the most important
short run.

libraries was demanded from the 5th
rk programme of research and
nt, *e.g.* for networking, drafting standards,
, and transferring information; there is no
ned library programme under the 5th
k programme

g-house to solve problems of long-term
ion should be founded.

oncerning permanent paper should be done
ean level.

nber states should take care of digitizing
ural heritage for future.

hould be studies and concrete support to
in licensing matters, which are - will be the
issue in library work.

cultural and information budget should be
to libraries as well, libraries and their co-
on should be taken in account in planning
ogrammes.

ms of legal deposit in international and
ational materials, especially in electronic
als should be solved.

ember states should provide all types of
s with modern equipment, particularly with
et connections.

f charge use of public libraries, in the spirit of
UNESCO Public Library Manifest, was
nded.

nd easy access via libraries to material produced
he aid of tax revenues was demanded.

nembers states should organize for their library
ssionals up-dating education and training.

it is packaged in such a way that, when it is needed, it can be found and put to use. No other institution carries out this long-term, systematic work.

Culture must be Nominated Especially: It has an important and unique role in mobilizing resources of human beings.

It has been described:

* To some extent, culture makes its influence felt more indirectly than knowledge, but it is impossible to imagine how people's creative powers could be fully activated without the impact of culture, which extends into the depths of the mind.

The challenge to modern societies is that the basic resource, knowledge, is developing from information in very individual, capricious and unpredictable process. It cannot be commanded. Still, societies can support this development, *e.g.* by offering acces to cultural and knowledge treasures. This can even be translated into economic language: to get out the best from the human resources in Europe, this resource must be feeded up with rich and various cultural and information contents! I would like to stress especially the idea of organising information by libraries. It is often shadowed by the second important side of library work: offering access. But in the life-long learning and new technology context just all forms of organising documents are getting more to the focus. This is clear to anybody who has tried to find something from not-so-often-used Internet websites.

New Lines in the EU - and in the United States

In accordance with these phenomenons, there are new political lines in the European Union: The Maastricht Treaty in 1992 launched the cultural aspects. This was only after a long discussion, which made it clear that we have to remember to separate the national view and the European view. The Amsterdam Treaty in 1997 declared citizenship as an important theme. A significant part of this are a.o. granting information skills and access to information to every European. In addition to this, the European future strategies need to meet the democratic aspects of the information society development.

One of the crucial points is again general access to information. Libraries, especially public libraries, are a good tool in all of these new areas. But the European union does not support whichever cultural or citizen concentrated projects in Europe. In the interests of the European Union there is always to find the European element. So, what can be done in library policy on the European level, taking in account that libraries are primarily a part of national education and cultural policies?

The own-initiative report "The role of libraries in modern societies", adopted by the European Parliament in October 1998, is the first effort to answer these questions.

The same topics have been dicussed in the United States. They have reached the point where especially the problems of those lacking access to digital resources have been studied. The report Falling Through the Net: Defining the Digital Divide by the U.S. Department of Commerce was released earlier in July 1999. The report finds that minorities, low-income persons, the less educated, and children of single parent households, particularly when they reside in rural areas or central cities, are risk groups.

The report calls for public policies and private initiatives to expand affordable access to critical information resources. But it also shows,, for the first time as far as I know, that libraries and community centres really can diminish the information gap between haves and not-haves. The 1998 data from the U.S. demonstrates very clearly that community access centers, primarily public libraries, are particularly well used by those groups who lack access at home or at work: *e.g.* unemployed groups used Internet in libraries three times as often as an average citizen.

Earlier Actions in EU

In the European Union, there have been some efforts to mobilize "the treasures of the European libraries" since the mid-80's. These discussions and resolutions led to two special library programmes under the 3rd and 4th Framework programmes of research and development. The later programme has been known as "Telematics for Libraries".

* A European Union focal point for libraries should be set up
* The member states should found European information points at libraries in countries where they do not yet exist.
* Library statistics should be better and more comparable both on national and European level.
* The national Parliament libraries should be opened to the MEP's in countries where this is not yet the practice.

In addition to these, the report strongly stresses that the library financing must be re-thougt in the information society. Without new resources libraries are unable to do everything they are expected to do! After the EP adoption of this report, the European Commission informed that it will next prepare a communication about actions to do. It was stated that the report had already served as a discussion paper, and so the need for the Green Paper had disappeared. The communication is in summer 1999 still under work in the Commission DGXIII/2.

Traditions and New Forms of Work in the Same House

The European Commission R&D framework programmes have concentrated in IT matters. The three cultural programmes, Caledoskope, Ariane and Raphael, have not been very useful for libraries, because their scope has been quite narrow, *e.g.* the books and reading programme Ariane has concentrated in translations. In the coming framework programme Culture 2000 libraries will have more possibilities to get support also for their cultural actions. What then will be the fate of the traditional tasks of libraries in general? Will the information society wipe out book loaning and poems? These elements will survive, but will get completed by new media forms. It was stated earlier that culture has a special role in building up the modern society and in mobilizing the capacity of its members The significance of reading is only growing in future. Demands to enlarge and deepen literacy skills get greater and greater.

Literacy has a special role in guaranteeing the basic citizen competence to everybody. It is in general interests of the society to offer possibilities to all people for maintaining and developing their literacy. In library work new technologies offer new possibilities to raise service level, too. Good examples can already now be found all over the world, mainly of course in those countries where Internet is used largely.

Some models: Library catalogues are available via Internet, the patron can check her/his loaning data from Internet, and even renew the loans a country/area wide information service via Internet and e-mail; there are versions for link libraries or virtual libraries, where libraries collect and describe high-level link-ups discussion lists of librarians, where they can share their professional skills and knowledge, even take part in developing the library policy of the country/area. There is one special comment concerning Internet which I have heard both from small libraries with rejected printed collections in Finland and from African libraries: In case you got reach in Internet, the resources your library can offer to the patrons are suddenly multiplied.

All of once we have exactly the same resource as British Library or the Library of Congress. It is amazing, it is revolutionary, and we can use it! In the complicated modern society libraries have many kinds of answers to many demands of the society, as well as those of the citizens. They have potential means to serve both the information society development and their traditional humanistic tasks. Maybe information technology will even make it easier to combine these elements in future than in the past!

PUBLIC LIBRARIES AND THE INFORMATION SOCIETY

On 14 and 15 October 1999 senior politicians and policy makers from 31 European countries met to consider the vital role of public libraries within the emerging Information Societies. Those attending the meeting heard about the key roles already played by many European public libraries in encouraging community identity, economic development, lifelong learning and cultural diversity. At the end of the meeting those present agreed the following declaration as a statement of intent for the future of public libraries across the continent of Europe.

In support of the:

* UNESCO Public Library Manifesto
* IFLA Guidelines on Public Libraries
* Report on the Role of Libraries in the Modern World of the Committee on Culture, Youth, Education and the Media of the European Parliament
* European Commission's study – Public Libraries and the Information Society
* Council of Europe Cultural Committee report: Library Legislation and Policy in Europe
* IFLA statement on Freedom of Expression

We declare the following as a common basis for national and European policies regarding public libraries:

ROLES FOR THE PUBLIC LIBRARY

We support the following roles for public libraries, highlighted in the Leuven Communique:

* *Democracy And Citizenship:* Public libraries have a strategic opportunity to increase quality of life and democratic possibilities for citizens of the Information Societies by providing free and equal access to high-quality information.
* *Economic and Social Development :* Public libraries support the growth of communities through the provision of information services designed to meet local needs. They are important tools for reducing disparity between the information rich and the information poor citizens of Europe.
* *Lifelong Learning:* Public libraries provide, through their widespread distribution across Europe, a cost-effective infrastructure for lifelong learning and easy access to the content of the virtual networks. They also support students at all levels of formal education.

* *Cultural And Linguistic Diversity:* Public libraries are cultural institutions in accordance with the cultural dimension of the EU-Treaty with a great responsibility for cultural heritage, literature and literacy.

Action by the European Commission

We call on the European Commission to support the European Parliament initiative 'The Role of Libraries in the Modern Society' by promoting practical actions to implement the recommendations of the report. These actions should stress the key role of public libraries in the emerging Information Society and the need for a European level information policy.

Action by National and Federal Governments

We call on all national and federal governments to take the following actions:

* Prepare a national information policy for the development and co-ordination of all relevant resources, in the public interest. This policy framework will recognise the vital and unique role of public libraries as access points for the majority of citizens and be supported by suitable library legislation.
* Create suitable networking infrastructure to support the development of a national information policy in the Information Age. The network infrastructure should draw together all information creating agencies, especially the traditional memory institutions to encourage information sharing and the creation of joint resources. The infrastructure should also encourage practical co-operation between public libraries.
* Implement a development programme for public libraries that ensure minimum standards of access to every citizen including appropriate information and communication technologies and suitable levels

of investment to meet those standards. This programme should reflect the need for there to be control of developments at the level of the local community through the relevant municipality or other organisation.

* Ensure that public libraries are equipped to provide maximum access to the new information resources for all citizens regardless of financial, physical or educational abilities and that those libraries have adequate resources to sustain the services over time.
* Lobby the European Parliament to place public libraries high on the social agenda now and in the future.
* Work to ensure that there is an equitable balance between the rights of the creators of information and the rights of citizens' access to the information that will help them to lead better lives.

Action by Public Libraries

* Be prepared to re-assess roles and resources and re-design services to respond to changing social needs.
* Work towards long-term co-operation and partnership with other memory institutions and those involved with community education.
* Ensure that citizens are aware of and feel able to exploit fully all the resources of the public library network by effective marketing of services to all sectors of the community.

SOCIETY LITERACY AND PUBLIC LIBRARIES IN INDIA

After Independence, India has experienced growing population of literate and educated citizens due to various efforts in universalisation of elementary education through programmes like:

* Sarva Shiksha Abhiyan (SSA),
* District Primary Education Programme (DPEP), and
* National Literacy Mission and so on.

On the other hand, for the facilitating educated citizens with the adequate documentary and knowledge resources, government and other agencies have established public libraries. The community information centres and village knowledge centres are the recent additions to this effort that would transform India into an information society, where information and knowledge resources are considered as critical ingredient for development. But problem is with the effective and efficient use, consumption and evaluation of information resources, so that informed citizen can take right decisions.

Here information literacy can play a vital role in educating the users of libraries on various information and documentary resources, where to start searching of information, what where and how to access them, how to assess and compare retrieved information, how to communicate their information or findings to the general masses and experts, and so on. In addition to borrow books for entertainment and leisure, public libraries can also disseminate information on community development, best practices, literature, culture, trade, education, etc. which may be further elaborated when needs arise.

Information seekers may want consolidated or exhaustive information. To provide right information to the users, public librarians should be trained to develop information literacy competency and should able to educate the user that will make user information literate. Before going into depth, we would like to know what is 'information literacy' and who are 'information literates'.

'Information literacy' is "the ability to recognize when information is needed and have the ability to locate, evaluate and use effectively the needed information". Information literacy embraces related concepts like 'user education', 'library instruction', 'bibliographic instruction' and 'library research', although 'information literacy' has broader perspectives and wider applications than these concepts. Information literacy competency development programmes and standards are designed to produce information literate. American Library Association Presidential Committee on Information Literacy defines 'information literates' as:

- "...ultimately, information literate people are those who have learned how to learn. They know how to learn because they know how knowledge is organized, how to find information, and how to use information in such a way that others can learn from them. They are people prepared for lifelong learning, because they can always find the information needed for any task or decision at hand."

Information Literacy Standards and Indicators

In 1998 American Association of School Librarians and Association for Educational Communications and Technology prepared a document titled 'Information literacy standards for student learning: standards and indicators', which is widely accepted worldwide as a set of information literacy standards that can be imparted to produce information literate citizen. The each standard has some indicators that show kinds of competency and parameters to accomplish that standard. As far nine standards are identified which have three broad spectrums, such as information literacy standards, independent learning standards and social responsibility standards.

Although these standards and indicators are initially developed for students, these can be equally applicable to the common citizens as well as public libraries users. The information literacy standards and respective indicators are shown in the tables. Table 2.1 indicates that information literates are also independent learners, and information literates who contribute positively to the community use information ethically and responsibly. We know that many public libraries cater information services to the higher learners and researchers.

It is also being said that one of the best research libraries in the world is New York Public Library. Table 2.2 indicates information literacy competency standards for higher education. American Library Association and other organizations endorsed these two standards.

Table 2.1. Information Literacy Standards and Indicators.

Standards	Indicators
Information Literacy Standards	
1. The person who is information literate accesses information efficiently and effectively.	1. Recognizes the need for information. 2. Recognizes that accurate and comprehensive information is the basis for intelligent decision-making. 3. Formulates questions based on information needs. 4. Identifies a variety of potential sources of information. 5. Develops and uses successful strategies for locating information.
2. The person who is inform-ation literate evaluates inform-ation critically and competently.	1. Determines accuracy, relevance, and comprehensiveness. 2. Distinguishes among fact, point of view, and opinion. 3. Identifies inaccurate and misleading information. 4. Selects information appropriate to the problem or question at hand.
3. The person who is informat-ion literate uses information accurately and creatively.	1. Organizes information for practical application. 2. Integrates new information into one's own knowledge. 3. Applies information in critical thinking and problem solving. 4. Produces and communicates information and ideas in appropriate formats.
Independent Learning Standards	
4. The person who is an indepe-ndent learner is information literate and pursues information related to personal interests.	1. Seeks information related to various dimensions of personal well-being, such as career interests, community involvement, health matters, and recreational pursuits. 2. Designs, develops, and evaluates information products and solutions related to personal interests.
5. The person who is an indep-endent learner is information literate and appreciates literature and other creative expressions of information.	1. Is a competent and self-motivated reader. 2. Derives meaning from information presented creatively in a variety of formats. 3. Develops creative products in a variety of formats.

(Contd...)

6. The person who is an independent learner is information literate and strives for excellence in information seeking and knowledge generation.	1. Assesses the quality of the process and products of personal information seeking. 2. Devises strategies for revising, improving,and updating self-generated knowledge.
Social Responsibility Standards	
7. The person who contributes positively to the community and to society is information literate and recognizes the importance of information to a democratic society.	1. Seeks information from diverse sources, contexts, disciplines, and cultures. 2. Respects the principle of equitable access to information.
8. The person who contributes positively to the community and to society is information literate and practices ethical behaviour in regard to information and information technology.	1. Respects the principles of intellectual freedom. 2. Respects intellectual property rights. 3. Uses information technology responsibly.
9. The person who contributes positively to the community and to society is information literate and participates effectively in groups to pursue and generate information.	1. Shares knowledge and information with others. 2. Respects others' ideas and backgrounds and acknowledges their contributions 3. Collaborates with others, both in person and through technologies, to identify information problems and to seek their solutions.
	4. Collaborates with others, both in person and through technologies, to design, develop, and evaluate information products and solutions

Table 2.2. Information Literacy Competency Standards for Higher Education.

Information Literacy Competency Standards	Performance Indicators
Standard One IL person determines the nature and extent of the information needed.	1. IL person defines and articulates the need for information. 2. IL person identifies a variety of types and formats of potential sources for information. 3. IL person considers the costs and benefits of acquiring the needed information.

(Contd...)

	4. IL person reevaluates the nature and extent of the information need.
Standard Two IL person accesses needed information effectively and efficiently.	1. IL person selects the most appropriate investigative methods or information retrieval systems for accessing the needed information. 2. IL person constructs and implements effectively designed search strategies. 3. IL person retrieves information online or in person using a variety of methods. 4. IL person refines the search strategy if necessary. 5. IL person extracts, records, and manages the information and its sources.
Standard Three IL person evaluates information and its sources critically and incorporates selected information into his or her knowledge base and value system.	1. IL person summarizes the main ideas to be extracted from the information gathered. 2. IL person articulates and applies initial criteria for evaluating both the information and its sources. 3. IL person synthesizes main ideas to construct new concepts. 4. IL person compares new knowledge with prior knowledge to determine the value added, contradictions, or other unique characteristics of the information. 5. IL person determines whether the new knowledge has an impact on the individual's value system and takes steps to reconcile differences. 6. IL person validates understanding and interpretation of the information through discourse with other individuals, subject-area experts, and/or practitioners. 7. IL person determines whether the initial query should be revised.
Standard Four IL person, individually or as a member of a group, uses information effectively to accomplish a specific purpose.	1. IL person applies new and prior information to the planning and creation of a particular product or performance. 2. IL person revises the development process for the product or performance. 3. IL person communicates the product or performance effectively to others.

(Contd...)

Standard Five IL person understands many of the economic, legal, and social issues surrounding the use of information and accesses and uses information ethically and legally.	1. IL person understands many of the ethical, legal and socio-economic issues surrounding information and information technology. 2. IL person follows laws, regulations, institutional policies, and etiquette related to the access and use of information resources. 3. IL person acknowledges the use of information sources in communicating the product or performance.

Information Literacy and Reading Habits

Present urbanized society observes a changing face of new generation, where children have access to various modes of entertainment and amusement. Every middle-class household in India equips with at least one electronic gadgetry, such as, television, music system, DVD-player, VCD-player, Internet, video games, etc. All these gadgets may be detrimental our new generations as well as older generations, that is one of the reasons for declining number of regular users of public libraries. We know public libraries build up collections of literature of local languages, national literature and world literature.

A public library user can get higher satisfaction if they read classic literature, contemporary literature and know cultural heritage of India and the state he/she belongs. Other than books on literature, many informative books and magazines that enhance knowledge levels of the users are available in the public libraries. Other useful documents, such as career handbooks, encyclopedias, directories, dictionaries, etc. are also accessible in public libraries. Reading habits not only help a person becoming knowledgeable, socially responsible and socially productive person but also help in personality development.

Information literacy competency development programmes may be initiated to impart necessary information skills and reading skills to public library users in maximizing utilization of public library resources. A public library may be participating a library resource-sharing network. The public library users should learn how to search union catalogues of the network, how to obtain documents from other participating libraries through inter-library loan service and document delivery service. This way the limitation of collection in one public library may overcome and users get satisfaction for this service. Public libraries also conduct various other extension programmes, like, quiz competition, story, poetry and essay writing competition, etc. that also aims to enhance reading habits of the users, specially younger users of the public libraries.

Public Libraries in India

Public libraries in India is spread all over the countries, consist of state central libraries in every state, district libraries, urban public libraries at the cities and rural public libraries at the villages. Public libraries are mainly supported by state governments and local authorities, and some times by the central government, developmental agencies, nongovernment organizations and private trusts. The Delhi Public Library (DPL), established in 1951 by government of India in collaboration with UNESCO, caters library and information services to the National Capital Territory of Delhi. It has 176 service points spreads over five regions and consists of branch libraries, sub-branches, community libraries resettlement colony libraries, reading rooms, mobile library points, Braille library and deposit stations.

The DPL is a recipient of books published in India as per the provision in the Delivery of Books and Newspapers (Public Libraries) Act, 1954. The DPL has collections about two million books and other documents. Raja Rammohun Roy Library Foundation (RRRLF) is the nodal agency of the Government of India to support public library services and system and promote public library movement in the country. The RRRLF undertakes different functions in each state and union territory through a State Library Planning Committee (SLPC) or State Library Committee (SLC).

Its headquarter is located at Kolkata and it has four zonal offices in Kolkata, Delhi, Mumbai and Chennai. RRRLF provides financial and technical assistance to public libraries and organisations engaged in the promotion of public library development through different schemes. Schemes of RRRLF broadly categorized as Matching Schemes and Non- Matching Schemes. Assistance under matching schemes is given from the resources shared on 50:50 matching basis with the state governments. Assistance under nonmatching schemes does not have share of the state governments. Table 2.3 shows the number of different public libraries in India. Table also indicates that there is lack of existence of public libraries in some villages even after 59 years of independence.

Table 2.3. Penetration of Public Libraries in India.

Demography of India	Number	Public Libraries	Number	Percentage covered
States and Union Territories	35	State Central Libraries	28	80%
Districts	592	District Libraries	451	76%
Talukas	3,987	Taluka Libraries	501	12.5%
Villages	587,226	Rural Libraries	28,820	4.9%

Library Legislation in India

Public library development in the state is the responsibility of the respective state government. Ten states in India have enacted Public Libraries Act in their states. The library legislation ensures the smooth functioning of the public libraries in the state. A state may have three tiers of public libraries in hierarchy. The apex body would be a state central library, the next tier consists of district libraries in all districts of the state, and third tier consists of rural and urban public libraries spread all over the state. Public Libraries Act also ensures each village or city at least have one government-aided public library. This Act also makes provisions of finances, human resources and other resources for the development and functioning of public libraries. Some state governments provide grants for the public libraries; some other state governments collect Library Cess from the taxpayers.

The states that passed Public Libraries Act are shown along with the year:

* Tamil Nadu (then called Madras Public Libraries Act, 1948);
* Andhra Pradesh (Hyderabad Public Libraries Act, 1955; then Andhra Pradesh Public Libraries Act, 1960);
* Maharashtra (Kolhapur Public Libraries Act, 1945; then Maharashtra Public Libraries Act, 1967);
* West Bengal (West Bengal Public Libraries Act, 1979);
* Manipur (Manipur Public Libraries Act, 1988);
* Kerala (Kerala Public Libraries Act, 1989);
* Haryana (Haryana Public Libraries Act, 1989);
* Mizoram (Mizoram Public Libraries Act, 1993);
* Goa (Goa Public Libraries Act, 1994).

Although other states as such have no Public Libraries Act, these states have government funded public libraries at the state and district levels; government aided public libraries at the rural and urban areas are mostly absent or having in an unorganised manner. The Delhi Public Library is located in Delhi, which is fully funded by the union government, so Delhi state has no such Act. For getting into the profession, public librarians should have formal training, at least a Certificate in Library Science (CLS) or Diploma in Library Science (DLS) for the rural libraries and Bachelor's in Library and Information Science (BLIS) for the district libraries. There is also provision of training of public librarians in the Public Libraries Act in some states, in the forms of orientation training, refresher training.

The public librarians should be aware of recent development in information sources and information systems, especially in the digital environment, as many public libraries worldwide are providing web-based library and information services to their users. Digital divide in the India can reduce significantly if they use computers and Internet technologies in the public libraries at the grass-root level. The users of public libraries then access digital information available through Internet to keep abreast of recent development in their areas of interest. Information literacy competency development programmes for public librarians and users can be a part of provisions in the Public Libraries Act of the states.

Role of State Level Library Associations

Library associations exist in most of the states and union territories of India. State level library associations are very active in public libraries development in their respective states. Some library associations also conduct certificate and diploma courses in library science that help the learners get into the profession. Some library associations also conduct refresher courses for the in-service public librarians, mostly in the areas of library automation, ICT applications in libraries, and other contemporary issues. Most library associations observe Library Day and Dr. S.R. Ranganathan's birthday. On those occasions they organize one-day seminars or lectures.

This way public librarians get informed about the recent development in the librarianship and public libraries movement in India and the states. Some library associations bring out their newsletters and bulletins for their member librarians and disseminate various professional information. Some library associations take up the issue of information literacy competency for the librarians and library users. Library associations in the state should come forward and develop information literacy competency of the public librarians through organizing training programmes, workshops and seminars. In December 2005, Indian Library Association had organized 51th All India Conference with the focus on "libraries, information literacy and lifelong learning", where many librarians felt the importance of information literacy in life-long learning and optimizing the usage of information in the libraries.

In October 2005, an international information literacy workshop was held at the Punjabi University, Patiala, India to promote information literacy in South and South East Asia, with the support of UNESCO and other partners. In September 2003 at Prague, the International Alliance for Information Literacy was formed where India's Networking Alliance for Voluntary Actions, a network of NGOs, became a member. In

India, a number of NGOs support public libraries and community information centres, where common people become users of these libraries. The state level library associations, NGOs and developmental agencies can collaborate amongst themselves to develop information literacy competencies of the librarians and library users.

Information Literacy (IL) Competency Development Programmes for Public Librarians and Library Users

Information literacy (IL) competency development programme for public librarians would be a kind of training course for the trainers. The public librarians would impart training to the end users of public libraries. Some of the skills required for the information literacy are already achieved by the public librarians through their formal degree or diploma courses; induction, orientation, and on-the job training programmes. Some librarians started their career before the introduction of information communication technologies (ICT) in library services and information handling. Such ICT skills, communication and teaching skills need to be obtained freshly through the refresher courses.

The aims of the information literacy competency development programmes for public librarians can be:

* The ability to apply the principles of scholarly communication to problems of information handling;
* The ability to locate, select and use appropriate information retrieval tools in order to obtain useful information in connection with studies or work of the end users, and when required;
* Confidence in using, and satisfaction in carrying out information searching;
* Confidence in communicating, instructing and educating the users.

Some of the objectives IL competency development programmes for public librarians are:

* Public librarians would be able to develop a systematic method of searching for information related to areas of studies of the users;

* They would be aware of wide range of sources available for finding information and select the sources which will best meet users needs;
* They would be aware of appropriate indexing and abstracting services and databases and understand the principles of their use;
* They would develop database searching techniques for accessing both web-based and CD-ROM databases;
* They would be able to use current awareness methods to keep up to date with the published literature;
* They would be able to use international academic networks for getting information;
* They would be able to use and create list servers, discussion forums, Internet chat services and bloggers for obtaining and disseminating information;
* They would be able to use local library network for sharing in-house resources and obtaining documents through inter-library loan and document delivery services;
* They would be able to compare and critically evaluate information obtained from various sources;
* They would be able to cite bibliographic references in the papers, objects, reports or theses;
* They would be able to construct an institutional bibliographic system;
* They would be able to motivate library users in accessing library resources and availing user services;
* They would be able to communicate, instruct and educate library users;
* They would be able to prepare learning and assessment modules both printed as well as web-enabled for the learners;
* They would be able to make strategies for influencing stakeholders; and prepare action plans.

Some of the aims and objectives of the IL competency development programmes can be considered for public library users, as some of the components of the programmes are common. These aims and objectives of the IL competency development programmes are not exhaustive; and some elements may be altered whenever needs arise. Public library authorities in India, like Raja Rammohun Roy Library Foundation, Delhi Public Library, state central libraries and library associations can introduce IL competency development programmes for public librarians objectives and aims. The changing library scenario, present and future public library systems in India should be considered when designing such courses.

3

Agencies in the Promotion and Development of Public Library System

STATE LIBRARY AGENCIES

Continuing education for professional and support staff in all the professions has been receiving increasing emphasis in recent years. The need to update current practice through new knowledge and insight of societal conditions and client needs has had its impact in the library and information science fields. The advances in automation and technology, the proliferation of knowledge, and the growing recognition of the need to provide access to the rapid delivery of information in many formats have given priority emphasis to continuing library education as a means of responding to the changes taking place in our society. State library agencies have a continuing responsibility for a planned approach to the development of library and information services in each state. This planned approach includes the need for the continuing education of library personnel to meet changing service demands.

This object reviews the background for the continuing education role of the state library agency, the development of continuing education for libraries, the implications of these developments, current programmes in progress, and trends which may indicate future change. Historically, state library agencies have had the responsibility for statewide library development, particularly public library development. The provision of advice, assistance and consultant services has been one of the primary means employed. Included in the advisory activities were the conducting of workshops and other educational and staff development programmes. State library agencies having responsibility for school library development as units of state departments of education carried on similar programmes and activities to improve school libraries.

Following the enactment of the federal Library Services Act (LSA), state library agencies moved into a new era of growth and influence. The requirement to develop state plans and the attendant emphasis on establishing libraries, creating library systems and extending library services created the need for staff development and continuing education activities as a major component in the achievement of desired objectives.

A U.S. Office of Education study of state library extension resources and services compares the data from 1955-56 prior to LSA with the re- sources and services of state library agencies in 1960-61. For the purposes of this chapter, the report of consultant activity and training programmes during this period is of interest. Forty-eight States reported 16,466 field visits compared to 6544 in 1955-56; 44 states held or sponsored some 1600 training programmes for over 56,000 persons from 1956 to 1961. These pro- grams served professional (36 %) and nonprofessional (22 %) personnel and public library trustees (26 %).

The responsibility of state library agencies for the planning and ad- ministration of federal funds under the Library Services Act of 1956 and the Library Services and Construction Act (LSCA) of 1964 gave added impetus to national documents and conferences concerned with improving the capabilities of state library agencies. These reports emphasize a stronger focus on goals, purposes and long-range plans with the attendant need for highly skilled consultants and related staff development activities in the field in order to implement the statewide programme.

All state library agencies view continuing education and consultant services as a major responsibility of the agency. In a recent survey, about one-half of the state library agencies considered the continuing education responsibility to be a shared responsibility and not solely the responsibility or of the state library agency. In recent years national activities of major importance have contributed to an increased awareness of continuing education responsibility and to an increase in planned activities of state library agencies.

In the regional hearing conducted in 1972 by the National Commission on Libraries and Information Science (NCLIS), one of the identified priorities was the availability of continuing education for the development and maintenance of competencies which are needed to deliver the library and information services required by the nation. Subsequently, NCLIS funded a study in 1973 to recommend a nationwide programme of continuing education which culminated in Continuing Library and Information Science Education. This report made recommendations which eventually led to the formation of the Continuing Library Education Network Exchange (CLENE). The NCLIS report outlines the development of library continuing education and comments on the necessity for continuing life- long learning.'

Based on responses from the field, an operational definition of continuing education was developed which includes the following:

* The implication that lifelong learning is necessary to keep the individual up to date,
* Assurance that the individual carries the basic responsibility for his/her own development,
* Diversification to new areas of interest, and
* Involvement in educational activities beyond those considered necessary for entrance into the field.

In comparison with other professions, the librarians felt that continuing education should be pro- vided for all levels of personnel, not solely professional, and that it not be limited to improved competence for the job held now or aspired to in the future. In its plan for continuing education, the report suggests roles and responsibilities of the individual agencies and organizations in order to coordinate efforts, including those of the individual employee, the employing library, the state library agency, the library schools, and state, regional and national associations.

Major responsibilities outlined for the state library agencies include coordination of continuing education programmes on a statewide basis, identification of continuing education needs of the state, provision of a link between librarians in the state and national and regional plans, and the appointment of a continuing education coordinator on the state library agency staff. The other major responsibility is three-fold: the planning, implementation and evaluation of statewide continuing education programmes based on identified needs.

These initial efforts to provide a suggested outline of responsibilities continued to receive attention through CLENE as a newly formed national organization. State library agencies which joined CLENE as sustaining members, as well as the state library agency directors and continuing education staff members, influenced some of the priorities of CLENE. In 1976 CLENE received a USOE, Title II-B grant to provide an "Extended Institute to Train State Library Agency.Personnel to Implement and/or Strengthen Statewide Systems of Continuing Education for Library/Information/Media Personnel." The workshop phase of the institute was held November 7-13, 1976, at the Illinois State Library. Continuing education personnel from twenty-five state library agencies met to develop planning and implementation skills in continuing education. For participating states the institute spurred development of statewide coordinated planning among providers of continuing education in the state.

During this period several regional consortia of states were formed with a primary concern for continuing education. CELS grew out of a survey of members of six state library associations where the need for Continuing education was strongly expressed. State library agencies are major financial contributors to this programme. The Western Interstate Commission on Higher Education (WICHE) had a major continuing education component funded in large part by five state library agencies. The Western Council of State Libraries has succeeded WICHE in this regional effort.

State library agencies were asked to report on activities in needs assessment, programmes in continuing education, the extent of cooperation of other agencies in planning and implementing continuing education programmes, recent changes and improvements in state library agency continuing education programmes, and trends and new developments in continuing education. Forty responses to the questionnaire were received. State library replies indicate that all state library agencies have a responsibility for continuing education. Several have stated that the agency statutes define this responsibility but most suggest that agency planning documents cover these functions.

Cooperation with other continuing education agencies is extensive; 63 per cent of the respondents work closely with state library associations, and 34 per cent with library schools. State universities, higher education commissions, state departments of education, and other agencies were also listed. State staff are active participants on the continuing education committees of other agencies, and either library associations or the state library agency has formed a continuing education committee for coordinated planning and programmes. The formation of continuing education planning committees representing all types of libraries is a recent development in many states.

These committees are in various stages of the development of guidelines, policy statements or state plans for coordinated continuing education programmes. Examples of plans underway can be found in Illinois, Michigan, Ohio and Louisiana. Oklahoma reported the formation of a state committee in 1978, Maryland in 1977. Pennsylvania is planning a special project in 1978 with a director and task force to develop continuing education coordination. States participating in the Western Council of State Libraries and CELS are the primary planners for the continuing education programme of the regional consortia. Coordinated planning appears to be one of the more significant activities now underway.

Continuing education needs were identified by the majority through surveys and questionnaires at state, regional or local levels;consultations with local staffs and "perceived changes in the library climate," evaluation of current programmes and of new national library trends and programmes were also cited. The responses did not indicate the types of libraries involved in the needs assessment process. The influence of continuing education committees and recently formed task forces has not yet been felt to any great degree in the development of continuing education programmes as reported.

The continuing education programmes sponsored by state library agencies are directed primarily to public library staffs, although programme offerings to reach a broader group were listed. All respondents listed public library directors and public library professional staff as participants; twenty-six listed nonprofessional public library staffs. However, twenty- one listed academic librarians;twelve, school librarians;twelve, multi-type participants; and two listed institutional and special library staffs.

Principal topics in continuing education programmes covered a wide range including copyright, networking, automation, planning, management, public relations and audiovisual materials. However, over one-third of the respondents offered basic or refresher courses to public library staffs in such areas as reference, children's services, storytelling, and young adult services. A few states mentioned law materials, oral history, censorship, and government documents. Workshops on community needs and development of special services to disadvantaged, senior citizens and other groups reflect the outreach programme priorities of some states.

Wisconsin reported a continuing education programme for public library and staff through the University of Wisconsin using the Education Telephone Network (ETN). Once a month for about two hours, several topics are discussed by a group or panel. Local libraries may purchase sets of materials related to the programme.

Topics covered in the last two years include:

* Networks,
* Censorship,
* School-public library cooperation,
* The independent adult learner,
* Deaf awareness, and
* Service to special groups.

Alaska and Hawaii reported the use of video cassettes to bring continuing education programmes to remote areas, and West Virginia reported that the capability now exists there to provide this form of continuing education programming.

Frequently, continuing education programmes sponsored by the state library agency are executed by contract with a university or other educational organization. Some states do this extensively; others use this method for institutes in such areas as management.

Recent changes and improvements in the continuing education activities of state library agencies reflected the increased emphasis and direction given a planned and coordinated programme. The establishment of a new position of continuing education coordinator was listed by five states; assignment of this responsibility to an established position was listed by many states. Several states were engaged in "train the trainer" programmes with the shift to local library systems of responsibility for staff development and training in their own institutions, particularly for nonprofessional staff. State programmes will provide for more advanced and intensive training and attempt to ensure continuity in programme offerings. At least two states - North Carolina and Maryland - provide reimbursement to public library staffs for attending out-of-state institutes.

The responsibility of the continuing education coordinator for developing and disseminating information on continuing education offerings in-state and nationally; for maintaining a master calendar; for providing continuing liaison with library schools, library associations and other educational agencies; and for assuring a programme of needs identification and developing plans to meet needs were mentioned. These activities reflect to a marked degree the influence of the CLENE report and subsequent programmes and activities of CLENE. It should be noted that state library agency personnel active in CLENE are frequently those most active in continuing education development in their respective states.

Several states commented that NCLIS and CLENE had provided the impetus for renewed continuing education activity at the state level; one saw CLENE as the key to noteworthy, effective state library agency work in continuing education. The continuing education programmes of CLENE itself provide state library agency personnel the opportunity to gain knowledge, exchange information, and encourage the further coordinated development of continuing education activities of state library agencies.

Changes and trends seen as important and needed for further development of continuing education include the development of more non- traditional methods for the delivery of continuing education programmes, as well as education techniques more suitable to adult learners. States ex- pressed the need for improved needs assessment and evaluation skills and techniques.

At least one-half the states were interested in a recognition system for continuing education. This seemed to be the national trend of greatest interest. Some states are currently using the continuing education unit (CEU) in institutions of higher education for library programmes. CEUs are directly related to certification in several states. South Dakota State Library provides voluntary certification for public libraries based on CEUs. Michigan and North Carolina have proposals for recertification of public librarians through approved programmes in continuing education and the CEU. The "college without walls" programme in New Hampshire and Vermont has prompted library staff to indicate that continuing education programmes should provide some academic credit.

A nationally recognized CEU programme for librarians was specifically cited by several respondents. The study recently completed by CLENE, Model Continuing Education Recognition System in Library and Information Science, was first discussed in January at a CLENE meeting and is to be further examined and discussed at a national convention sponsored by NCLIS in June 1978. State library agencies will need to give the proposal and comments from the field serious study, since it has implications for an increased state library agency role.

This object has attempted to provide a summary of the development of continuing education responsibilities in state library agencies as viewed in the literature and reported from the agencies themselves. A few other points and issues need to be raised. State library agencies have a continuing responsibility for the improvement of the quality of library services in the state. In that respect they are in a unique position to assess the impact of continuing education programmes on library services in the state, and have a responsibility to do so. There is no documentation to determine whether this is being done, but the need to develop the evaluation and performance criteria for this purpose is evident. In the author's opinion this would lead to fewer programmes of longer duration, involving participants in more appropriate learning situations and plans for implementation in their libraries.

Another issue is the responsibility of the individual for his own continuing education and for the pursuit of programmes that satisfy individual needs and interests. State library agency programmes are geared primarily to the perceived needs of the institution and to the priorities of the state library plans and objectives. To the extent that these coincide with individual needs and interests and that participation is voluntary and encouraged, the interests of both can be served.

By publicizing continuing education programmes at state, regional or national levels, state library agencies are helping individuals to become aware of other opportunities. Each state library agency needs to define its own role in continuing library education in relation to those of library schools, library associations and other providers of continuing education programmes.

State library agencies should continue efforts to make possible situations in which innovators and practitioners can reach each other, invent ways to be mutually instructive and supportive, define steps by which to strengthen the drive towards improved continuing education programmes, and undertake cooperative endeavours that ultimately may matter greatly in the capacity of library personnel to deliver the library and information services needed in today's society.

EMERGING ROLE OF PUBLIC LIBRARIANS AS E-GOVERNMENT PROVIDERS

In an effort to become more efficient, governments are moving more information and services to the Internet. As part of this transition, some agencies have begun to use technology and EGovernment to justify the elimination of staff, many of whom provide face-to-face programme support. The result is fewer agency staff able to assist government programme applicants and beneficiaries. This increase in E-Government at the expense of agency staffing raises a number of issues regarding government service delivery and support. In particular, as fewer government agency staff are able to assist existing and potential beneficiaries, citizens seek a range of assistance elsewhere.

One such institution is the public library. As local agency offices close, more citizens use the public library to: use free access to computers and the Internet; receive computer and Internet skills training; search for government servicerelated information and forms; seek government programme assistance; and receive assistance in accessing government websites, navigating programme requirements, and completing online forms. In short, the need for government agency programme and service support has not diminished, but rather, it is possible that some agencies shifted the burden of support to other entities. Although E-Government offers the potential to increase the efficiency and effectiveness of government services, E-Government as a means to reduce staff and service support may limit this potential. This is particularly the case if local agencies such as public libraries – where staff members are neither programme experts nor case workers – are expected to compensate for the reduction in government agency staff and services.

This chapter presents findings from an exploratory study that assesses the impact of E-Government on public libraries, the E-Government support roles of public libraries, and citizen expectations from public libraries regarding E-Government services. For the purposes of this chapter, the term "citizen" will be used to represent all residents of the state of Florida, regardless of nationality or country of citizenship.

Role of Public Libraries in E-Government

The E-Government Act of 2002 states the goal of E-Government as enhancing "governmental functions and service," achieving "more efficient performance," and increasing "access to Government information, and...citizen participation in Government". Since the passage of the E-Government Act, E-Government has quickly become an increasingly popular element of service delivery at the federal, state and local levels. If E-Government services are planned and executed well, they allow government agencies to increase effectiveness and efficiency, and can increase citizen trust in government.

The challenges that libraries encounter in providing E-Government vary geographically, as planning and execution of E-Government service varies between states, municipalities, and counties. Even different agencies within county governments approach E-Government in a number of different ways, and with varying levels of success. In addition to increasing effectiveness and efficiency of services, governments have increased their use of E-Government in an effort to cut operating costs. The Florida Department of Children and Families' (DCF) eliminated almost ten thousand staff positions between 1999 and 2007 with the introduction of its ACCESS Florida E-Government programme, three thousand of which are attributable directly to the ACCESS Florida initiative. The DCF ACESS programme is a "modernized public assistance service delivery system... based on streamlined workflows, policy simplification, technology innovations and partnership with local community organizations".

This programme largely eliminates DCF offices, instead, funneling applicants and programme participants to a network of Community Partners for assistance with applications and administration of accounts. DCF now counts public libraries among its Community Partners – agencies and organizations willing to provide Internet access and service assistance applicants. A close examination of the DCF Community partners list reveals that, in most counties, libraries are the only partners charged with providing free Internet access to any citizen who enters requesting service. Other partners are limited to specific constituencies. Since 1994, the Information Use Management and Policy Institute at Florida State University has conducted a national survey of public library internet connectivity. Between 1994 and 2007, Internet availability in libraries grew from approximately 21% to over 99%. Bertot, Jaeger, Langa and McClure write, "...by meeting user information needs through public access computing and Internet services, public libraries were able to serve a larger community need for access to e–government services and resources".

The 2008 national survey found that approximately 95% of public libraries provide asneeded assistance to patrons with understanding and using E-Government resources, while 69% help with E-Government applications and services. Sixty three per cent of respondents indicated that the public library was the only free public internet access point in the surrounding community. Thus, public libraries provide substantial E-Government service and resource support. One can view Government to Citizen EGovernment as a three-part system comprised of the public, the government agency involved and the networks and points of access that allow citizens to participate in EGovernment with that agency. By seeking

EGovernment information at the library and requesting assistance from librarians, citizens have added a fourth component to the system: the local librarian as a surrogate agency service provider.

In this capacity, the librarian facilitates what ideally develops into discourse around the design of the E-Government implementation in question. As library activities write:

"To develop citizen-oriented EGovernment services that achieve cost savings implies that governments...actively seek to discover what citizens want from E-Government"

Some provides a useful framework for understanding the implications of this "fourth party" service provider. The object outlines a four-part chain of interaction in E-Government development that includes developers (agencies), local designers (developers), service providers (libraries) and citizens.

The framework proposed by the library activities it is in the best interest of all parties to collaboratively develop effective ways to collect and channel patron feedback for successful, iterative development of the E-Government system. Citizens in need of government services do not bear sole responsibility for involving librarians in EGovernment service. Some agencies refer citizens to public libraries to access web-based forms or applications that are not available in their offices. The DCF ACCESS website encourages applicants to "apply for public assistance (food stamps, temporary cash assistance, and Medicaid) using the internet wherever it is available including home, a library, or a school". Because they are, in many cases, the only organizations offering free Internet access in their communities, the public library plays an instrumental role in leveling out differences in citizen access to personal computers and the Internet, moving the E-Government system away from exclusion of segments of the population, and towards "design for all".

In this role, many libraries have begun to evolve into "one-stop shops" that now include assistance with government service programmes, access, and delivery. This is a substantive departure from a longstanding role of public libraries that serve as access points to government information and forms (*i.e.*, tax forms during tax season). For example, though librarians provided tax forms in the past, they did not serve as tax accountants who assisted patrons complete and file their taxes. Now, citizens come to the library seeking government programme and services assistance, not simply access to information. This shift seems to occur in direct relation to government agencies cutting back in their provision of programme support services due to the adoption of E-Government technologies.

PURPOSE AND OBJECTIVES

The purpose of this exploratory study was to identify the E-Government related needs of citizens who access government related information at the library, and to identify current library E-Government practices in order to provide practical guidance to public libraries in meeting the needs of local community members they serve.

Specifically, the study addresses the following questions:

* What E-Government services and resources do public libraries typically provide?
* What types of E-Government assistance and/or resources do members of libraries' community members request?
* Why do citizens seek E-Government services and resources at the public library?
* What barriers and issues do librarians face in providing E-Government services and resources?

Answers to these questions can help ascertain EGovernment needs from a user perspective, but also foster understanding the impacts of E-Government on community-based support organizations such as public libraries.

The study was exploratory and used an iterative multi-method approach.

Limited to public libraries in the state of Florida, the study used:

* Interviews with public librarians. The interviews explored and identified the E-Government services

public librarians provided, and the issues encountered by public librarians in providing EGovernment services and resources.

* E-Government workshops. The study team conducted five E-Government workshops in key geographic regions to explore E-Government service provision by libraries in the regions.
* Survey of workshop attendees. The survey asked librarians to identify the most frequently provided E-Government services, and to identify issues encountered by patrons seeking E-Government assistance in local libraries.
* Librarian-maintained reference log files. The log files captured specific E-Government service and resource transactions provided to users in libraries.
* User survey. The survey explored the reasons why users came to the public library for E-Government services and resources, library services requested and used to engage in E-Government services, and issues encountered while engaging in E-Government services. The survey was available in English, Spanish, and French Creole. The survey was primarily in print format, though a web-based Survey Monkey version of the survey was available in English.

The interviews and workshops informed the development of the log file and user surveys. User surveys and log files were pre-tested to ensure their usability and ability to capture valid and reliable data.

Sampling Strategy and Data Quality

The study team employed a combination of purposeful and cluster sampling for the study's data collection efforts. The study team identified and selected public librarians who provided E-Government services in their libraries, both face-to-face and through developed web sites that contained a range of information regarding federal, state, and local government services. The study team also conducted workshops in four key geographic regions throughout the state of Florida to explore library E-Government involvement and services. Given the diversity of the state of Florida and its various communities, the regional workshops provided the study team with variations in E-Government services due to user needs in each of the regions. The individual interviews provided more in-depth information regarding librarian efforts to develop and offer E-Government services and resources in their libraries.

For the librarian logs and user surveys, the study team developed a cluster sampling approach to select libraries for participation based on:

* Library diversity *e.g.*, urban, rural, and suburban; and geographic spread throughout the state of Florida;
* Community diversity *e.g.*, poverty, immigrant, language, and a range of other library community factors; and
* Willingness to participate.

In all, 74 libraries agreed to participate in the study by maintaining library logs and distributing user surveys. The study team provided surveys in multiple languages based on librarian indications of the communities that the libraries served. The user surveys and log files were maintained and available for two weeks in March 2008. Overall, the study team interviewed nine public librarians individually, conducted workshops with 145 public librarians throughout the state, and received 415 librarian logs, and 210 usable user surveys. A total of 46 usable librarian surveys were collected during workshops. The data are limited due to the exploratory nature of the study and the purposeful and cluster sampling approaches. The five methodologies, however, provided detailed and overlapping findings regarding issues associated with providing E-Government services and resources in public libraries. By using an iterative and multi-method approach, the study team identified and triangulated perspectives on E Government in public libraries from both the public library and user populations.

Findings

The following is a brief summary of survey and librarian log data. Figure 3.1 illustrates participants' reasons for accessing E-Government information at the library, as opposed to other locations. Fifty two per cent of respondents selected "I don't own a computer," followed by "I don't have access to the internet at home or at work". The next most frequently selected response was "The internet at the library is free". Besides the given options, the two most commonly mentioned other reasons were "The library has better Internet access/ computer equipment than I have at home or work" and "the library has books/resources that I need to access for other reasons."

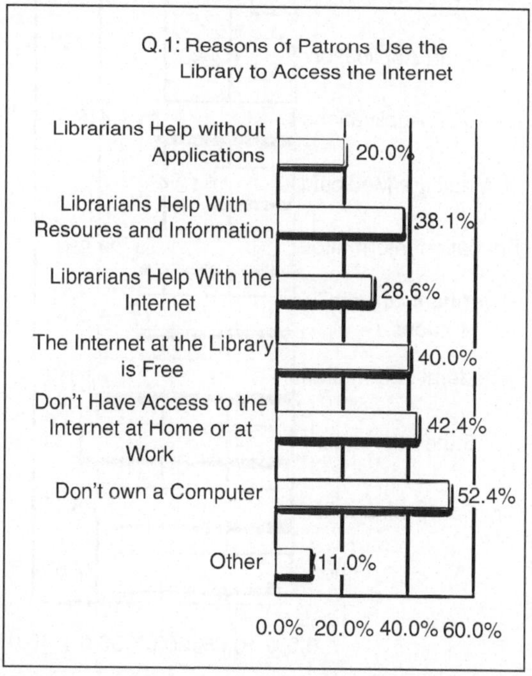

Fig. 3.1 Reasons Patrons use the Library to Access the Internet.

Figure 3.2 illustrates respondents' most frequent searches for E-Government information. Roughly 33% of respondents reported that they use the library to search for state E-Gov information, while almost as many reported that they searched for Federal (31%) and City/County Information (28.1%). Approximately 21% of respondents surveyed indicated that they used library computers to search for information on the Florida Department of Children and Families. The most commonly stated "other" responses included "research" and "e mail".

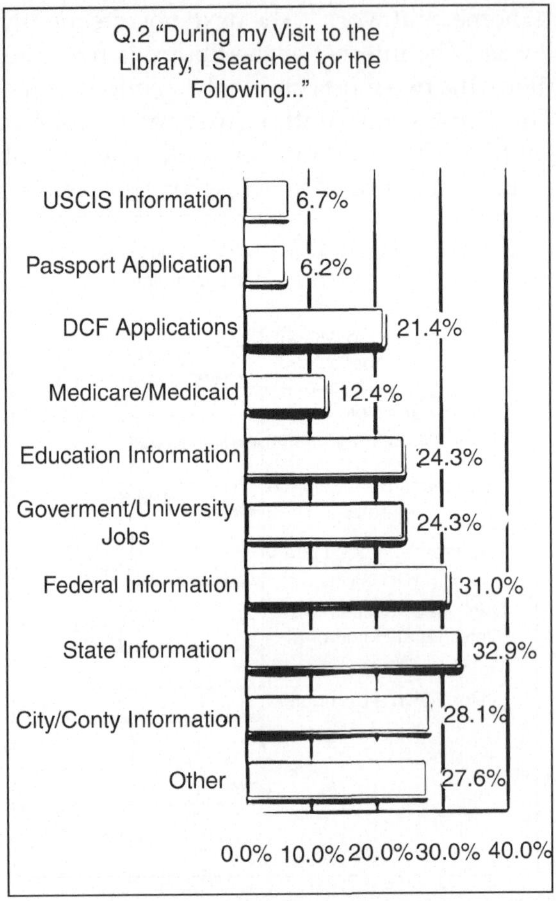

Fig. 3.2 Patron Searches by Subject.

Figure 3.3 describes problems patrons encountered in searching for E-Government information at the library. The most frequently selected response for this question was "I needed help with the Internet". Almost as many respondents mentioned that time limits on library computers presented a problem for them while searching for E-Gov information. Four per cent of respondents responded that they felt that library staff did not have sufficient knowledge to help them complete their searches. The majority of respondents who indicated "other" responded that they had no difficulty seeking government information on the Internet at the library.

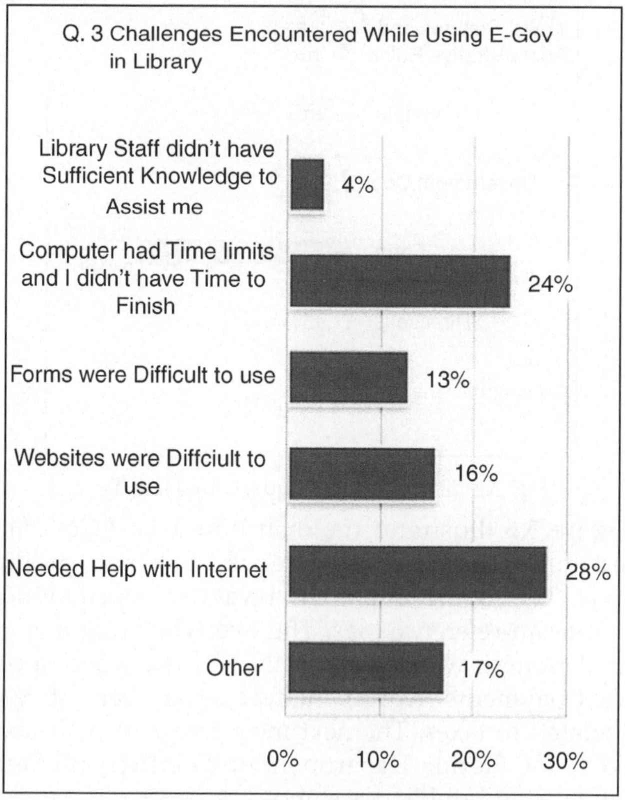

Fig. 3.3 Patron E-Gov Challenges

Figure 3.4 illustrates the type of E-Government data requested by library patrons. Only instances of requests for specific types of information were counted. Requests for general information related to E-Government topics were not counted. Approximately 40 per cent of all patron requests were related to finding or completing online government forms and/ or applications. The next most frequently requested type of information was contact information, followed by websites.

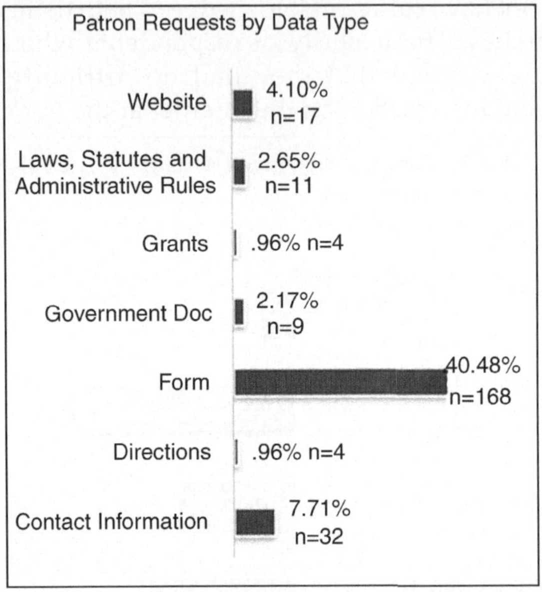

Fig. 3.4 Librarian log: Requests by Data Type

Figure 3.5 illustrates the distribution of EGovernment-related questions at the reference desk and public use terminals. The coding for this chart was developed inductively from librarian reference logs. The overwhelming majority of recorded requests were related to the IRS, taxes, and upcoming stimulus payments. Approximately 39 per cent of requests were related to taxes. The next most frequent requests were related to the Florida Department of Children and Families, food stamps and public assistance.

Approximately 15 per cent of logged requests were DCF related. In addition to these two agencies, which represented a large portion of the requests made, a number of other agencies and services emerge. Education related requests; legal advice, forms and information; United States Citizenship and Immigration Services requests; County-level property searches and ownership information; and government job searches all hovered between 3 per cent and 6 per cent.

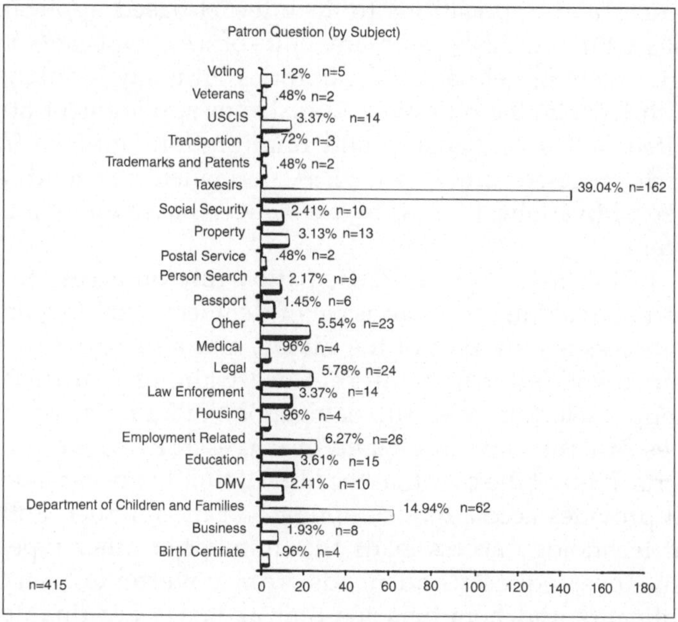

Fig. 3.5 Librarian Log: Patron Questions by subject

Key Issues

The study found a number of issues raised due to local, state and federal E-Government implementations.

Access and the Digital Divide

The transfer of some services from face-to-face to Internet-only highlights the gap between those who have and do not have access to the Internet. The digital divide continues to exist, to the detriment of citizens without access. In many communities, public libraries provide the only free access to the Internet, and thus the only link to E-Government. In some cases, E-Government is a matter of convenience. Some patrons seek websites and forms that make application for a service simpler than walking into an agency office or calling a phone number. In other cases, E-Government is the only option. The

Florida Department of Children and Families, which deals primarily with a low-income constituency, has moved its services and applications to an Internet-based application system. Since DCF closed many of its offices, applicants have begun seeking help at public libraries. In many locations in South Florida, the only way to make an appointment at the United States Citizenship and Immigration Service office, which processes immigrant visas, permanent residence and citizenship applications, is to use the web-based appointment system.

ECitizenship and E-Participation rely on access to the Internet, making access an issue of democratic participation. But access is only part of the divide, and a basic one. Users require computer and Internet use training, information resource selection, web site navigation, and a range of other types of assistance to engage in successful E-Government efforts. It is not the case that the library simply opens its doors and provides access to a computer and the Internet. Rather, that technology access leads to a number of other types of assistance requests and needs from government service applicants and beneficiaries that agencies are unable or unwilling to provide.

Resolving Life Events: The Evolving Role of the Librarian as Case Worker

The increased emphasis on E-Government in public libraries threatens to alter the role of the librarian from neutrally situated information provider to that of social worker. Instead of being asked to provide information, reference staff report being asked to help patrons resolve problems, advise patrons on which forms they need to use, and at times, assist patrons in completing applications. Patron requests ranged from help with enrolling children in childcare, to finding family members, to setting up businesses, to help going through the trademark process.

Increasingly, librarians are taking on the role of the social worker, referring patrons to one agency or another, and becoming more involved in patrons' personal lives. In addition, the needs of citizens change over the course of the year. Librarian surveys, conducted in late 2007, suggested that the greatest volume of EGovernment services were provided on behalf of the Department of Children and Families. In contrast, librarian log data collected in early 2008 suggested that most E-Government services were provided on behalf of the IRS. Together, the data demonstrate that E-Government related information needs change fluidly with external life events, such as tax season, and DCF application deadlines.

This evolution of librarian as information provider to case worker has multiple and profound implications. Not only is this a substantial shift in librarian duties, but it also requires librarians to become facile with multiple agency programmes. And, given that user life events can cut across multiple agencies, programmes, and eligible benefits, the knowledge and skills librarians need are numerous. A number of librarians commented that they had no training in being a social case worker and felt uncomfortable serving in that role.

Skills and Training

Librarians expressed concern and anxiety that they are unprepared to provide the services requested by users. While some agencies have made significant efforts to reach out to libraries and community centers that serve their target populations, many have not made any efforts to provide training to nonagency staff. As a result, libraries that embrace the role of E-Government service provider must pour significant resources into training staff, most often without assistance from local agencies. In short, librarians that engage in the provision of EGovernment services and resources are self-taught and can often lack an essential programmatic perspective.

There is a need for increased communication and cooperation between libraries and the government agencies on state and local levels. Local agency offices are often unaware of the level of service libraries are able to offer, and direct patrons to the library for services they may not provide. They also argued that state agencies often shut down local offices without consideration for the restrictions of the local library's funding, resources, or space. To some degree, librarians do not have a choice whether to assist or not assist someone needing help in using E-Government resources or services. If the person is present and needs assistance then the librarian will likely try to assist them as best they can – regardless of the level of training the librarian has received regarding E-Government. Thus, an area for additional research is the quality of the EGovernment services that librarians can provide – especially in the current Florida context of severe budget cutbacks, reduced library hours of operations and increasing overall library use.

Liability

As library staff members are asked to assist patrons with forms and applications, and to handle more sensitive personal information, librarians and administrators grow more concerned over possible liability issues. This anxiety includes civil and criminal concerns. Fear over possible lawsuits against library staff, administrators, and city/county councils, and criminal consequences associated with entering false information on behalf of library patrons lead some libraries to avoid EGovernment altogether. A few local library administrators restrict librarians from providing assistance with E-Government forms. In some cases, library staff members are instructed to limit EGovernment help to locating forms as requested, and to provide no help in interpreting or completing applications. But overall, there are no clear guidelines as to "how much assistance" in filling out forms requiring a range of personal information and explanation is too much assistance on the part of the librarian.

Forcing Technology Management Changes

Library public access computer and Internet resources are not limitless. Libraries only have a certain number of public access computers available for use. Indeed, 82.5% of libraries report that they have insufficient public access computers some or all of the time and 93.4% have time limits on workstation use. Given this, libraries have had to purchase, install, and maintain public access management software that manages user workstation registration process, enforces time limits, and resets the computers after each session. Time limits, imposed to alleviate public access computer and Internet access demands on limited library resources, are often in direct conflict with E-Government services requirements, which can often take considerable time and effort. Librarians either have to try and remove the time limit features, set up E-Government workstations, or risk the loss of E-Government application and other information by users. Thus, EGovernment service provision can impose a substantial management and infrastructure burden on libraries.

An Unfunded Mandate: Resources and Burden Shifting

When state and federal agencies send citizens to county-funded public libraries to access EGovernment forms, schedule appointments and seek information instead of providing that information in the traditional office setting, they add to an overall increase in the number of patrons requesting EGovernment services. Library services are provided by local tax revenue and libraries' budgets are significantly stressed. The increase in EGovernment users taxes the human and financial resources of already strained local libraries, increasing costs associated with staff time, computer equipment, and Internet bandwidth.

Although Florida's budget reductions represent an extreme case, reduced library funding is a national issue, made worse by downturns in the economy Agencies that choose to exchange face-to-face services for Internet based services are, in many cases, actually shifting personnel and operating costs to locally funded organizations that provide "free" public Internet access and assistance. Local agency offices are often unaware of what level of service libraries are prepared to offer, and direct patrons to the library for services they may not be in a position to provide.

State agencies often shut down local offices without consideration for the restrictions of the local library's funding, resources, or space. While some local libraries are able to absorb the costs associated with a spike in use, others cannot, and risk closure when local agency offices close their doors. This burden shift amounts to an unfunded mandate from state agencies to local, city and county governments that fund local library systems. Libraries are put in the position of providing services that they may not have the staff, expertise, equipment, or funding to deliver, or risk the ire of a patron base that provides the library's funding. Because public libraries are not legally mandated, community support is sometimes the only protection a library has at its disposal to maintain its operations. The extent to which reductions in state staffing at DCF, for example, have resulted in increased costs for public libraries in Florida, reductions in other library services, and staff time to meet E-Government service demands is an area for future investigation.

4

National Library Policy and Library Legislation

NATIONAL POLICY ON PUBLIC LIBRARIES IN INDIA

Pre–Five-Year Plan Period

The programmes executed by provincial and central governments since 1910 for the social and adult education of the populace have paved the way for the enactment of library laws and rules for grants-in-aid in the country. Hence, public library finance is part of the education budget. The level of literacy in 1941 being as low as 16 per cent, universalization of elementary education and eradication of illiteracy in the nation were the aims of the education policy of the government. To fulfil this goal, a variety of programmes were undertaken such as extension services, continuing education, social education, part-time education, refresher courses, non-formal education, and adult education.

In order to accelerate the pace of socio–economic development, the government considered public libraries to be an integral part of development projects. In 1948, the first public library bill was passed in the state of Madras, mainly due to the efforts of the eminent librarian S.R. Ranganathan. One of the earliest Advisory Committees-the Sinha Committee, appointed in 1957-recommended that public libraries be developed on the basis of a hierarchical network. The hierarchy should have the national central library at the apex, followed by state central libraries, district libraries, block libraries and panchayat libraries. This is the foundation upon which the public library system has been built.

First Five-Year Plan (1951–1956)

The first plan provision was ₹ 140 million for social education, physical education, and youth welfare, out of the total budget for education of ₹ 1.33 billion. Libraries were considered to be part of social education. ₹ 5 million was set aside for establishment of the national central library, but this sum was not used.

Improvement of library services was mentioned in this plan for educational development. The essence of the scheme was to establish district libraries in each state, which were to be supplemented by a state central library. The government of India also initiated a scheme, "Integrated Library Service," with the support of the state government. The scheme targeted units in every area selected by the governments for intensive educational development.

The experimental project was meant to monitor the impact of a number of educational institutions in areas covering 100 villages. Each area was to have five model community centers, plus a main library with branches to distribute books to 20 villages. This pilot project was implemented in 29 areas in the country. Nine states made plans to open state central libraries, and some others were in the process of setting up district libraries in about 100 districts. This cost approximately ₹ 10 million, of which nearly two–thirds was contributed by the government of India. Thus, libraries were considered to be an essential part of the Community Development Programme that was launched during the first plan period.

Other important developments included establishment of the Delhi Public Library in 1951. The Central Reference Library in Calcutta was established in 1955. Connemara Public Library, in Madras became the State Central Library in 1950 under the provisions of the Madras Public Libraries Act of 1948; in 1955, it became one of the three depository libraries. At the end of March 1954, the country had 32,000 libraries with a book stock of about 7.1 million volumes; an amount of ₹ 9 million was spent on library services. By 1951, the level of literacy had risen to 18.33 per cent.

In 1954, the Delivery of Books Act was passed to include newspapers. The act obligated every publisher in India to deposit a copy of its publication with the National Library in Calcutta; the Asiatic Society Library, Bombay; Connemara Public Library, Madras; and the Delhi Public Library. On the basis of books received under this act, India has a national bibliography which is published by the Central Reference Library, Calcutta. The bibliography, however, does not include textbooks, musical scores, maps, and atlases.

Second Five-Year Plan, (1956–1961)

Of the ₹ 2.040 billion budgeted for education, ₹ 100 million was proposed for social education, physical education, and youth welfare. This plan contained the same provisions as the first plan, plus additional provisions for establishing integrated library service. There were three objectives. First, state and district libraries were to be set up in each state. Second, the library services were to be organized on the basis of legislation. Finally, district libraries were to form the link between the state central library and village libraries. As a result, nine states in India established state central libraries and 254 district libraries. But the national central library was still not established. In 1960, the state of Andhra Pradesh enacted library legislation.

During this plan period, a total of ₹ 2.040 billion was spent on educational development, of which ₹ 9 million was spent on library development. Even though ₹ 18.6 million was provided, the states only used 48.6 per cent of this amount. Thus, the number of libraries nearly doubled in 1964 as compared to 1951, and the expenditure on public libraries in this period increased three–fold. A UNESCO report published on the occasion of the Public Library Seminar held at Delhi in 1955, India had 24,086 public library service points at the time. The level of literacy in 1961 increased to 28.31 per cent.

The Advisory Committee for Libraries was appointed in 1957 by the Government of India, with K.P. Sinha as the chairman.

The committee drafted a Model Library Bill and drew up a 25-year plan. In 1959, the committee submitted a report with recommendations, some of which follow:

* Enact library legislation, in all constituent states, to establish public libraries;
* Build nationwide library service with detailed suggestions for financing through the state and central governments;
* Extend public library service to the blocks, panchayats, and villages; and,
* Create an independent Department of Social Education and Libraries.

Third Five-Year Plan, (1962–1967)

The amount of ₹ 5.6 billion was budgeted for education in this plan period, but the amount to be spent on libraries was not clearly indicated in the plan. Of this amount, ₹ 620 million was expected to be available for social education. During this plan period, the system of central government assistance to the states was changed, and funding for libraries was kept to a bare minimum.

Thus, it was up to the individual states to take the initiative and develop their public libraries. With the beginning of this plan period, the scheme to assist state governments in establishing state central libraries, district central libraries, and block development libraries was abandoned. The central government decided to let the states decide on the development; the decision was a major setback that hindered the development of public libraries.

During this plan period, four national libraries were to be established at Delhi, Calcutta, Bombay, and Madras.

District–level libraries were to be established in all the states. A sum of ₹ 32.3 million was made available to the states for this purpose.

In 1962 the central government sent a model Public Libraries Bill to those state governments which had not adopted any library legislation, hoping to persuade these states to show an interest in passing the legislation.

A Working Group on Libraries was appointed by the Planning Commission in 1964. Group recommendations included:

* By the end of the Fifth Five Year Plan, set up libraries at block headquarters and in every village having a population of 5,000;
* Encourage the Programme of Adult Education to use the services of the public libraries to eradicate illiteracy.

As of January 1, 1965, according to the information received from the states by the Working Group:

* Twelve of 18 states/UT had state central libraries;
* 205 of 327 districts had district central libraries;
* 1,394 blocks of 5,223 had block development libraries;
* 28,317 villages out of 566,878 had village libraries.

Library legislation was passed in two states during this period: Karnataka in 1965, and Maharashtra in 1967.

Fourth Five-Year Plan, (1969–1974)

The education budget was estimated at ₹ 7.120 billion of which the social education component was ₹ 100 million. Thus, the tempo that had built for the development of library services slowed. However, ₹ 130 million was provided in this plan period for provision of information services, which included information centers, radio transmitters, film production, mobile cine vans, and other media. The literacy level rose to 34.45 per cent in 1971.

In 1972, the Working Group on Development of Public Libraries was constituted by the Government of India Planning Commission to make recommendations for library development. These recommendations were to be included in the Fifth Five Year Plan.

The group submitted detailed proposals for:

* Allotment of ₹ 310 million for the development of public libraries; but the amount actually provided was a meager ₹ 20 million;
* A network of libraries to cover the whole country, and other recommendations similar to those made earlier by the Advisory Committee.

Figures provided in 1973 concerned the number of public libraries, and read as follows:

* Fifteen of 21 states/UT had state central libraries;
* 235 of 376 districts had district central libraries;
* 1,500 of 3,100 sub–districts had sub–district central libraries;
* 50,000 villages of 566,878 had village libraries;
* 1,800 of 2,641 towns had town libraries.

In 1972, during this plan period, the central government established the Raja Rammohun Roy Library Foundation. The foundation was created as an autonomous body under the Department of Culture, controlled by the Ministry of Education, for the development of public libraries in India. This foundation matches the funds of the states for purchasing furniture and books, organizing conferences and seminars, and providing mobile library service to the rural areas. It also advises the central government on all matters relating to library development in the country.

Fifth Five-Year Plan, (1974–1979)

An adult education programme was the emphasis of this plan. The programme was to be supported by a network of libraries at the village and block levels, and various community centers. Thus, steps were taken to strengthen not only the village and block libraries, but also the central and state libraries, and the district libraries. The states were assisted by the Raja Rammohun Roy Library Foundation, which was established in 1972. During this plan period, the amount of ₹ 15.620 billion was allocated for general education, and ₹ 350 million was budgeted for social education.

The only state that enacted a public library law during this plan period was West Bengal, in 1979. In 1978, the government adopted the National Adult Education Programme, but it did not recognize the public library as an agency that could be assigned a role in solving the literacy problem. Rather, the public library was relegated to the role of post–literacy work. This view was also promulgated by the Draft National Policy on Education (NPE), 1979. However, the need for the rural public library system to play a role in continuing education in the villages and rural areas was recognized.

In 1979, the Ministry of Education in the Department of Culture established a library section under the charge of an under secretary. The goal: to promote development of public libraries in India. Since then, libraries have not been part of the social education budget. Instead, they have been included in the art and culture component of the budget.

Sub–Sixth Five-Year Plan, (1980–1985)

This plan emphasized minimum essential education of all adults, to be achieved by inter-sectoral cooperation and interand150; agency coordination. These efforts were to be supported by post–literacy, continuing education through a network of rural libraries as well as instructional programmes conducted through mass communication media. The amount allocated for general education was ₹ 21.622 billion. The art and culture component was ₹ 839 million.

During this period:

* Twenty–six states/UT out of 31 existing in 1982 had established/designated state central libraries;
* Out of 401 districts, 291 had district central libraries;
* Out of 5,027 blocks, 1,798 development blocks had block libraries;
* Out of 575,936 villages, 41,828 had village libraries;
* Out of 2,643 towns, 1,280 had town libraries.

Of the 29 metropolitan cities with a population of 400,000 and above, only four — Madras, Hyderabad, Bangalore, and Delhi — have city public library systems with central libraries, branches, and deposit stations. Thus, it is estimated that approximately 20 per cent of the literate population has access to public library service.

A Working Group on Modernization of Library Services and Informatics in the Seventh Plan was appointed by the Planning Commission in 1983. In its 1984 report, the group recommended formulation of a National Policy on Library Services and Informatics in support of similar recommendations made earlier by other committees.

From its establishment in 1972, to 1982, the Raja Rammohun Roy Foundation provided funds of ₹ 250 million to assist 15,000 rural libraries. In 1982, the Delhi Public Library became a copyright library. The level of literacy increased to 43.56 per cent in 1981.

Seventh Five-Year Plan, (1985–1990)

During this Plan period, the Planning Commission's objective was to address the needs of 90 million people, ages 15–35, in the Adult Education Programme. The network of libraries was to play a role in the development of literature for neoliterates. Library systems were to be strengthened with specific attention given to improvement of facilities at the national-level institutions. The general education budget was ₹ 47,753 million; ₹ 4.821 billion constituted the art and culture component.

An important development during this period was the 1986 adoption of the National Literacy Mission, which emphasized the education of women and also the establishment of rural libraries.

In 1989, there were 7,180 main libraries and 18,000 service points. The collections of the National Library of Calcutta were increased significantly. The Central Secretariat Library started creating a database on the epic "Mahabharata." The Raja Rammohun Roy Foundation set up an "Integrated Research Cell-cum-Computer Unit" for promoting research in librarianship, and also started a database of public libraries in the country. A Committee on National Policy on Library and Information System was appointed in 1985 by the Government of India, Department of Culture. The resulting final report was submitted in 1986. This policy stressed the need to establish strong links between a village's community library and primary school. If the school lacked a library, the community library was to provide the children with adequate resources. Furthermore, a children's section was to be organized in every public library.

The National Policy on Education, 1986 barely mentions libraries. It states that a nationwide movement for improvement of existing libraries and the establishment of new ones will be taken up, provision will be made in all educational institutions for library facilities, and the status of librarians improved. The school library programme, "Operation Blackboard," was initiated with the provision of essential teaching and learning materials.

The National Book Policy–1986 also had an impact on libraries, as it recommended:

* Provision of reading material for children by all the agencies involved;
* That 10 per cent of the annual education budget of the governments be used to purchase books for libraries.

During this plan period, these states passed library acts: Manipur in 1988, Assam in 1989, Haryana in 1989, and Kerala in 1989.

Eighth Five-Year Plan, (1992–1997)

The money allocated for this period for general education is ₹ 168.133 billion; for art and culture, ₹ 7.276 billion has been allocated. Universalization of elementary education, eradication of illiteracy in the 15-35-year age group, and strengthening of vocational education in relation to emerging needs in urban and rural settings are the major thrusts of the plan. These goals are to be achieved by using formal, non-formal, and open channels of learning. The plan states that in those states with an advanced library system, rural libraries should become the focal points for post–literacy and continuing education programmes.

Book promotion is also emphasized in this plan, to be promoted by the organization of a National Centre for Children's Literature, which should produce 3,000 titles annually. Important books are to be translated into the various Indian languages, and books for neoliterates published. Publishers and voluntary agencies will be given assistance, and the school library programme, undertaken as part of the "Operation Blackboard" scheme of the National Policy on Education-1986, will continue.

Public libraries of national importance are to be provided funds for improvements/innovations such as the following:

* The Khuda Baksh Public Library proposed establishment of an Institute of Oriental Studies and open regional units for research on Indo-Islamic and comparative religion;
* The Rampur Raza Library would acquire sophisticated equipment for preservation of its collections;
* The Asiatic Society, Calcutta, is to open an art gallery, introduce a desktop publishing system, and construct a new building;
* The National Library proposed making microfilms available, producing a national union catalogue, and providing book production statistics;
* The Central Reference Library is to be reorganized into a National Bibliographical and Documentation Center with a computer center; and,
* The Delhi Public Library is to open two new libraries within its service area.

The Raja Rammohun Roy Foundation proposes assisting state central libraries in their quest to obtain reprographic equipment. The Foundation also hopes to assist certain libraries in the processing of rare books, and to provide assistance to rural libraries, and to those public libraries that have completed 100 years of service.

The Model Public Libraries Act is based on the national seminar on this subject, which was held February 14, 1990, in New Delhi. The seminar was organized by the Indian Library

Association in collaboration with the Raja Rammohun Roy Library Foundation. This excellent document encompasses all aspects of legislation important to the establishment of public libraries.

The National Cultural Policy, 1993 is the new policy designed by the Government of India. It was created by merging the National Policy of Library and Information Science, the National Book Policy, and other related policies dealt with by the Department of Culture of the Ministry of Human Resource Development.

LIBRARY LEGISLATION

The Nature of the Problem

It would appear at first sight that provision and public maintenance of a system of public libraries would be an obvious step in any country where education and the promotion of literacy were considered important. Education, after all, is not an end in itself; the individual must not only have access to the printed word during his period of formal education, he must have the means of enlarging his experience after school and university, and this necessarily implies organized collections of printed materials. If a library is an essential adjunct to school or college, it is an essential adjunct in the world outside.

One would also think that the legislative base for such a system of public libraries would be a comparatively simple matter, and that those libraries would automatically be free for all to use. It is almost universally recognized that education should be compulsory, and that it should be free up to a certain level. True, cost can be a limiting factor but few countries today do not devote a large proportion of their resources to educational provision. Neither of these assumptions is in fact correct. Systems of public libraries, as against individual public libraries, have only recently been recognized as essential, even in advanced countries, and many countries, some with a secure basis of culture and education, do not have generally applicable public library legislation. Examples are France,

Belgium, the Netherlands and Italy. Even where public library legislation has been long established, it can be seen from the examples studied here that, in the framework of the modern State, public library law is noticeably defective. The development of public libraries has probably been hampered by the paradox that they were in fact recognized as instruments of popular education and social welfare long before the conception of compulsory education and before the legal framework of the modern State was established. The concept of the public library has been essentially that of a local community project.

All countries have public libraries, buildings where books are provided for general reading, either free of charge or for a small subscription. They have been provided in thousands all over the world by charitable bodies, educational, social and religious organizations, by philanthropic individuals, as memorials to a person or to commemorate an occasion. The public libraries in England and the United States in the early nineteenth century were typical, but they are not always a passing phase of development. The traveller interested in the phenomenon will come across examples almost anywhere: in Asia, for example, the Hardinge Library in Delhi, the Connemara Library in Madras, the Raffles Library in Singapore; in Africa, the King George VI Memorial Library in Tanga, the Connaught Library in Nairobi. Some become moribund. Some are being or have been incorporated by good fortune into a national or local public library system. Some operate even today with some success. But they are not public libraries in the modern accepted sense, nor were they, for that matter, in the nineteenth century.

Edward Edwards, pioneer of the public library in Great Britain, summed up their built-in failure over a hundred years ago, in evidence to the Select Committee on Public Libraries of the House of Commons in 1849:

* Without some assured provision of the means of continued increase, as well as simple preservation-no man ever secured to posterity the true advantage of a public library. To those persons, therefore, who

took thought of such matters, two principles to start with seemed plain. The one that new libraries should be formed in a catholic spirit. The other, that they should be freed from all dependence either in gifts or in current 'subscriptions', for their permanent support. The first principle involved the corollary that the new institutions and their management should stand entirely aloof from party influences in politics or religion. The second principle involved the corollary that the maintenance must be by rate, levied on the whole tax-paying community, and administered by its elective and responsible functionaries.

This statement quite obviously implied that a legal basis was necessary, if the public library was to be a permanent institution and on the implications of this statement most of the public library legislation of the nineteenth century and early twentieth century was founded.

In 1949, Unesco issued the first international declaration on the need and the functions of the public library, and in it was contained the same principle:

* This manifesto, by describing the potentialities of the public library, proclaims Unesco's belief in the public library as a living force for popular education and for the growth of international understanding and thereby for the promotion of peace.
* The public library is a product of modern democracy and a practical demonstration of democracy's faith in universal education as a lifelong process.
* Though primarily intended to serve the educational needs of adults, the public library should also supplement the work of schools in developing the reading tastes of children and young people, helping them to become adults who can use books with appreciation and profit.
* As a democratic institution operated by the people for the people, the public library should be: established and maintained under clear authority of

law: supported wholly or mainly from public funds: open for free use on equal terms to all members of the community, regardless of occupa-tion, creed, class, or race.

The manifesto goes on to define the purposes and list some of the services of the public library. It did not, however, attempt to deal with a problem that was already engaging the attention of public librarians and those concerned with the spread of education and literacy, that there must not only be a legal base, but that that base must give equal opportunity to all citizens to use the services of public libraries. In other words, the legislation must be mandatory and cover the whole of the area falling within the scope of the legislation. The legislation must also provide for something more than opportunities for voluntary co-operation between libraries-it must provide for a nation-wide service, even though the public library remains a locally rooted institution. In 1953, Unesco organized its first seminar on public libraries in developing countries, at Ibadan, in Nigeria. Eighteen countries were represented, mostly in West Africa. Legislation was one of the primary subjects discussed, and in the general report of the seminar, the following statement of principles was included:

* Only legislation can empower the appropriate authorities to provide the service and ensure adequate financial support and efficient administration according to a national standard. Only legislation can define the functions of the providing authority, create the conditions in which it may fulfil those functions, and ensure development.

Library law for national schemes should include the following elements:

* General authorization of expenditure without fixing a maximum.
* Compulsory implementation whenever conditions become favourable. The basis of favourable conditions, it is suggested, is the possession of necessary finance and all requisite material by the

providing authority, the existence of a tested organization and the presence of trained and experienced personnel. Compulsory provision is never likely to precede compulsory primary education.

* The obligation to employ only qualified and trained personnel as librarians, and to authorize development only when professional librarians are available to administer the service.
* Service for the entire population in some form or other.
* The inter-lending of books between libraries so that the book resources of the whole territory shall be available to all.
* The book stock shall embrace every shade of opinion, without prejudice to anyone.
* The national scheme in all its parts shall aim at free service.

An addendum to this statement pointed out that there was great difficulty in arriving at a conclusion regarding compulsory legislation, since it was recognized that permissive legislation might well allow for a high standard to be set by enthusiastic authorities, which would act as an inspiration to others. This, and other proposals of the Ibadan seminar, were an act of faith at the time they were published, in view of the conditions of West Africa at the time, just beginning to emerge from colonial rule, with very few African librarians. But the statement was the beginning from which can be traced the rapid development of public library services in Ghana, Eastern Nigeria and Sierra Leone, based on simple but mandatory legislation. In 1955, the Public Libraries Section of the International Federation of Library Associations published a memorandum on the development of public library services, of which one section was devoted to legislation:

Each State should adopt library laws which will include the following provisions:

* Appropriate local authorities must be empowered to expend public funds for public library purposes.

* The amount of local expenditure should not be limited: local authorities should be able to expend as much as they are willing and able.
* The public library purposes for which funds may be expended shall be so defined as not to restrict development.
* Local authorities should be empowered to enter into arrangements with other local authorities for joint schemes for providing the whole or any part of the service, and to contribute to the cost of schemes for cooperation and mutual assistance.
* Each local authority should appoint a library committee directly responsible to the local council.
* Each local authority should have power to appoint staff who shall be employed in accordance with the conditions and regulations applicable to other local government officers.
* The use of all the services provided must be available to all inhabitants free of any charge whatsoever.
* Though each local authority provides services primarily for the use of its own inhabitants and those who work or study in its area, other persons living outside that area should be able to use those services if they wish... when adequate library services are provided generally in a country or region, however, they should be available to all, regardless of place of residence, without payment.

As soon as practicable, all appropriate local authorities should be legally obliged to maintain adequate public library services. The document was adopted as a statement of policy, with the recommendation that it be sent for study to all governments and appropriate agencies concerned. One further example may be given of the continuing concern with the importance of library legislation. In October 1955, Unesco organized a further seminar on public libraries, this time at Delhi, India, where a successful demonstration project had been founded. The seminar was held in the Delhi Public

Library and twelve Asian countries were represented by forty-six librarians and educators. Again, public library legislation and its nature were under discussion, and the following proposals were accepted:

Over-all control and co-operation of development, to provide for a permanent and progressive national public library service, can be obtained only by legislation, which should provide for the following:

* Opportunity for the development of public library service which will be available to all people on the basis of free and equal access.
* An independent service, and not one attached to another department.
* The constitution of a governing body, to be referred to in this report as the central library board, or in a federal state a number of such bodies, subject to a national body with advisory functions.
* Provision for adequate public finance.
* The constitution of district library boards responsible for administration of units of public library service.

Other parts of the report pay tribute to the work done by private bodies in founding and maintaining public library services, but affirm that planned direction and control are now required, and that these cannot be achieved by subsidy to private organizations. On finance the report states: It is of fundamental importance that finance should be by public funds, whether national, state or local, or a combination of these... differences in the structure, powers and financial resources of government at local, state, and national level are such that a simple statement of general applicability cannot be made. It can be said however that sources of finance must be adequate for the support of the service established. The proportion of local funds to national or state funds is a matter for decision by individual governments.

On the unit of service:

* At an early stage in the establishment of a national public library service, the question arises of the convenient administrative unit. This may be defined

> as the smallest autonomous unit of public library service... the selection of this unit as the real basis for the development of public library service, is a matter of some importance. It should be a viable area as regards finance and administration, and should conform as for as possible to existing local government boundaries... for ideal development, the area chosen should contain both rural and urban districts.

It is illustrative of the complexity of the problem that these four authoritative statements on public library development, issued over a short period of time, should vary so greatly in their emphasis. The Unesco Manifesto concentrated on the value and use of the public library, but said nothing about its financial or legislative base. The Ibadan seminar defined as a first principle that only legislation could provide the necessary secure and permanent foundations. It said nothing about the administrative unit on which implementation must depend, or financial problems, but it did prescribe mandatory legislation under favourable conditions.

The IFLA statement, though it defined the nature of public library service, proposed what was in fact permissive legislation, and it did not make any proposals about central control, the size of the administrative area, or financial viability of local authority areas. Although it said there should be no upper limit on expenditure, it did not mention the vital problem of minimum expenditure. The Delhi seminar proposals, with the previous statements before it, went much further, and proposed legislation which would provide for over-all control, viable areas and financial support at national and local level. But it found itself in difficulties when it attempted to define the nature of the viable area. Any acceptable general statement must be vitiated by the enormous differences between countries in national administrative and executive structure, local government and its relationship to central government, the powers existing at different levels of government, and above all, the financial capacity of these different levels.

The stage of educational and technical development of a country must also be taken into account, but this is possibly not quite as important as it may appear. While literacy is obviously a primary requirement of public library use, most countries now have an extensive programme of primary and secondary education, and in many countries, too, advanced technology exists side by side with primitive standards of living in some areas. It should also be remembered that in the last century, in some countries, notably the United Kingdom, public library legislation actually preceded general legislation on education. It would be a mistake, also, to assume that the problems of public library legislation are confined to the developing countries. If there is one thing that emerges quite clearly from this study of public library law, it is that the problems of an adequate and effective library law are just as great in the more advanced countries as in the developing ones, apart from the fact that some advanced countries do not yet have a general public library law.

In some countries, such as the United Kingdom, the United States and Canada, the problem is primarily one of reshaping law which is defective and inadequate to meet the need of the user of the public library in the twentieth century, who requires access to the enormous and increasing flood of printed material, numbered in books by the hundred thousand, and periodicals by the thousand. These requirements create in their turn a need for more and more specialized and trained personnel. The search is for a legislative base for viable units which can meet the readers' needs, and provide not only the material, but the technical services, equipment and staff required.

In other advanced countries, such as Norway and Denmark, the problem is not one of the viable unit, which in fact cannot be provided, but of compulsory co-operation to give the same results. The problems facing the developing countries may be different, but not so very different. It has often been stated that in social legislation, some African and Asian countries are at the stage others had reached in the nineteenth century. This is only superficially true. We are all living in the twentieth century. If the legislation of the nineteenth century is to be repeated, there is a long road to travel. Not only long, but unnecessary. The example of the past is to be learned from, not repeated.

Basic Principles and Practical Considerations in the Framing of Legislation

Assuming for the purpose of this chapter that new legislation is being considered, the first consideration in the framing of legislation is, of course, the nature of the State itself and the place that legislation takes in its structure. Particularly in social legislation such as the establishment of public libraries, which has primarily a local impact, account must be taken of the nature of the authority by which national government passes on its responsibilities, the basis of taxation at local and national level and in a federal State, the constitutional rights of established organisms within the State. Even where there is no general legislation, in countries where the doctrine of ultra quires does not apply and organs of local government may establish any service they are not specifically forbidden to do, public libraries may exist perfectly legally by local legislation, and this in turn will cause difficulties in framing a general law.

This is the case in the Federal Republic of Germany, and to some extent in the Netherlands and Belgium. Apart from this, there are patterns in the relationship of local government to national government which must be taken into account. H. F. Alderferl in his study of local government in developing countries, identifies four basic patterns, which are established in developing countries either through adoption or by passing on of previous colonial development. The French pattern, which exists in a large part of Africa, carries the doctrine of ultra vires much further than in England or the United States. Local government has no powers not granted to it by constituted authority.

Local government also is subject to executive jurisdiction which is independent of the administrative and legislative branch to a great extent. Generally, he states, French local government is characterized by centralization, chain of command, hierarchical structure, executive domination and legislative subordination. The English pattern, as defined by Alderfer, is characterized by decentralization, with local decision-making bodies with more or less independent powers, as against concentration, in the French pattern, where all power lies with the central government with local units acting as agents.

The English pattern generally implies also legislative dominance, the committee system and voluntary citizen participation. The Soviet system is one of 'democratic centralism', with all organs as links in one continuous chain of governmental power. Communist Party direction and leadership exist at all levels, and local agencies are not law-making or executive bodies in their own right, but subject to correction not only at the next higher level but at other levels. The 'traditional' form of local government is non-Western, though in Western forms there are traditional residues. The pattern is one of a chief or local leader, or a group of people, having jurisdiction over a village or group of villages. Essentially the form is non-urban, but it has deep roots and cannot be ignored as a working unity.

The Indian panchayat system of local government is an example of a traditional form being incorporated into the local government system of a modern State, organized generally on the English system. The clash between two systems, and the different types of law that may be produced, was illustrated in Africa when, at a UNESCO seminar at Enugu in 1961, the question of a model Act for African countries was discussed. The Act proposed was on the English model. This was simple and mandatory, giving almost unlimited authority to an independent board, subject to central government control. It was this type of legislation which has been successful in practice in Ghana, Eastern Nigeria and Tanzania.

The delegates from the French-speaking countries could not accept this since it was not an acceptable type of legislation for their countries, and they proposed a different model Act for their purposes. Without quoting this in full, it can be said that it was at once more detailed and less specific. Though it set up a directorate attached to the Ministry of Education, and advisory bodies, it could be said to be rather a statement of intention than a legislative instrument. Subsequent decrees in the various territories have similar structure. Thus, the decree for the Ivory Coast goes into some detail on expenditures and staff required, but does not provide for means of raising the necessary funds or an organization charged with continuous development.

The differences may be more apparent than real, given a determination to create a public library service, but it does seem that in Europe, the Scandinavian countries, the United Kingdom and Ireland have been more successful, through planned co-operation between local and national government, than for instance, in France. A recent survey in Le Monde of the public libraries of Paris showed enormous variations in expenditure on libraries in the various communes, with seemingly no co-operation or standards imposed centrally. A generous system of subsidies for building is offered by the central government, but there does not appear to be any way of forcing local authorities to take advantage of them if they do not wish to provide their share.

There are other, important factors to consider in pre-consideration of legislation. Some investigation must be made of the practical problems, and a body of facts built up. While the survey is important, it must be a practical move towards action, and not an end in itself or a means of delaying action. One of the most successful librarians in charge of a library service in a developing country has said that until a service is provided it is impossible to say what sort of service is needed. A careful analysis at grass roots level involves a detailed statistical examination of a community-its growth rate, its educational levels, its literacy rates; it involves the testing of different types of reading materials and a survey of existing places for reading and studying.

Such an approach overlooks the complete lack of basic statistics on which to base the survey. And above all, it ignores the sense of urgency which permeates any developing country trying to pull itself into the twentieth century by its bootstraps.

I am sure that these critics would produce a magnificent report. . . and that report would probably conclude that the contemplation of any form of library service was premature. By the time it appeared it would have been overtaken by events, such is the speed of development of Africa today. This may be overstating the case against survey, but it is true that a survey should be made after decision-to discover specific problems and how they might be overcome.

These problems can be summarized as follows:

* *Educational Situation:* The provision of libraries depends on adult literacy, and is also concerned with the provision of primary education. Literacy rates based on averages are deceptive-for instance, the adult literacy rate in India is less than 20 per cent, but in Delhi in 1954 it was nearly 40 per cent and is now over 50 per cent. The Government of India report of 1959 did not consider that a literacy rate of 20 per cent was any barrier to a nationally organized public library service, but of course one would assume that a low average literacy rate would suggest concentration on urban areas. In terms of cost relative to use, there would be no point in providing for an elaborate system of mobile libraries to serve rural areas.
* *Language and Book Production:* The number of languages in use and their relative importance is a factor in pre-consideration. Allied to this is the matter of book production. Lack of book production in the national language is an extreme limiting factor, though the establishment of public libraries may well stimulate production and in fact has done so in some countries. But it must be observed that the success of public library development in some African countries has been due largely to the fact that English is the established language of communication, thus giving immediate access to an abundant source of material.
* *Population Density and Concentration:* It goes without saying that a rural and scattered population is more

difficult to provide for than an urban one. The problem therefore is not one so much of over-all density as of concentration, and this can well affect the unit of administration

* *Communications:* This also affects the matter of the unit, and administrative arrangements. Decentralization may well be necessary. This may be a problem of organization rather than legislation, but it must be considered.
* *Income and tax structure:* This affects the time factor during which legislation can be expected to come into effect, and also the proportion of cost to be met from various sources.
* *Existing Legislation:* This may exist nationally or locally, and consideration must be given to its possible incorporation in new legislation. In some countries, Ceylon is an example, effective public libraries exist in some areas through local legislation, and a new library law must take into account their existence and their legislative base.
* *'Trained Librarians and Training Facilities:* While most countries will have trained librarians, though not in public libraries, pre-consideration must take into account the availability of trained librarians to implement legislation. Opportunities for training abroad must also be considered. While it is an important consideration, the availability of trained librarians is no more than a temporary limiting factor, since there is little point in training unless there are opportunities for employment. In India and Pakistan, facilities for training and qualification are in advance of employment possibilities in the public sector-not only bad planning but wasteful public policy.

These are some of the major items For pre-consideration and survey. The objective is to determine what a country can afford, how great is the need, what structure is required, and how legislation can assist rapid development, without placing too great a burden on financial ability or the administrative structure. None of them should be over-emphasized. The objective remains the same; the limiting factors affect how it is to be attained and at what speed. In this connation, the object by E. M. Broome repays careful study. Nearly all these limiting factors were present, but none of them deterred the Government of Tanzania from passing legislation and implementing it with determination and success.

As was reported at the Delhi seminar:

* In all countries represented at the seminar, public library service is already being provided in some degree, and the time is ripe for further development. In no country do the material difficulties appear to be unsurmountable, nor is a low literacy rate a decisive adverse factor. The rate of development may vary with the speed of overcoming these problems, but the basis for public library services should be laid now. The major deficiencies in present provisions are: lack of over-all control, and the existence of small unco-ordinated units; lack of, or deficiencies in, existing legislation; lack of sufficient funds and government interest; and lack of trained and experienced librarians.

Practical Considerations in Framing Legislation

It has been said that it is easier to pass a law than it is to change it, and this is a lesson to be learned from existing legislation. In the United Kingdom, for nearly seventy years only minor amendments were made to the enabling legislation, despite the fact that under the existing law there was no means by which county councils could set up public library services for rural populations. Legislation should therefore be flexible and allow for changes in social conditions, in local-government structure and in the tax base. It should be capable of immediate application, but with progressive application. Study is made of the comparative merits and defects of existing legislation, but certain basic problems can be enumerated for primary consideration.

The Public Library as an Independent Service or Part of a National Library Service

In any country which can even consider the foundation of a public library service, there will already be in existence many libraries of high standard: university libraries, libraries of institutions, government departmental libraries, technical libraries and almost certainly a national and probably state libraries. It is tempting to think that there is an advantage in creating an integrated library service of which such libraries are a part. But it must be remembered that public libraries are for the whole community, whereas all other libraries are designed to serve a section of the community for a special purpose, and that purpose must be their prime consideration. Techniques are similar, but basic purposes are different. Uniting all libraries in one piece of legislation at an early stage is hardly practical, since not only would it tend to stifle the growth of the public library, but it would also entail bringing independent libraries under the legislation, and this would undoubtedly be resisted.

At the same time, there is an obvious need for provision for cooperation and some co-ordination, probably best organized around the national library. Bibliographical and interloan functions should be of value to all libraries. The national library could therefore be usefully linked to the central public library authority.

The Central Authority

The need for a central authority charged with carrying out the provisions of legislation is clear. Should it be an independent body or one linked to, or subordinate to, a government department? This is a matter for decision at governmental level. There are advantages in making the central authority part of the department of education, with a department for libraries and controlling body, which should have more than advisory functions. The central board or authority is a modern device of government much used in developing countries, and experience of its past success in other circumstances will affect legislation for public libraries. But the implementation of legislation should not be left to any other body but education, and if education is chosen as the implementing and organizing department, then a section including trained librarians is essential, with advisory and inspecting functions.

Permissive or Mandatory Legislation

It has been shown that permissive legislation is of limited effectiveness, even when accompanied by financial inducements. Legislation should therefore require action to be taken, wherever the ultimate source of action. But provision should be made for progressive implementation at a rate to be determined by resources.

Relationship Between Local and Central Authority

It is generally accepted that the public library is a local community service. In fact, this becomes less and less true with the explosive growth in production of information material and technical developments in library organization. The answer must be sought in the local government structure of the country concerned. In some countries, a nationally controlled public library service has been created, with provision for some devolution to local government at later stages. The existence of federally organized states also presents some problems. But it must be stated that local interest is desirable and must be stimulated. This implies the passing over of some authority, or the creation of local advisory bodies.

The Size of' the Unit

Assuming that local authority interest is essential, the question then arises: what unit, what size and with what authority? The lbadan seminar, speaking for the situation in Africa, concluded that since recognition of local authority was only beginning, the sole public authority should be the national or state agency. At the same time, the appropriate local authority must eventually be given a responsible place in any national scheme of book service. The roots of the service must be in the local community rather than in the state, regional or national headquarters.

The size and authority of the local unit are important questions, even when there is a suitable urban authority. An urban authority should never be the sole local unit, since its economic and social catchment area is equally important for public library purposes. The requirements for a viable unit, as we have seen, were well stated in the report of the Delhi seminar, but it is already clear, fifteen years later, that they are expanding. In developed countries for example, much larger units than previously thought necessary are now postulated, and the basing of a service on too small a unit can be disastrously hampering in later development. Apart from size, there are other considerations. Whatever the attachment at national level, it is generally conceded that at local level the public library service should be executively independent of other agencies, whether education or other departments such as cultural affairs or social education.

The public library serves all, but is not solely a part of any, SO it should remain independently governed and administered. The question of policy control is a matter of the form local government takes. There is much to be said for the board system, independent but responsible to the local-government system, but this is not always legally possible. But it should be possible at all times to bring into consultation persons of knowledge and goodwill.

Finance

It is generally now accepted that financial support for public libraries should come from public funds, that is, taxation. It is also generally recognized that the service should be free to the user, though this is not always the case in practice. In most developing countries, this means major support at national level, with assistance at local level so far as practicable, having regard to the limitations of local taxation in most developing countries. The acceptance of this principle has been a major limiting factor in public library progress, even in advanced countries, as will be demonstrated in study of existing legislation. It follows, therefore, that any unit at local level must be a tax-raising body, and provision for funds from taxation at a national level must be written in to any legislation. In a federal system, of course, another stage of financial support will be introduced.

Various calculations of the cost of a public library service have been made, but they are of little value in view of changing needs, and could not sensibly be included in basic legislation. No one would expect a public library service to spring armed and ready from the ground, like Jason's dragons' teeth, and financial provision must depend on the rate of implementation of legislation. The Government of India report of 1959 postulated a period of twenty-five years for the creation of a full service, but its calculations as to cost are already completely out of date. Given progressive implementation, standards of service required are also a matter for progressive regulation, and not a suitable one for inclusion in legislation. The power to make regulations on standards and other matters should, however, be given.

Other Considerations

There are several other considerations which may have to be taken into account in framing legislation, but their importance will vary according to country. In some countries, there will be a problem of fitting in private or subscription libraries to the system. There must also be some provision for co-operation between libraries, but this again will vary with the primary decisions already taken. If a linkage with the national library, for instance, is envisaged, or if the unit of service is the whole country, then these provisions can be taken care of automatically under regulation. But if existing resources, as provided by various agencies, are to be fully utilized, then some provision for co-operation and inter-lending must be made. Although university and institutional libraries may not be fully integrated, their resources, after their first priorities are met, should be circulated generally. Whether library education, or the encouragement of library associations, should be incorporated in legislation is a moot point.

It could be fairly argued that if opportunity for employment of qualified people is given by the provision of a public library service, then educational institutions will provide the necessary further education facilities for training librarians and technicians, without any legal requirement to do so. Library associations, also, should not be too dependent on legislative assistance. Again, the provision of a service will itself exert the necessary stimulus for the creation of an active body of professional librarians. And if such associations are to encourage further progress and technical improvement, they should be independent. All these problems and others applying to particular countries will need to be closely considered before framing suitable legislation in terms which will create a permanent, expanding public library service available to all people, whatever their age, status or geographical situation.

The way in which the problems have already been approached and the answers embodied in legislation is the subject of the next stage. There are many lessons to be learned, and the gap between intentions and results is often a depressing commentary on how the goodwill of legislators can be frustrated by circumstances unforeseen or unsuspected. Government and legislation are, alas, by no means an exact science. But in the framework of the modern State, legislation as an instrument of authority is necessary. In the case of public libraries it can truthfully be said that no successful public library system can exist without legal authority, but that many devices have been necessary to get round defective legislation. Public libraries happen to be the subject of this study, but no doubt authorities on law and government could produce better examples of problems caused by legislation rather than solved by it.

The Pattern of Legislation Comparative Solutions

The main body of this study consists of summaries of the existing legislation in fourteen countries, and taking into account the federal countries, twenty Acts are considered, with others mentioned in passing. More could have been chosen, but in fact, not more than thirty countries have effective general library legislation, less than a quarter of the independent nations of the world. Of the countries chosen, four are developing countries, two are countries with centrally planned economies and three are federally organized.

This, therefore can be considered a reasonably representative sample, ranging from the most advanced countries, where coverage is complete and basic standards established, to a country which has only just become independent, Botswana. They all have one thing in common; in none of them is legislation, even now, entirely satisfactory and effective, in that it encourages development to the point of greatest efficiency and maximum results. All have problems to some degree, despite the fact that in most of the countries considered there has been revision of law in the last ten years. The advanced countries, most of which have had public library legislation in some form for many years, but with varying effectiveness, have no great problem of financial ability to provide a nationwide system of public libraries, if that ability can be brought to bear.

The problem is rather one of an inadequate and unsuitable local-government structure, and the supplementation of local resources, or in some examples, replacement of local initiative, by central-government intervention. A pattern clearly emerges in nearly all recent legislation, first of a search for a larger and more viable unit of service, which must be both geographically and financially able to deploy larger resources for public library service, and second of the creation of a central advisory body to encourage improvement of public library service. One can see similarities in the solutions adopted, but there are also wide variations.

It is proposed in this chapter to show by comparison the major similarities and variations of the law as it stands in advanced countries. There are important lessons to be learned by the developing countries in framing their own legislation, and it appears that the advanced countries could also learn from their neighbours. In making these comparisons, it must of course be borne in mind that though public library law is evolutionary in character, it cannot be separated from the general body of law of a country, and it must be set in the executive, social and geopolitical structure of the country concerned.

The fact that some countries with a high educational and cultural standard have not so far been able to enact general mandatory legislation on public libraries proves this to be the case. Permissive legislation has been replaced by mandatory legislation in most countries. The appropriate local authorities are now required rather than permitted to provide a public library service.

In some countries, notably the United Kingdom, Finland and Sweden, mandatory provision is not necessary, since coverage is already complete. In Norway, obligatory provision is laid down in the Act, and in Denmark a date is set for all communes to provide public libraries. In Canada and the United States, though provision is not mandatory, the problem is no longer one of provision but of viability, and this could be said generally of all the countries considered, except the countries having centrally planned economies, where the law has nothing to say on this. But it would appear that in Hungary, at any rate, there is complete coverage.

Central Government and Advisory Bodies

In all countries, the intervention of the central government, either at state or federal level, or both, has led to the setting up of a central body to guide future progress, and this is the most common feature in all recent legislation. These central bodies may take many forms, either advisory or executive. They may be independent, or responsible to a department of State. Their membership may be drawn from organizations or individuals. Their constitution and powers can be summarized as follows:

Czechoslovakia

The Central Library Council is an advisory body in the Ministry of Education and Culture. There are two bodies, one for Bohemia-Moravia and one for Slovakia. Membership consists of representatives of authorities and expert librarians.

All proposals concerning libraries are submitted to them, and they have the right to initiate proposals themselves.

Denmark

The Library Council consists of sixteen members representing all sections of the Danish Library Service. They are appointed by the Minister of Cultural Affairs, are consulted in all matters of importance to the working of the Libraries Act, and have the right to initiate representations. The chairman is the Library Director, head of the State inspectorate.

Finland

The library delegation is an advisory body responsible to the Central Board of Schools. There are twelve delegates, representing the Department of Education, local authorities, library training and other organizations working for libraries and adult education. The delegation can take the initiative in submitting proposals to the Central Board of Schools.

Hungary

The National Council for Library Activity, responsible to the Ministry of Culture, has a section for public libraries. It has also a working organization, the State Institute of Libraries, similar in some respects to the State inspectorates of Scandinavian library systems. The functions of the National Council are advisory and technical, but being a direct organ of central government, it obviously has great prestige.

Ireland

The Library Council has as its main purpose the operation and supervision of the Irish Central library, and a secondary purpose of assisting local library authorities to improve their services. Its membership is by nomination, and a majority of the members are nominated by universities or the National Library. The powers of the Library Council are considerable, since it considers applications for grants from local authorities and its functions are much more than advisory. In view of the form of local government in Ireland, it can be said to be an executive body with potentially great powers. In fact, the original secondary function has become the primary one.

Qntario

The Provincial Library Council is an advisory body responsible to the Minister for Education, and it consists of nine members appointed by the minister, and one for each regional system. It has certain functions under the Act and may also make recommendations regarding development and co-ordination of library service.

Quebec

The Quebec Public Libraries Commission is responsible to the Minister for Cultural Affairs. Its membership is six persons nominated by the minister, whose qualifications shall be their interest in the development of public libraries, and the Director of Public Libraries of the Province. The powers and duties of the commission are wide, in that it is generally charged with the study of the best means of developing public library services, and it must report every three months on its findings regarding the working of the Public Libraries Act.

United Kingdom

The Library Advisory Councils, set up by the Minister of Education under the 1964 Act, one for England and one for Wales, have no set number of members, nor any stated qualifications for membership. They are nominated directly by the minister, and actually the representatives are drawn from local authority members, university and public librarians representing all the major interests of local government and various sizes and types of library. The function of the councils is purely advisory, and their main work is in connexion with the achievement of standards and the general working of the Act. But by their existence, they have become the advisory bodies for libraries in general, and on such matters as librarianship training.

Washington State

The State Library Commission is an executive commission appointed by the Governor, and responsible for administration of federal and state funds for improvement of public library services. It operates through the state library and appoints the state librarian, who acts as secretary to the commission. Though its main functions are executive, it also has advisory responsibilities. The functions of these bodies are mainly advisory, and as will be seen generally from their constitutions, are intended as a source of expert opinion on public library development.

They are useful bodies, but equally important, their existence creates a secretariat, and that secretariat, whether clearly laid down in legislation as in Quebec, or not, as in England and Wales, inevitably assumes supervisory functions. Those functions can be of inspection and control, as in Finland and Denmark, or they can be limited to advice to the appropriate minister and the right to ask for regular reports and give advice to individual library authorities. Even where there is no central coordinating body, there is invariably a central coordinating government department.

In Norway, the State inspectorate is recognized by the Act, and the State Inspector is a direct appointment of the Crown, though responsible to the Ministry of Church and Education. In Sweden, there is a Library Section of the Central Board of Education, and its functions include supervision of State grants, approval of building plans, and supervision of the School of Librarianship. With the change in local government law, its functions are now more limited, being more advisory than supervisory.

In the United States, in addition to the state departments concerned with public libraries, now established in most states, there is an office in the Department of Education in Washington charged with supervision of the very substantial grants under the Library Services and Construction Act. Except in Scandinavia, where they have been in existence for many years, the emergence of these bodies and the departments attached to them is comparatively recent, and their influence on public library development is bound to increase. It will be noted that the usual attachment of the library councils and their civil-service bureaux is to the Ministry of Education, in some cases to the Minister of Culture. But this attachment at central-government levels does not necessarily imply any attachment of public libraries at lower levels of government to any particular department.

Provision for Co-Operation

In most countries, legislation shows a marked preference for the provision of public library services within the existing local-government framework, and an equal reluctance to interfere with those existing agencies, even when they are clearly not viable. The only exception to this in recent legislation, where smaller authorities are required to give up their powers, is in England and Wales, where there is provision for the compulsory surrender of library powers by authorities of less than 40,000 population.

Even here, the clauses have not so far been used, since a major local-government reform is expected to make them unnecessary. Local-government reform in Sweden and Denmark is also making the problem less urgent, though it will still exist. Failing the forcible creation of larger public library authorities, the search for the larger unit must take the form of co-operation, and recent legislation is characterized by the creation of a superstructure of co-ordination, often at two or three levels, either mandatory or permissive. Library authorities are either to be persuaded to join with others in a library system, or a superstructure of co-operation is created above them, in which they have the opportunity, or are compelled, to take part. Financial assistance is usually given. Some examples of this kind of provision are as follows:

Denmark

A number of suitable libraries are designated as county libraries, serving a district. Their functions are to assist the local libraries in the district by lending or obtaining for them books and other suitable materials they cannot provide themselves, and by giving advice and technical assistance. In the present legislation, the Library Director recommends which libraries shall be recognized as county libraries, and the minister shall ensure that the district served is of a suitable size and that the county library is able to carry out its functions. In the past, it is thought, too many county libraries were designated, and the districts were too small. The provision is mandatory, that is to say, all libraries must join a district, and an advisory committee is formed to direct the work. National grants are made to the county libraries, and the county or counties must also contribute at rates laid down. The communes themselves do not contribute directly.

Norway

The system of regional central libraries is similar, except that the designated libraries have wider functions in supervision of their local libraries. The problems of establishment, and suitable areas, are very great in Norway, and though nineteen regional libraries have now been established, they vary greatly in resources. Again the inclusion in an area is mandatory, and grants are made to meet the cost, with supplementary grants from the areas covered.

Sweden

In addition to the establishment of county libraries on similar lines to Denmark and Norway, a further superstructure has been added of three inter-library loan centres, which lend to the county libraries and receive grants for their services from the State. It must be emphasized that in the Scandinavian countries, the aid-giving libraries are the larger libraries in their area, and though they may establish special departments for their additional functions, in no sense, except in a limited way in Norway, do they administer or supervise the other libraries in their area.

Quebec

The regional libraries in Quebec are quite different from others, and serve a different purpose. They are intended, not to superimpose an additional system, but to encourage the provision of public library service in those sparsely populated areas which cannot provide for themselves, even with grant aid. The system is fully described in the appropriate section, but briefly, when a minimum area containing 25,000 inhabitants can be defined, an ad hoc committee is formed. The kind of service depends on the size of the area and other factors, but generally, grant is 85 per cent of the total cost. Such a system is only required under extreme adverse conditions, but the similarity to the Norwegian system in its northern area is obvious.

Ontario

The Ontario method of creating larger areas is in effect a three-tier system. In a county, a combined library system can be formed at the request of 75 per cent of the authorities in the county, then a county library service is formed, and a separate public library board set up. But it is only responsible for that part of the county which has asked for inclusion. The system has obvious defects, but it does have the effect of helping some at least of the smaller authorities to combine. Superimposed on this system of county libraries and independent libraries is provision for regional library systems, working roughly on the Scandinavian pattern, and having similar responsibilities. Substantial grants are available from state funds, but regions are not necessarily inclusive of all the libraries in their area since, throughout the legislation of Ontario, there are no mandatory powers.

United States of America

There are no mandatory powers in the United States, and most recent legislation, both federal and state, has written into it an injunction that the independence of the community library is to be respected and preserved. The creation of the larger unit therefore is by the voluntary amalgamation of independent libraries into 'systems', in which service is often provided by contract between one library and another. It is interesting to note that current thinking puts the minimum viability of a system at 150,000 population.

United Kingdom

A voluntary system of co-operation has existed for many years, with member libraries paying subscriptions usually on a per capita basis. The country is divided into fourteen regions for this purpose. The 1964 Act legally recognizes this system, and provides for compulsory membership by all library authorities, and for amalgamation of the regions where necessary. Two of the largest regions, comprising London and the south-east of England, have already amalgamated, with the authority of the Ministry of Education. The purpose of the regions is principally inter-library co-operation, and for this purpose provision is made in legislation for bringing into the system other than public libraries.

LIBRARY LEGISLATION IN INDIA

India became an independent republic in January 1950. It is a federal union of states, there being seventeen states and ten union territories. The form of government is democratic, with a president and two Houses of Parliament. The Upper House, or Council of States, is indirectly elected, the members being elected by the legislative assembly of each state. The Lower House, or House of the People, consists of 500 members directly elected by adult suffrage. Each state has its own legislature, directly elected. Certain legislative powers are retained by the central government, but education, the most important function so far as libraries are concerned, is reserved to the states, though there is a central Ministry of Education with co-ordinating powers, including that of making grants for specific purposes.

These powers have been increased by the very large sums made available under successive Five-year Plans. The area of India is 1,262,275 square miles, and its population approximately 5II million.

Local Government

Local government is in the hands of some 2700 municipal authorities which have primary functions relating to their own areas and frame their own budgets, though usually, however, these require approval at state level. For rural areas there is a three-tier system of panchayats, or local councils-at village, block and district levels. Generally speaking, the block panchayats consist of groupings of village panchayats, but this does not apply to the whole of India, There are nearly 4000 block panchayats, and some 212,000 village panchayats. The district is the taxing authority below the state. The system is virtually complete and one can therefore say that local administration proceeds from state to city, district or municipality, and right down to its roots in the villages.

Education

The literacy percentage is approximately 24 - men 34.5, women 13. Despite this very low rate of literacy, very great progress has been made in education, and the rate has been improved by 8 per cent since 1951. Over ₹5,000 million were spent on education in 1964 and over 750,000 primary and secondary schools were in operation. The official national language under the Constitution is Hindi, but under the Official Language Act of 1963, English will continue to be used as an official language for an indefinite period alongside Hindi. The regional language of the state is also taught at various levels. There are fourteen officially recognized regional languages.

Library Provision

In the light of the facts the problems of public library provision are very great. India is a very large country with a predominantly rural population, a small per capita income and a number of recognized languages. There are other problems, arising from the local-government system and the relations of the central government to the states. India is a federal State and, as in Canada and the United States, provision of public libraries is reserved to the states and is their sole responsibility. Even grants under the Five-year Plans, given specifically in the past for public library development, were changed under the third plan to block grants to be spent at the discretion of the states. The central government has therefore no coercive powers to enforce legislation by the states, or to dictate the form of such legislation.

The legal powers to take over the many private or association libraries are also limited. To bring them into the public sector would require separate legislation which is unlikely to be voted. In view of the numbers of such libraries, this is important. Given a government determined enough to create a nation-wide public library system, the position could, of course, be changed. There is a national Ministry of Education, and it could be given coordinating functions. In fact, the Advisory Committee of I 959 proposed this in the form of an All-India Library Advisory Council, with an executive committee nominated by the Minister of Education, and a secretariat consisting of a division of libraries in the Ministry of Education.

It also suggested that the Government of India should contribute to the library funds of the state an amount equal to funds raised by property tax. Presumably, these proposals would require legislation at national level. Despite many obstacles, India has a strong and continuing literary tradition, and there is a thirst for knowledge which is evidenced by the fact that over 10,000 periodicals and newspapers are published in India. Book production, although its organization is chaotic, flourishes and there is not in fact, any shortage of libraries. Very few Indian towns or even large villages are without a library of some sort, provided by a charitable foundation, by an educational organization or by executive action on the part of state, municipal or district authority.

Very few of these institutions are well endowed, many are little more than reading-rooms. In this connexion, the statement by the Advisory Committee on Libraries, which reported in 1959, is of value in estimating the true position:

* In India the phrase 'public libraries' is used in a very loose sense. It is used to denote any library which permits members of the public to use its material for reference or borrowing on payment of fees or rent. In this sense, all kinds of libraries, national, university, schools and subscription libraries, etc.,

would be public libraries. Because of the loose connotation of the term, it would appear from the statistics published by Unesco in 1956 that India leads the world in the number of public libraries, which is given as 24,086. The statistics are flattering; they express the aspiration rather than the achievement of the country. The internationally accepted definition of a public library is that it is a library which is:

- Is financed out of public funds;
- Charges no fees from readers and yet is open for full use by the public without distinction of caste, creed or sex;
- Is intended as an auxiliary educational institution providing a means of self education which is endless;
- Houses learning materials giving reliable information freely and without partiality or prejudice on as wide a variety of subjects as will satisfy the interests of readers. Were such a definition adopted, the number of public libraries in India could not be counted by tens, let alone by hundreds or thousands.

A framework of library provision does, however, exist, and it has been expanded by grants under successive five-year plans, at national level. In the first five-year plan, 1951-56, a scheme of improvement of library service was included calling for a network of libraries to be spread over the whole country. The kernel of the scheme was the establishment of district libraries, which would circulate books throughout the district. These were to be supplemented and supported by a central library for the whole state, or for a whole linguistic region. A supplementary scheme to set up integrated library units was also commended to state governments in connexion with the areas selected for intensive educational development. Under successive Five-year Plans, the schemes have been developed but have not so far been backed up generally by a legislative base, despite strong recommendations by the Advisory Committee in 1959.

These recommendations were for a comprehensive state library law, which would provide for free library service for all. Funds would be provided by a library rate on property tax, the income to be covered by a matching State grant. The unit of library service would be the district. Proposals were also made for legislative action by the Government of India to collate the various Copyright and Book Deposit Acts and to make them viable for a national library service. The Act should also provide for assistance to state governments for public library service. Since provision of public libraries by executive action is an important feature in public library provision in developing countries, a typical example in India, that of West Bengal, is worthy of brief examination.

West Bengal Library System

West Bengal not only contains the largest city in India, Calcutta, but also India's National Library. Its population is over 65 million, and the principal language is Bengali. The literacy rate is 30 per cent. The first public library was opened in Calcutta in 1836 and it was followed during the nineteenth century by the founding of many other libraries on a subscription basis. After independence, small grants were made by local authorities and from state funds, and in 1950, about 1,000 subscription libraries were receiving small grants. In 1956, a coordinated scheme was sponsored by the state government, with financial assistance on a 50 per cent basis from the Government of India.

In 1969-70 a sum of ₹4,313,000 was given in annual grants. All the districts of West Bengal now have a district library and much progress has been made in the provision of buildings, furniture and equipment. A reasonably coherent library system has now been established, with a state central library in Calcutta, over 68 district and area libraries and 579 rural libraries, with total staffs of over 1500. Many of the libraries are still subscription libraries, and grants in fact are still given to many subscription libraries outside the system. While it is a source of satisfaction that public library service has been created, it cannot be denied that it is far from ideal. Since the entire service is under the Department of Social Education, district librarians have no real executive powers, and there appears to be little co-ordination of book stocks. Above all, the lack of a legislative and tax base necessarily makes for uncertainty in future planning.

The Delhi Public Library

Another example of executive action is the Delhi Public Library. This was founded by joint action of the Government of India and Unesco as a demonstration project applying Western concepts of book provision, furniture and equipment in a developing country.

In the final terms of agreement between Unesco and the Indian Government, the terms of reference for the project were set out:

> "It shall provide a public library service for the people of the City of Delhi and shall be a model for all public library development in India, and in all other countries where similar development of public libraries can be undertaken. The library shall be designed to carry out the policy of the Unesco Public Libraries Manifesto and to serve the needs of popular education."

The organizers of the library had, therefore, to plan for a library which would have complete open access to the shelves, which would make no direct charge to readers, and would be organized not for preservation, but for use by readers of all ages and all levels of education. These concepts were not new to India. They had been propagated by the devoted work of Dr. Ranganathan and his disciples. But between concept and execution there was still a wide gap, and the Delhi Public Library was the first in India, and probably the first in Asia, to apply these principles. The library was opened in 1951 by the Prime Minister, Mr. Nehru, and the present author was consultant to the project during the first year of its life. The government of the library is by the Delhi Library Board, an autonomous body acting on behalf of the Ministry of Education.

It is a well-balanced body, now with fifteen members. The Ministry of Education, the Finance Ministry, the Delhi

Municipal Corporation, the Delhi Administration and the New Delhi Municipal Committee are all represented and four experts with technical qualifications or library experience are co-opted.

The director of the library is secretary of the board and ex oficio member of it. Finance was jointly from the two sponsoring bodies in the first two years, but is now the sole responsibility of the Indian Government, with small grants from the municipal bodies. The story of the Delhi Public Library has been told many times, and it is not proposed to repeat it here. From its inception it was an enormous success, enrolling over 10,000 members in the first few months and lending over 70,000 books.

In 1966-67, membership had increased to 136,000 and annual issue of books to nearly 2 million volumes. Book stocks have increased from 14,000 to 350,000. It is still, in the words of a recent Indian writer, 'the only public library in India worth the name.' In 1955, the author was invited by Unesco to make a detailed evaluation of the project. This was published by Unesco in 1957. In 1956, the Government of India notified its acceptance of this evaluation, the preamble of which began with the statement: 'During this period of five years the library has made gratifying progress and it has, therefore, been decided to place it on a permanent basis. ' After twenty years of existence, this statement is still the only basis on which the library operates.

Its functions have never been more clearly defined than in the original terms of reference as a pilot project, and it is still not a statutory body. More curious still, though it spends over I million rupees a year, by far the greatest expenditure of a single Indian public library unit, it still has not been given over-all responsibility for providing public library service in Delhi.

In 1964, a further evaluation of the library was made by the board itself, which has this to say about the area of the library's responsibility:

> "A rather peculiar feature of the situation regarding public library service in Delhi is that in addition to the

Delhi Library Board, three other bodies, *viz.*, the Delhi Administration, the Delhi Municipal Corporation and the New Delhi Municipal Committee operate a few libraries and reading rooms, and the New Delhi Municipal Committee proposes to open small lending libraries in the area within its jurisdiction. There is no co-operation at all between the several authorities administering these libraries. The fact is stated here because of a possible wasteful duplication of effort and money."

The fact that Delhi is the seat of government and has no state administration possibly accounts for the perpetuation of this rather odd situation. But one would have thought that a short enabling Act would have been possible giving the Delhi Public Library responsibility for providing all public reference and lending services in the Delhi area. Nevertheless, the Delhi Public Library has shown and continues to show that a modern public library can exist and can flourish in India.

Model Libraries Bill

In 1960, following the recommendations of the Advisory Committee on Libraries, the Government of India appointed a committee for drafting a library bill. This was submitted to the Ministry of Education in 1963 and in 1964 the ministry circulated the bill for comments to the various state governments and professional organizations. No further action has yet been taken. The bill is intended for adoption on a nation-wide basis. It would therefore need to be adopted by each state and presumably general legislation by the Government of India would be necessary to define the rights of the citizen to access to libraries, similar to those he has to education, to provide for some form of co-ordination of the various state library services and to provide for financial assistance for the state public library services as envisaged in the Model Bill.

The exact form of such legislation, in view of the states' rights, is difficult to foresee, but a similar problem was solved in the United States with the Library Services Act. A long process of legislation is therefore obviously involved, and an equally long process of organization. The integration of the present systems of public libraries provided by executive action will in itself present certain problems.

State Legislation

The Model Bill has been discussed at length because it is presumably the basis on which future legislation will be founded for all the states. But four Indian states have already passed legislation: two, Madras and Andhra Pradesh, before the publication of the Advisory Committee Report and the Model Bill, and two, Mysore and Maharashtra, after the publication of the Model Bill.

Madras Act

Madras State (capital: Madras) has a population of 37 million. The literacy rate is 30 per cent. Tamil is the principal language. Madras was the first state to pass legislation to create a public library system, in 1948. This was largely due to the unremitting efforts of Dr. Ranganathan, but the bill was watered down in its various stages to make it acceptable and it is generally agreed that in its present form not only is the Act defective but that its implementation has been unsound.

In the words of S. K. Mookerjee:

> "The Madras Act and its implementation in the sphere of library organization have taught us all a very good lesson. It has shown how completely the intentions of the legislature can be flouted and the public needs neglected when such implementation is entrusted to the wrong agency."

The main provisions of the Madras Act are as follows: A state library committee is formed for the purpose of advising the government. Its membership includes the Minister in Charge of Education, who is to be president of the board, representatives of universities and local library authorities and three persons nominated by library associations in the state. But the Director of Public Instruction is named as being ex officio Director of Public Libraries and a 'Special Officer' assisting the director in the administration of the Act is secretary of the committee. It is quite clear that it is not intended that the special officer shall be a librarian and there is no place in fact in the Act for a state librarian with technical qualifications.

It has been stated that the 'Special Officer', not a librarian, was in fact appointed with some haste. The Director of Public Libraries is charged with managing the State Central Library, superintending the work of local library authorities and superintending and directing all matters relating to public libraries in the state. The Act creates local library authorities, one for the City of Madras and one for each district, each district authority being given full powers of management of libraries within the district.

This is a much more sensible arrangement than the one in the Model Bill, in that it creates, in theory at any rate, more viable authorities. There are thirteen districts in Madras, so the average effective literate population of a district is around I million. The powers and duties of district library authorities do not, however, include provision for the appointment of a librarian, and there is no provision for a librarian on the committee. The power to make regulations also includes clauses: to 'provide for the admission of the public to public libraries in its area on such conditions and on payment of such fees as it may specify'; and 'requiring from persons desiring to use such libraries any guarantee or security against injury to, misuse, destruction or loss of the property of such libraries'.

These sections of the Act do, of course, nullify the whole function of public libraries if acted on, although they are permissive. Each local library authority is empowered to levy a library cess in its area, of six paise per rupee. This can be increased by an authority with sanction. The principal defects of the Act, apart from the omission of a requirement for trained staff with some status and the out-of-date provisions for access to the libraries, are that the Act does not in any way create a system of libraries. The State Central Library has no duties in relation to the district libraries and the district libraries have no duties in relation to each other. A parallel system of libraries is also created under the Act, since one of the duties of the director is to declare what libraries are eligible for government aid.

In the rules made under the Act, the director is to maintain a register of such libraries and conditions are laid down for eligibility for grant. There appear to be no provisions, as in the Model Bill, for eventual merging of these libraries within the public libraries administered by district authorities. Despite the defects of the Act, and its slow implementation, in recent years the public library service has obviously made some impression. In 1965, total expenditure reached over 7 million rupees as against I,685,000 in 1957, and of this sum I,897,000 was raised in library cess. Over half the total expenditure in 1965, however, was by special grant, under the five-year plan, and it is not known whether this has been maintained since. Book stocks are reported as being nearly 2,500,000, visitors to the libraries nearly 18 million. But one notes with surprise that there are in the whole state only 15,000 registered borrowers and only 143 trained library staff, of whom only I have full library qualifications. But however suspect some of the statistics, and it must be noted that criticism of the Madras library service by Indian librarians has been very severe, it is undoubtedly true that some progress has been made which would not have been made without a legislative base.

It is to be hoped that the efforts of Dr. Ranganathan and others to improve the Act will eventually bear fruit and that Madras may then emerge as not only the first, but also the foremost, Indian state with a tax-based, legally founded, public library service.

Andhra Pradesh

Andhra Pradesh was a linguistic state formed from Hyderabad and parts of Madras State. A Telugu-speaking area, it has always had a strong library and literary tradition. In the words of an Indian librarian, 'the library movement has had a vast influence on the social and political life in Telugu land'. The population is over 40 million. When the new state was formed, there was already an Act in force for Hyderabad, while the parts of Madras taken over were covered by the Madras Act. In 1960 an integrated Act was passed for the entire state. In many ways the Act is similar to the Madras Act, in the provision of a state library committee, the constitution of local library authorities, the levying of library cess and the matching of the funds raised in this way by grants from the state government. But generally the Act is a great improvement on the Madras Act, and corrects many of its defects.

The Act creates a separate department of public libraries, although the Director of Public Instruction may be the director in charge of the department. But the librarian of the State Central Library has a place on the State Library Committee. In the provisions for the district authorities and the city authority it is laid down that the District Librarian and the City Central Librarian shall each be secretary of the respective committee. The amount of library cess is fixed at four paise, which may be increased to eight paise at the discretion of the district authority. It is prescribed in the Act that no fees for admission to any public library shall be charged, but it is not clear whether a fee can be charged for borrowing of books. Again, a parallel system of libraries is formed, since under the definitions, a public library can be 'a library established or maintained by any local body or co-operative society and declared open to the public', or 'a library declared to be eligible for aid and receiving aid from the Government or from the Library Fund'.

The duties of the Director of Public Libraries also include a declaration of what libraries are eligible for aid and under the rules of the Act conditions for such aid are laid down. It is clear that these are libraries outside those provided directly by the library authority, but there are no provisions, as in the Model Bill, for taking them over. The Act has been rapidly implemented, and appears to be working fairly satisfactorily.

Mysore Act, 1965

This Act has taken features from the Madras Act, the Andhra Pradesh Act, and the Model Bill and is a great improvement on all of them. Mysore is a Kannada-speaking

State formed under the States Reorganization Act. The capital is Bangalore and the population is approximately 27 million. The literacy rate is 25 per cent (36 % males). The preamble of the Act states that it is:

* 'To provide for the establishment and maintenance of public libraries and the organization of a comprehensive rural and urban library service for the State of Mysore.'

The State Library Authority includes a member representing the State Library Association, but the State Librarian, though *ex officion* secretary of the authority, is not a member. A department of public libraries is formed under the Act, with the State Librarian at its head. This clause takes the administration of the public library out of the province of the Department of Education. The State Librarian is also specifically stated to be a whole-time officer with qualifications to practise as a librarian. All posts in the Department of Public Libraries are to be filled by appointment of persons employed by the state library service. This may seem supererogatory, but is obviously intended to prevent appointment of persons already in other departments of the civil service. It is one of the grievances of Indian librarians that posts are often filled by people without library qualifications, coming by promotion from such departments as social education and community development.

Local library authorities are specified for cities and urban areas with populations of more than 100,000, and for each district authority. The chief librarian of the city or district is *ex officion* secretary of the local library authority. Development plans are to be prepared for each district and advisory committees formed by branch libraries and mobile libraries under the plan. The library cess is not confined to a levy on property, but is also levied on other taxes in city areas. It is limited to three paise in the rupee, subject to increase at discretion, with an upper limit of six paise. It will, of course, raise much more money, though the rate is the same, than property tax.

The grant from the state to districts is met from land revenue tax, at the rate of three per cent. In addition the whole of staff salaries in the library authority is met by the state. The State Central Library has, among other functions, the task of providing facilities for the blind. This is not mentioned in any other Act. The Act also specifies a number of public libraries owned by societies which are to be taken over under the Act. Whether this is by prior agreement or not, it is an immense step forward. The Mysore Act, it will be seen, is in many respects an improvement of the Model Bill, particularly in its creation of an independent library service and the widening of the tax base for urban libraries. The provision that all staff are employees of the state library service and paid by the state creates, for the first time in any of the Indian legislation, an integrated library system with the State Central Library at its head.

Maharashtra, 1967

Maharashtra, a Marathi-speaking State has a population of 46 million. Literacy is 30 per cent (males 42%). The Maharashtra Act, passed in 1967, has some of the features of the Mysore Act in that it creates a state library council, with a director of libraries who is a member of the council, acts as its secretary and must be a qualified librarian. A department of libraries is established and a state library service with staff salaries to be paid from state funds. There the resemblance to the Mysore Act stops.

A state library is to be established and a divisional library for every division. But provision for library service in a local area can only be made if the director is not satisfied that a local authority, society or trust is willing or competent to provide a public library service. No such library however shall be established without an opportunity being given to the local authority, society or trust to show because why the state authority should not establish a library. The Act gives no powers of taxation; the Library Fund is made up solely from general and special grants, and central government grants. The general state grant is to be not less than 2,500,000 rupees, not a large sum. It is difficult to see from this how the Act can work satisfactorily, even though a functioning department and qualified staff are provided for.

SUMMARY

The Indian position has been dealt with at some length because of the variety of existing legislation and the fact that for the greater part of India there still is no legislation. This is not for want of trying. There must be few countries where there has been so much effort, so many reports, such unremitting lobbying of politicians. Dr. Ranganathan has devoted a lifetime to the problem, as well as gaining an international reputation for his contributions to librarianship, and nearly every Indian state has been in consultation with him at one time or another over legislation.

All states have active and persistent library associations, hampered by lack of funds it is true, but making up for it in publications and conferences. The will is there, the sympathy is there, but results have been more than disappointing. The main problem is, of course, one of taxation. The states' governments are reluctant to pass mandatory legislation that will increase the tax burden; the rural and urban areas have not sufficient potential revenue to provide library services; and the states themselves have a limited amount of revenue to disburse.

Finally, the central government, although it has distributed large sums for libraries under successive five-year plans, is reluctant to make permanent commitments. But eventually the problem must be solved by central government contributions to make up the deficiency in the states. It has been suggested that 5 per cent of the amount spent on education should be aimed at as the total. This would not provide expensive buildings and equipment, but it would provide a basic public library service. The difficulty is that the longer the central government hesitates to insist on mandatory state legislation, the more difficult it will be to provide this basic service.

A start must sometime be made on bringing the many semi-public libraries into a system and possibly channeling and consolidating the small sums they spend. Grant-in-aid to them altogether must amount to a respectable sum and a large part of it is wasted so long as these libraries are independent, using untrained staff and decrepit premises. The attitude is that they are better than nothing, but this is not true if they give the impression that they are a library service. There is also a danger that more states will pass defective legislation, and the more that do, the longer it will take to bring them into line.

The only Act which is reasonably acceptable so far is the Mysore Act and it is the only one to create a state-wide service. It is now nearly ten years since the Advisory Committee reported and gave a comprehensive view of the situation. It is surely time for the Government of India to make a definite move, if only because otherwise they may be faced with a series of defective and conflicting Acts by the states.

5

Resources and Services of Libraries

For this chapter information was collected from library staff using a questionnaire about the administration, organization, resources, services and facilities of libraries of colleges of education under study. An attempt was also made to ascertain the problems being faced by them in managing these libraries.

YEAR OF ESTABLISHMENT

Libraries constitute an integral part of colleges. These are supposed to be established simultaneously with their parent institutions. Realizing their crucial role in education, all the libraries have been established together with the inception of colleges. All libraries, except one had been existing for more than 30 years. Library of University College of Education (UCE) came into existence in 2001 along with the college.

LIBRARY STAFF

Library is the trinity of collection, staff and readers, where staff brings together other two elements. Qualified and adequate staff is pre-requisite for effective functioning of libraries.

Librarians

Libraries need the services of professionally qualified librarians for proper administration of the system. A library having good collection and adequate staff may not essentially provide effective library services, unless it is managed by a professionally qualified librarian having managerial capabilities. All the colleges, except UCE had sanctioned posts of librarians. The UCE library had a post of an assistant librarian as incharge, which was lying vacant since the establishment of college in 2001. It was being managed by a library assistant. Two Government. Colleges of Education (GCE) had two posts of librarians each. Out of these, in a college a post was vacant and one librarian was managing library. Table 5.1 reveals the prevailing position of librarian's posts in colleges under study.

Andhra Pradesh

Table 5.1. Prevailing Position of Librarians Posts

Sl. No.	Particulars	No. of Libraries	Percentage
1	Permanent Librarians	13	72.22
2	Adhoc based librarians	01	05.56
3	Post vacant	04	22.22
	Total	18	100.00

It is evident from Table 5.1 that out of the 18 libraries having sanctioned posts of librarians, 13 (72.22%) libraries had permanent librarians, whereas, a government aided college appointed a librarian on adhoc basis. In four (22.22%) colleges posts of librarians were lying vacant. Out of these, a government. aided college appointed a professional and designated her as an assistant librarian, inspite of the fact that the college did not have any sanctioned post of an assistant librarian. The remaining three libraries were being run by restorers. The National Council for Teacher Education (NCTE) required each college to have a full time librarian. Analysis of the responses revealed that libraries of six (31.58%) colleges consisting of four Government. Aided Colleges of Education (GACE), one government. college of education and UCE did not meet the NCTE norms about full time librarian.

Educational Qualification of Librarians

Educational qualifications of librarians influence the organizational health of libraries. Higher academic and professional qualification leads to better library management, ultimately better library services.

Table 5.2 shows that out of 15 librarians serving 14 libraries, six (40.00%) possessed master's degree in arts/science and bachelors' degree in Library and Information Science (LIS), while four (26.66%) librarians had master's degrees in arts/ science in addition to masters' degree in LIS. Three librarians had bachelors' degree in arts/ science and master's degree in LIS.

Table 5.2. Educational Qualification of Librarians.

Sl. No.	Qualification		No. of Librarians	%age
	Academic	Professional		
1	M.A./M.Sc./M.Ed./ M.Com.	Ph.D.	01	06.67
2	M.Phil/ Ph.D.	B.Lib.& I.Sc.	01	06.67
3	M.A./ M.Sc.	M.Lib.& I.Sc.	04	26.66
4	M.A./ M.Sc.	B.Lib.& I.Sc.	06	40.00
5	B.A./ B.Sc.	M.Lib.& I.Sc.	03	20.00
	Total		15	100.00

A librarian possessed Ph.D. degree in the subject of History and bachelor's degree in LIS. Only one librarian had Ph.D. degree in LIS and master's degree in another discipline. Out of the seven librarians having master's degree in LIS, three had qualified National Eligibility Test (NET) for Lectureship, while a librarian qualified State Eligibility Test (SET) for Lectureship. It has been found that all three librarians serving GCE libraries had bachelor's degree in LIS, whereas all the librarians having master's degree in LIS were serving at GACE. The NCTE has revised its norms regarding qualification of librarians. These are now only bachelors degree in Library and Information Science whereas as per NCTE these were "As prescribed by State Government/UT Administration concerned." The qualifications laid by State Government were as per University Grant Commission. But the qualifications prescribed by NCTE are only B.Lib. & I.Sc. Therefore, this amounts to the degradation of librarians and eventually libraries.

Table 5.3 depicts that out of 15 librarians, 09 (60.00%) had experience of more than 20 years. Out of these, 07 librarians possessed bachelor's degree and two had master's degree in LIS. Five (33.33%) librarians had experience of less than 10 years, while a remaining librarian's experience ranged between 16-20 years. All three librarians serving GCE had experience of more than 20 years each. Analysis of the responses tabulated in tables reveals that all the librarians having only bachelor's degree in LIS were appointed more than 20 years ago. On the other hand, all the librarians appointed thereafter had master's degree in LIS.

Table 5.3. Experience of Librarians.

Sl. No.	Experience in Years	No. of Librarians	Percentage
1	Up to 5	02	13.33
2	6-10	03	20.00
3	11-15	—	—
4	16-20	01	06.67
5	21-25	03	20.00
6	26-30	03	20.00
7	More than	30 03	20.00
	Total	15	100.00

Refresher Courses Attended

Librarians were asked if they had attended any refresher course, orientation programme, workshop, etc. Responses revealed that out of 15 librarians, 07 (46.67%) attended refresher courses, two (13.33%) had attended orientation programmes and a librarian also participated in a workshop. It has been found that about 50% librarians had not participated in refresher courses and workshops, which are imperative for updating professionals and essential for Continuous Professional Development.

Library Assistants

The UCE and a government aided college had a post of library assistant each. Out of the two library assistants serving respective libraries, one possessed bachelors' degree in LIS, while another was only matriculate not having any degree or diploma in LIS.

Library Restorers

Thirteen (68.42%) libraries had sanctioned posts of restorers, while remaining six (31.58%) did not. In 12 (92.30%) of 13 libraries, restorers were working against the sanctioned posts, while in a government college library post was vacant. Two colleges out of the six not having sanctioned posts, appointed restorers on adhoc basis, while remaining four had not made such effort. All the GCE had sanctioned posts of restorers. About two-thirds of the library restorers serving libraries possessed either diploma or bachelor's degree in LIS, while remaining five did not.

Library Attendants

Eight (42.10%) libraries did not have sanctioned posts of library attendants. In two libraries, out of the 11 (57.90%) having sanctioned posts of attendants, posts were vacant. All the GCE had sanctioned posts of library attendants. But it was shocking to find that in Desh Bhagat Pandit Chetan Dev Government College of Education, Faridkot the previous principal had assigned the job of a 'gardener' to a graduate library attendant and replaced him with an illiterate peon in the library to provide library services to the users. This shows the ignorance and lack of importance of libraries on the part of authorities. Out of the nine attendants serving libraries, one third had either degree or diploma in LIS, whereas, the remaining two third did not.

LIBRARY COMMITTEE

Generally, library committee comprises of three types of authorities, principal as the chairman of committee, librarian as secretary and teachers and students as members. Keeping in view its significance, librarians were asked about the existence, structure and functions of library committees.

Existence of Library Committees

Out of a total 19 libraries, 18 (94.73%) had library committees, whereas a government aided college did not. In a college it was named as 'Book Purchase Committee'.

Chairperson of Library Committee

Table 5.4 reveals that in 12 (66.67%) libraries out of the 18 having library committees, principals were serving as the chairpersons of the committees, whereas in two GACE libraries, librarians themselves led these. In two colleges, lecturers were the heads of committees. Out of these, a college did not have regular principal. In two colleges, library committees did not have any chairman. In one of these, college principal was the convener of committee and librarian and lecturers were members, while in a remaining library, committee comprised of members only.

Table 5.4. Chairperson of Library Committee.

Sl. No.	Chairperson of Committee	No. of Libraries	Percentage
1	Principal	12	66.67
2	Librarian	02	11.11
3	Lecturer	02	11.11
4	No Chairman	02	11.11
	Total	18	100.00

Secretary of Library Committee

It is worth mentioning here that in majority of the libraries *i.e.* eight (44.44%), librarians were serving as secretaries of the committees, while in six (33.33%) libraries lecturers did the job table 5.5 . Four libraries did not have any secretary of the library committees. In a library, it comprised of principal as convener and librarian and lecturers as members, while in two libraries these had only members including librarians. In a remaining library, where librarian was head of the committee, it consisted of lecturers as members. Survey revealed that only one library had students' representatives as members in the committee.

Table 5.5. Secretary of Library Committee.

Sl. No.	Secretary of Committee	No. of Libraries	%age
1	Librarian	08	44.44
2	Lecturers	06	33.33
3	No One	04	22.23
	Total	18	100.00

Nature of Work of Library Committee

In majority of the libraries forming 66.67%, library committees were advisory bodies. In remaining one third libraries these were executive in nature because of lack of full time librarians.

COLLECTION DEVELOPMENT

The Working Group on Libraries set up by National Knowledge Commission emphasized for collection building based on the information needs of users. In its recommendations the Group added: "To fulfil its role in the present and changing context, each library must have a well-rounded collection relevant to its user community". A balanced and need based collection, adequate to meet the present as well as future information needs of users depends upon a well prepared collection development policy. Library staff of ten colleges responded that they had prepared and were following collection development policy, while staff of remaining nine libraries responded otherwise. It was very disappointing to find that none of the libraries had any written guidelines for collection development.

Who Makes Selection of Subject Related Books

Subject books are meant to meet the curriculum based information needs of users and enable them to explore the concerned subjects in depth. Library staff was asked to give ranking in order of preference to the different authorities mentioned in Questionnaire I, according to their role in selection of subject books (Table 5.6).

Table 5.6. Selection of Subject Related Books.

Sl. No.	Persons who Select Books	Scores	Ranking
1	Teachers	66	01
2	Principal	60	02
3	Library Committee	43	03
4	Librarian	39	04
5	Others (students and college management)	15	05

Sum total of the scores assigned to different options on the basis of ranking given by librarians reveals that teachers occupied the leading role in selection of subject books, followed by the principals and library committees respectively. Librarians attained the fourth position in order of ranking for subject related document selection, while others earned least scores.

GENERAL AND REFERENCE COLLECTION

As in case of subject books, scores have been assigned to the different authorities involved in selection of general and reference collection also, which are tabulated in table 5.7:

Table 5.7. Selection of General and Refrence Books.

Sl. No.	Persons Who Select Books	Scores	Ranking
1	Teachers	62	01
2	Principal	60	02
3	Librarian	45	03
4	Library Committee	43	04
5	Others (students and college management)	05	05

Table 5.7 shows that teachers have earned the highest scores in selection of general and reference collection too.

Principals and librarians were given second and third preferences, while library committees and others attained fourth and fifth positions respectively. Analysis of the responses given in tables makes it clear that the teachers and principals played a leading role in selection of subject related as well as general and reference collection.

Document Selection Tools

Scores have been assigned to the various document selection tools on the basis of preference ranking given by librarians. Rank '1' was given the highest score '8' followed by others in descending order of 1 score at each stage.

Table 5.8 depicts that teacher's suggestions have earned the highest scores as sources of document selection, while publisher's catalogues and student's suggestions earned the second and third position respectively. Book reviews and other bibliographical tools were given least ranking as document selection tools.

Table 5.8. Document Selection Tools.

Sl. No.	Sources of Book Selection	Scores	Ranking
1	Teachers' Suggestions	132	01
2	Publishers' Catalogue	101	02
3	Students' Suggestions	71	03
4	Books on Approval	54	04
5	Book Sellers' List	42	05
6	Book Exhibitions	40	06
7	Book Reviews	16	07
8	Other Bibliographical Tools	11	08

COLLECTION OF LIBRARIES

Among three components of libraries i. e. collection, staff and readers, collection occupies the key position. It is collection which determines the use of a library. Collection is a wider term covering books, periodicals, microforms, electronic form documents, etc. Information was gathered about the nature and size of collection of libraries under study.

Total Book Collection

Responses received about the total collection of libraries were arranged into different ranges of 5000 each. It is evident from table that majority of the libraries under study *i.e.* 10 (52.63%) possessed 15,000-25,000 volumes, while four (21.06%) libraries had 10,000-15,000 books table 5.9. Only two GCE libraries crossed the figure of 30,000 volumes. The UCE library had less than 5000 volumes due to its recent origin in 2001. The GCE were found rich in collection size than GACE and UCE. Main factor affecting this was that GCE received recurring grants for reading material from both the University Grants Commission (UGC) and the State Government, while GACE got grants for library from UGC only.

Table 5.9. Book Collection of Libraries.

Sl. No.	Total Number of Books Possessed	No. of Libraries	%age
1	0-5000	01	05.27
2	5000-10000	02	10.53
3	10000-15000	04	21.06
4	15000-20000	05	26.31
5	20000-25000	05	26.31
6	25000-30000	—	—
7	More than 30000	02	10.52
	Total	19	100.00

The NCTE require each college to have a minimum 1000 titles and 3000 books for B.Ed. Course and minimum 2000 titles for M.Ed course in libraries to get recognition. The UCE had less than 5000 volumes though it was offering both B.Ed. and M.Ed. courses. The NCTE further mentioned that a library should add 200 titles annually wherever B.Ed. course is being run. In addition it requires annual addition of '100 quality books' where M.Ed. course is also being run. It has been found that libraries of only two GACE were fulfilling the NCTE norms for M.Ed. course. Whereas, for B.Ed. course libraries of total seven colleges were adding 200 volumes annually on an average including the two mentioned earlier.

Text Book Collection

Table 5.10 shows the textbook collection of libraries of colleges of education in Punjab.

Table 5.10. Text Book Collection of Libraries.

Sl. No.	Number of Text Books Possessed	No. of Libraries	%age
1	0-4000	06	31.58
2	4000-8000	07	36.84
3	8000-12000	03	15.79
4	12000-16000	03	15.79
	Total	19	100.00

Table 5.10 reveals that majority of the libraries had 4000-8000 textbooks. Six libraries had less than 4000 volumes and three possessed 8000-12000 textbooks. Three libraries had 12000-16000 volumes of textbooks. It is evident from the table that textbooks constitute a large part of the total collection of libraries.

Reference Collection

A good reference collection is the soul for sound reference service. It has been observed that all libraries maintained separate reference sections. Responses received about the strength of reference collection are shown in table 5.11.

Table 5.11. Reference Collection of Libraries.

Sl. No.	Number of Reference Books Possessed	No. of Libraries	%age
1	0-200	02	10.53
2	200-500	05	26.31
3	500-1000	02	10.53
4	1000-1500	03	15.79
5	1500-2500	03	15.79
6	More than 2500	04	21.05
	Total	19	100.00

Table 5.11 depicts that five (26.31%) libraries possessed 200-500 reference volumes, while other five had 500-1500 books. About 21.05% libraries had more than 2500 volumes in reference sections. In majority of the libraries, the reference collection was found to be satisfactory in proportion to their total collection. It was noticed that though the libraries of two GCE were richest in their total collection, still libraries of four GACE had more volumes in reference sections.

Book Bank

Fifteen libraries (78.94%) had book banks to help poor and needy students, while remaining 04 did not. Out of the 15 libraries, 14 maintained separate book bank sections, while a librarian shared that they did not have any separate book bank section, but lend books to needy students for the full session from text books section. Table 5.12 furnishes the number of volumes in book banks of 14 libraries.

Table 5.12. Size of Book Bank Collection.

Sl. No.	Number of Books in Book Bank	No. of Libraries	%age
1	0-500	04	28.58
2	500-1000	04	28.58
3	1000-2000	03	21.42
4	2000-3000	01	07.14
5	More than 3000	02	14.28
	Total	14	100.00

Table 5.12 discloses that out of 14 libraries having separate book bank sections, eight had less than 1000 volumes in their respective book banks. Four libraries had 1000-3000 books and two possessed more than 3000 volumes. It was learnt that majority of the libraries added only gifted books to book banks.

Non-Book Material

Non-book material constitutes an important source of information. The NCTE also requires libraries to have electronic publications (CD-ROMs) in collection. But, it has not gained the desired momentum in the libraries of colleges of education. It was found that only nine libraries had non-book material in meager quantity. Out of these, seven libraries possessed a few CD's and one had cassettes that came free with books. Another library had approximately 400 maps.

Dissertations

Out of 15 colleges running M.Ed. course, libraries of 13 had dissertations. Eight libraries possessed less than 300 dissertations and three had 300-400 titles. Two libraries possessed more than 400 dissertations. Number of the dissertations possessed by libraries varied according to the year of starting M.Ed. course. The University College of Education, Bathinda and SDS College of Education, Lopon started M.Ed. courses during the academic sessions 2006-07 and 2007-08 respectively. Libraries of both of these colleges did not have dissertations.

Periodical Literature

Periodical publications serve the purpose of both information and recreation. These include journals, magazines and all other publications, which are issued at regular intervals.

Journals

Journals are the subject specific periodicals, usually containing primary information. Table 5.13 represents data about the number of journals on subscription of libraries.

Table 5.13. Number of Journals on Subscription.

Sl. No.	Number of Journals	No. of Libraries	%age
1	0-10	04	21.05
2	11-20	10	52.63
3	21-30	03	15.79
4	More than	30 02	10.53
	Total	19	100.00

Table 5.13 reveals that majority of the libraries forming 52.63% were subscribing to 11-20 journals. Three libraries had

21-30 journals on subscription, while two libraries were subscribing to more than 30 journals. Only one library subscribed two international journals. A government aided college library was subscribing to merely two journals. The NCTE has prescribed for B.Ed. and M.Ed. colleges to subscribe to a minimum of 10 and 15 journals respectively. But libraries of two colleges offering B.Ed. course and three colleges offering M.Ed. course in addition to B.Ed. also did not meet these standards. The NCTE provided revised norms regarding journals for M.Ed. course. It requires each library to have subscription to at least one international publication.

Back Volumes of Journals

Back volumes of journals are the vital sources of information for furtherance of research. All the libraries except one had back volumes of journals.

Table 5.14 depicts that eight (44.44%) out of a total 18 libraries having back volumes of journals had less than 100 back volumes, while three (16.67%) had 100-200 volumes. Three libraries possessed 200-400 volumes, whereas other three libraries were having more than 400 back volumes of journals. One librarian had not specified the number of back volumes of journals available in library. Survey brought to notice that back volumes of journals were not properly organized as six libraries had loose issues, while in three libraries these were partially bound.

Table 5.14. Back Volumes of Journals.

Sl. No.	Number of Volumes	No. of Libraries	%age
1	0-100	08	44.44
2	100-200	03	16.67
3	200-400	03	16.67
4	More than 400	03	16.67
5	No Response	01	05.55
	Total	18	100.00

Magazines

In addition to journals, libraries provide general magazines to users for reading. Majority of the of libraries i. e. 13 (68.42%) were subscribing to less than 20 magazines, while four had 21-30 magazine titles on subscription. Two libraries were making available more than 30 magazine titles for users.

Newspapers

Sometimes, newspapers contain information not available from other sources. Fifteen libraries were subscribing to 05-10 newspaper titles, whereas two had 05 or less newspapers on subscription. A library was subscribing to more than 10 newspapers daily in English, Punjabi and Hindi.

LIBRARY BUILDING

Libraries are dynamic institutions which continue to grow in terms of collection, staff and readers. In order to tackle the resultant growth it becomes necessary to house a library in an independent, functional and modular building. Keeping in view the significance of library building, query was made to ascertain whether libraries have their own independent buildings. Responses revealed that only one government aided college library had an independent building used exclusively for library purpose. The remaining 18 libraries were housed in buildings forming part of college premises. During visit, it was observed that library of GHG Khalsa College of Education, Gurusar Sadhar was sharing building with canteen. Library was located on first floor while canteen was sited on ground floor, causing disturbance to library users.

Majority of the libraries i. e. seven (36.84%) were housed in single rooms, while six (31.58%) libraries had two rooms each. Three libraries consisted of four rooms and one had more than five rooms. It was astounding to find during visit to Khalsa College of Education, Mukatsar that a teacher was taking class in library.

When asked, assistant librarian shared that it was a usual practice. Majority of the libraries were housed in one or two rooms, which can not be considered sufficient for effective functioning of libraries. The NCTE norms about library building need to be revised. These require each college to have "a library-cum-reading room."

Separate Reading Room

A separate reading room with sufficient seating capacity and free from disturbance is the essence of all types of libraries. Survey revealed that only five (26.31%) libraries had separate reading rooms for users, while in remaining libraries chairs were arranged within stack area. Similarly, five libraries had separate librarian's offices to perform the documentary work. In remaining libraries these were in the form of tables or cabins in corners of libraries.

USERS' VISIT TO LIBRARIES

Libraries exist to meet the information needs of users. The strength of users, their information needs and subjects of study, etc. greatly influence the resources and services of libraries. Table 5.15 reveals the average number of visitors to libraries.

Table 5.15. Average Number of Visitors to Libraries.

Sl. No.	Number of Visitors	No. of Libraries	%age
1	0-40	03	15.79
2	40-80	06	31.58
3	80-120	06	31.58
4	More than 120	04	21.05
	Total	19	100.00

It is evident from the table 5.15 that six (31.58%) libraries were being visited by 80-120 users and other six libraries were visited by 40-80 users everyday. Four libraries were visited by more than 120 users daily on an average. In three libraries less than 40 users were visiting a day. The number of daily visitors to libraries varied due to variation in the students' strength with colleges.

SEATING CAPACITY

A library is supposed to provide adequate seating arrangement to users for reading inside library premises.

Following table reveals the seating capacity of libraries. Table 5.16 shows that majority of the libraries had seating capacity for 26-50 users, while 04 libraries could accommodate 76- 100 users at a time. Three libraries had less than 25 seats each for users.

Table 5.16. Seating Capacity for Users.

Sl. No.	Number of Visitors	No. of Libraries	%age
1	0-25	03	15.79
2	26-50	08	42.10
3	51-75	03	15.79
4	76-100	04	21.05
5	More than 100	01	05.27
	Total	19	100.00

A library had seating arrangement for more than 100 users. Six libraries had separate seating arrangement for M.Ed. students, while libraries of remaining nine colleges offering M.Ed. course did not have such facility. Ten libraries had separate seating arrangement for teachers. The NCTE prescribed for each college to provide seating arrangement in libraries for at least 25% of their B.Ed. students and for 10 students of M.Ed. course, but 08 libraries did not meet this requirement.

NCTE has revised norms regarding seating capacity of libraries for B.Ed course. It requires libraries to have seating arrangement for at least fifty per cent of B.Ed students. Only one library had drinking water facility for users. Similarly, Library of DAV College of Education, Abohar had toilet facility for faculty members. Students were not allowed to use that.

LIBRARY BUDGET AND SOURCES OF FINANCE

The impact of Information and Communication Technologies (ICTs) on libraries has brought structural changes to library practices. Effective library management and provision of services depends upon the availability of adequate funds.

It was disappointing to find that none of the libraries except one had provision for library budget. Only UCE,

Bathinda had provision of ₹ 50,000 each year for reading material. But since its establishment in 2001 no increase has been made in this amount. Libraries of GCE and GACE mainly depended up on the UGC grants. Moreover, NCTE is silent about the financial provision for libraries. In libraries of colleges of education under study, the sources of finance varied considerably.

Major sources of finance for purchase of reading material are given below:

* University Grants Commission (UGC) Grants
* Library Fees
* Library Development Funds and
* Amalgamated Funds

UGC Grants

The UGC plays a significant role in funding libraries through out the country. An attempt was made to find whether libraries have received any grant from UGC during the period 2002-2007. Only 13 (68.42%) libraries responded.

Table 5.17 shows that out of 13 libraries, 10 (76.92%) received recurring grants under tenth five year plan, while a library got nonrecurring grant from UGC during the period 2002-2007. Office superintendent of the government aided college shared that the college had received special grant for library meant for 'Backward District College'. Libraries of two colleges including UCE and a government aided college had not received any recurring or non-recurring grant from UGC. The government aided college had not demanded grants from UGC because of the conflict between members of college management committee.

Table 5.17. Type of Grants Received from UGC.

Sl. No.	Type of Grant Received	No. of Libraries	%age
1	Recurring	10	76.92
2	Non-Recurring	01	07.70
3	No Grant	02	15.38
	Total	13	100.00

Amount of Grants Received by Libraries

Librarians were asked to mention the amount of grants received from UGC during the period 2002-2007. Responses received were arranged into different ranges of one lakh each.

Table 5.18 reveals a considerable variation in the amount of grants received by 11 libraries. Majority of the libraries received less than ₹ 01 lakh as UGC grant for purchase of reading material under tenth five year plan, while 36.36% received 1-2 lakhs. A library received grant of more than rupees three lakhs from UGC.

Table 5.18. Extent of Grants Recevid.

Sl. No.	Amount of Grants Received (Rs)	No. of Libraries	%age
1	Up to one Lakh	06	54.54
2	1-2	04	36.36
3	2-3	—	—
4	3-4	01	09.10
	Total	11	100.00

Grants from State Government

None of the libraries under study received grants from the State Government during the period 2002-2007. The State Government had earlier given grants to libraries of GCE only, as reported by librarians.

Amalgamated Fund

Amalgamated fund is collected from students each year at the time of admission to colleges. This amount is to be used for various purposes i. e. cultural activities, games, library and for some other similar purposes. Allocation of amalgamated funds towards library depends upon the discretion of the principals of colleges.

Library Fee and Library Development Funds

As like amalgamated fund, Library Fee and Library Development Fund are also charged from students at the time of admission to colleges. Out of the 13 responding colleges, eight charged library fee at varying rates from Rs.200-400. In four colleges it was termed as 'Books and Journals Fee'. Similarly four colleges charged library development fund from students at different rates of 100-200. In a government aided college it was being charged under the head 'Books Replacement Fund'.

Overdue Fine

The negligible amount of overdue fine can not be considered as reliable and sufficient source of funds for libraries. In UCE, the amount of overdue fine goes to the University Account.

TECHNICAL PROCESSING

Technical processing of documents takes place after accessioning. It covers all the activities related with their classification, cataloguing and physical processing. Classification provides systematic order among documents and catalogue guide the users to retrieve needed documents easily from large collection, through various access points.

Classification

Collection has to be classified and the classification scheme has to be user friendly. Survey revealed that out of a total 19 libraries, 18 had classified their collection. On the other hand, in the library of Dev Samaj College of Education for Women, Ferozepur City that was established in 1942, collection was not classified at all. Almirah numbers were written on catalogue cards instead of call numbers. The following table furnishes data about the extent of classification of documents in libraries:

Table 5.19 reveals that in majority of the libraries i. e. 11 (57.90%) collection was fully classified, while in seven (36.84%) libraries it was classified partially. In a remaining library documents were not classified at all. It has been found that all libraries were using Dewey Decimal Classification (DDC) scheme ranging from 16th to 21st edition to classify collection. Earlier UCE library was using Colon Classification (CC), but later on it switched over to DDC. Three librarians responded of facing problems in classifying collection. A librarian having 18th edition of DDC shared that the respective library had an old edition of DDC which did not contain detailed class numbers for the subject of Computer. Librarian of Government College of Education, Jalandhar said, "It becomes very difficult to decide the main class of a book in case of interdisciplinary subject books". A librarian stated lack of professionally qualified staff as one of the obstacles in organizing collection.

Table 5.19. Status of Classification of Collection.

Sl. No.	Extent of Classification	No. of Colleges	%age
1	Fully Classified	11	57.90
2	Partially Classified	07	36.84
3	Not At All Classified	01	05.26
	Total	19	100.00

Cataloguing

Survey revealed that 11 (57.90%) libraries had partially catalogued their collection, not providing access points for all documents in possession. On the other hand, eight libraries had fully catalogued their holdings. Majority of the libraries *i.e.* 11 (57.90%) were following Anglo American Cataloguing Rules-II and remaining eight (42.10%) libraries were using Anglo-American Cataloguing Rules-I for cataloging. This reflects the popularity of dictionary catalogue over classified catalogue among college libraries.

Number of Entries Prepared for Each Document

Users may approach a document through different access points *i.e.* subject, author, title, etc. Table shows the number of entries prepared for each volume in libraries to provide access to their holdings.

Table 5.20 reveals that in nine (47.37%) libraries, only two entries, and in six libraries only one entry for each document was prepared. Three librarians responded that they prepared all possible entries for each book in possession. Librarians were further asked to state the time taken to process new arrivals.

Table 5.20. Number of Entries Prepared for each Document.

Sl. No.	No. of Entries Prepared	No. of Libraries	%age
1	One Entry	06	31.58
2	Two Entries	09	47.37
3	Three Entries	01	05.26
4	All Possible Entries	03	15.79
	Total	19	100.00

Table 5.21 depicts that in eight libraries, it was taking 1-2 weeks to process new arrivals, whereas, in other eight libraries books were being processed with in a week. Three librarians responded of taking more than two weeks to process documents, due to inadequate staff. All libraries maintained card catalogue. Eight libraries using computers also prepared computer-based databases of books. Five librarians mentioned the problems they faced in cataloguing, whereas, remaining majority responded otherwise.

Table 5.21. Time Taken to Process Books from Date of Acquisition.

Sl. No.	Average Time Taken	No. of Libraries	%age
1	Less than a Week	08	42.11
2	1-2 Weeks	08	42.11
3	More than Two Weeks	03	15.78
	Total	19	100.00

Three librarians complained of lack of professional staff and one of them further added that his college principal did not sanction funds even to purchase catalogue cards and cabinet. A librarian responded that they did not have catalogue code to get clarity in case of any doubt about cataloguing rules, while another shared that their library did not have standard subject heading list and they faced problem in assigning subject headings.

STOCK VERIFICATION

Stock verification, also known as physical verification brings to light the number of volumes missing from a library. It also helps to rectify the misplaced documents, and enable to take out books for repairing and binding. It has been found that 18 libraries were undertaking stock verification regularly, whereas in the library of UCE it was done since its establishment in 2001.

Frequency of Stock Verification

Responses revealed that out of 18 libraries, 11 (61.11%) undertook stock verification once in two years, whereas in seven (38.89%) libraries it was undertaken every year. Majority of libraries i.e. 15 did stock verification during vacations and a library carried out it during the period of examination. A librarian responded that, "It depends upon the availability of time" and another preferred to perform this job before the commencement of the new academic session. There are various tools to undertake stock verification i.e. stock taking registers, accession register, separate sheets with accession numbers, computers etc.

Table 5.22 depicts that out of the 18 libraries, 88.88% were using stock verification register for this purpose. A library was using accession register for stock verification, while in a government aided college library computer was used for the purpose.

Table 5.22. Method used for Stock Varification.

Sl. No.	Method of Stock Verification	No. of Libraries	%age
1	Stock Verification Register	16	88.88
2	Computer	01	05.56
3	Accession Register	01	05.56
	Total	18	100.00

Average Loss of Books

Librarians were asked to mention the quantum of loss of documents suffered annually on an average. Responses received are shown in table 5.23:

Table 5.23. Quantum of Loss of Books.

Sl. No.	Average Loss of Books	No. of Libraries	%age
1	0-20	05	27.77
2	21-40	07	38.89
3	41-80	01	05.56
4	No Loss	01	05.56
5	Loss Not Calculated	01	05.56
6	Not Specified	03	16.66
	Total	18	100.00

It is obvious from Table 5.23 that out of 18 libraries, in 07 (38.89%) libraries average loss of collection per year ranged from 20 to 40 books, whereas in 05 libraries it was below 20 documents. In a library average loss of documents went beyond 40. Three librarians had not specified any number representing loss of book, but responded that it was very low. A librarian responded that they never found any book missing from library. Another shared that they did stock verification every year, but never calculated the loss of books because of shortage of time and adequate staff, which makes stock verification useless.

Responsibility for Loss of Books

Responses revealed that in 14 libraries out of the 18 undertaking stock verification, missing books were written off against loss of books, while staff of four libraries responded that they were held responsible for the loss. On asking about the policy for writing off books, staff of 16 libraries responded that maximum three books were being written off for every thousand books with the permission of library committee. Whereas two librarians responded, "there is no such policy, library committee takes the decision for writing off books".

CIRCULATION SERVICE

Circulation is highly used service of a college library. Survey revealed that in two libraries 'demand boxes' were placed for B.Ed. students. The students were required to put slips in demand box giving details of needed books and their identification. The demand boxes were being opened next day morning to take out the needed books from almirahs for lending to students. Similarly, a library adopted slip system for lending books to B.Ed. students. In these libraries the M.Ed. students were entitled to borrow books at any time. The remaining 16 libraries had practice of lending books on the spot when demanded.

Number of Books Users were Entitled to Borrow

An attempt was made to find the maximum number of books that a user could borrow from library at a time. Responses received are organized according to category of users.

B.Ed. Students

No uniformity was found among libraries on the number of books that users were entitled to borrow at a time. Majority of the libraries *i.e.* 11 (57.90%) entitled users to borrow three or less books at a time, whereas remaining eight (42.10%) libraries had this limit between books.

M.Ed. Students

Total 5.24 colleges were offering M.Ed. course in addition to B.Ed. In libraries of 12 (80%) of these colleges, users were entitled to borrow 04-06 books, whereas in two libraries they were allowed to borrow up to three books only at a time. In a government aided college library M.Ed. students were entitled to borrow up to 10 books at a time.

Table 5.24. Number of Books Entitled to Borrow (M.ED. Sutdent).

Sl. No.	No. of Books Being Issued at a Time	No. of Libraries	%age
1	1-3	02	13.33
2	4-6	12	80.00
3	7-10	01	06.67
	Total	15	100.00

Teachers

Table 5.25 reveals that eight libraries had no limit over the number of books a teacher could borrow at a time. Six libraries entitled teachers to borrow 06-10 books, while a library gave privilege to teachers to borrow up to 30 books at a time in case he or she was guiding M.Ed. students for dissertation.

Table 5.25. Number of Books Entitled to Borrow (Teachers).

Sl. No.	No. of Books Being Issued at a Time	No. of Libraries	%age
1	1-5	—	—
2	6-10	06	31.57
3	11-15	03	15.79
4	15-20	01	05.27
5	20-30	01	05.27
6	No Limit	08	42.10
	Total	19	100.00

Loan Period

Students

It has been found that majority of the libraries were lending books to B.Ed. and M.Ed. students for 14-15 days. In a government aided college library users were entitled to keep books with them for seven days only. In case of M.Ed. students, a library had practice of lending books for a month.

Teachers

Ten (52.63%) libraries had not fixed any loan period for teachers. They were entitled to keep books with them as long as desired. Four libraries had practice of lending books for one month, while in three libraries teachers were privileged to retain books with them for the full session. A library had practice of lending books to teachers for the period of one year, while another fixed loan period as three months.

System of Circulation

It is evident from the Table 5.26 that 17 (89.48%) libraries were using ledger system for circulation of books, while one was using Browne system. In library of a government aided college computer was being used for circulation. In two libraries, B.Ed. students were allowed to borrow books during particular fixed time only. In a government aided college library books were issued to students during the period of tea break and lunch break only, while in another library circulation time was fixed as 11 a.m. to 3.30 p.m., though the library was kept open for 9 a.m. to 4 p.m. In remaining libraries there was no such restriction of time for lending books to students. A few libraries had fixed days for different sections of students for circulation.

Table 5.26. System of Circulation.

Sl. No.	System of Circulation	No. of Libraries	%age
1	Ledger System	17	89.48
2	Browne System	01	05.26
3	Computer	01	05.26
	Total	19	100.00

AVERAGE NUMBER OF BOOKS ISSUED DAILY

B.Ed Students

Table 5.27 shows that in five (26.32%) libraries up to 30 books were being issued daily. Four (21.05%) libraries were lending 31-60 books and other four were lending 61-90 books to B.Ed. students per day on an average. In 04 (21.05%) libraries more than 120 books and in two libraries 91-120 books were being issued everyday. The variation in number of books being circulated by libraries was caused by variation in student's strength with colleges also.

Table 5.27. Number of Books Issued Daily.

Sl. No.	Average Number of Books Issued	No. of Libraries	%age
1	0-30	05	26.32
2	31-60	04	21.05
3	61-90	04	21.05
4	90-120	02	10.53
6	More than 120	04	21.05
	Total	19	100.00

M.Ed. Students

In case of M.Ed. students, five libraries were lending 21-30 books and other five were lending 11-20 books daily. Responses revealed that two libraries were lending more than 30 books everyday. In proportion to the strength of M.Ed. students considerable number of books were being circulated daily. In two libraries dissertations were also being issued to M.Ed students for two days only.

Teachers

In 11 libraries up to 10 books and in seven libraries 11-20 books were being issued to teachers daily. A library was lending more than 20 books to teachers on an average.

Return of Books

Responses revealed that in 17 libraries students return books in time with in the prescribed loan period, whereas two librarians responded otherwise. The majority of the libraries had not fixed any loan period for teachers, therefore no question of timely return of books by them arises. Responses revealed that out of remaining nine libraries having prescribed loan period, teachers of five colleges did not return books by the due date.

OVERDUE FINE

Sixteen (84.21%) libraries were charging overdue fine from users for return of books after due date, whereas remaining 03 libraries did not. Out of the 16 libraries charging overdue fine from students, 15 could not dare to charge it from teachers. Only UCE library was charging overdue fine from teachers for late return of books.

Rate of Charges

Majority of the libraries were charging overdue fine from users at a nominal rate of ₹ 1 or less per book per day. It is interesting to mention here that in a government college library overdue fine was being charged from students @ Rs.10 per book per day.

RESERVATION OF BOOKS

Librarians were asked whether they had provision for reservation service in case the needed books were already issued to other users. Response revealed that majority of the libraries comprising 17 (89.48%) were providing reservation service to users, while remaining two libraries did not.

MOST USED COLLECTION

Responses revealed that in 17 libraries textbooks were used by students and teachers more frequently than other documents. Of remaining two libraries, a librarian responded that books of all categories were used equally, while, another shared that text books and reference books were used more frequently.

EXPECTATION OF THE INTERNET CONNECTIVITY

Responses of the library staff revealed that the users of 12 libraries did not expect the Internet connectivity in libraries because of its availability in computer labs, whereas seven librarians responded that users do expect this service. Six libraries were already providing the Internet service to users. Librarians responded that users expect the Internet in libraries for academic purpose *i.e.* to access research papers and objects in the subject of education.

SERVICES

Our education system is becoming more and more complex. The classroom instruction alone cannot be considered sufficient to attain educational objectives. College libraries exist to supplement their parent institutions in achieving educational goals. Therefore, these are expected to provide the necessary services and facilities to users. Services provided by libraries under study are discussed here.

Opening Hours of Libraries

Opening hours of libraries have direct bearing on the use of their resources and services. Survey brought to notice that 15 (78.94%) libraries were being kept open for 6-7 hours a day, while remaining 04 (21.06%) libraries were being opened for

7-8 hours daily. Working hours of majority of the libraries coincided with class hours. All libraries remained closed with colleges on Sunday and holidays, but were kept open during vacations.

It has been found that during vacations also majority of the libraries were kept open for 6-7 hours a day, while a library remained open for 4-5 hours only. Three librarians shared that there was no specific timing for opening libraries during vacations.

REFERENCE SERVICE

Responses revealed that all libraries were providing reference service. Librarians were further asked to indicate the type of reference service being rendered.

Table 5.28 makes it clear that 17 libraries were providing only short-range reference service while two librarians accepted of providing long-range reference service also in addition to short-range reference service.

Table 5.28. Provision of Reference Service.

Sl. No.	Type of Reference Service	No. of Libraries	%age
1	Short Range	17	89.48
2	Short Range and Long Range	02	10.52
	Total	19	100.00

Current Awareness Service (CAS)/Selective Dissemination of Information (SDI)

Current Awareness Service is aimed at keeping users abreast with the latest developments in concerned field. As reported by librarians, 11 libraries were providing CAS, while remaining 08 did not. None of the libraries had provision for SDI service. Librarians were further asked about the methods of providing CAS.

The responses received for multi-choice options are given in Table 5.29:

Table 5.29. Method of Providing Current Awareness Service.

Sl. No.	Methods of CAS	No. of Libraries	%age
1	Display of List of Recent Acquisitions	03	27.28
2	Recent Acquisitions Display	06	54.54
3	Routing of Periodicals	05	45.46
4	Verbal Discussion with Users	01	09.10
	Total	15	100.00

Table 5.29 reveals that majority of the libraries were providing CAS through display of recent acquisitions and 03 were rendering it by display of recent acquisition lists. Five libraries were circulating periodicals among teacher. A librarian shared that he provided CAS through verbal discussion with the users. But on the other hand, only one student of a college was familiar about this service.

Book Exhibitions

Only four libraries were organizing book exhibitions. Two librarians responded of organizing these on the 'important occasions' *i.e.* Gandhi Jayanti, Maharishi Dayanand Anniversary etc. A library organized book exhibition on the occasion of annual convocation, while remaining one arranged that on the college functions. A few librarians invited booksellers to organize book exhibitions in their libraries. Three librarians responded of providing bibliographical services, while remaining responded otherwise.

Photocopy Service

The NCTE provided in its norms and standards that a college library shall have photocopying facility. Only 08 (42.10%) libraries had provision of photocopy service, while remaining majority *i.e.* 11 (57.90%) did not. In majority of the libraries it was offered at a genuine rate of 50 paise to ₹ 1 per copy, whereas in a library photocopy charges were fixed @ ₹ 1.50 per copy for students and ₹ 1 for teachers. All libraries except one had no limit over number of pages a user could get copied at a time. The remaining library had fixed this limit to a maximum of 20 flashes.

Resource Sharing

Resource sharing enables libraries to provide access to the users to the resources and services beyond their means and help to overcome the problem of paucity of funds. Only five libraries of GACE were participating in resource sharing programmes with other libraries. It has been found that resource sharing was limited to books only. These libraries were co-operating with the libraries of other institutes run by the same management.

Referral Service and Newspaper Clipping

Referral service is very useful as no library can acquire all the available information. Survey revealed that 14 libraries were providing referral service, while library staff of remaining five libraries responded otherwise. Staff of all libraries except one library had maintained newspaper clipping files of important newspaper objects on education and of news related to NCTE and their colleges.

ORIENTATION

Responses revealed that library staff of all libraries, except one was giving orientation to users towards libraries. Library staff was asked about the method of providing orientation. *Response received is tabulated below table 5.30:*

Table 5.30. Methods of Providing Orientation.

Sl. No.	Method Used	No. of Libraries	%age
1	Lecture	10	55.56
2	Visit Around Library	03	16.67
3	Notice Board	01	05.55
4	Lecture and Visit Around Library	03	16.67
5	Other Method	01	05.55
	Total	18	100.00

It is evident from Table 5.30 that in 55.56% of the 18 libraries giving orientation to users, it was provided through lecture method, while in three (16.67%) libraries users were taken around libraries. In three libraries, a combination of the aforesaid methods was used to give orientation. In UCE library users were given orientation individually at the time of giving them membership.

Access

Open access is essential to facilitate maximum use of library collection. It gives users opportunities to browse documents on their own and enable them to find most relevant information. Survey brought to notice that only five libraries had open access system and eight libraries were providing partially open access. The remaining six libraries had close access to collection. Fear of theft and lack of adequate number of staff members were the main reasons for following close access. During visit to DAV College of Education, Abohar it was observed that books were kept in almirahs touching the ceiling of library, leaving no scope for browsing.

USE OF COMPUTERS

The ICTs has greatly enhanced the efficiency of library services. Computers are used to provide various library services and perform the routine, repetitive and clerical jobs. The functioning of all types of libraries is influenced by this vital machine. Libraries of college of education are also adapting to this need of the day. It was found that out of total 19 libraries, 10 libraries had computers, while remaining nine did not.

Eight libraries were using computers for automation, and one had two computers to provide the Internet service. In a library computer was kept aside in a corner without any use as library did not have any library automation software and the Internet connectivity. Librarians were further asked to indicate the softwares being used for library automation. The responses received from library staff of eight libraries using computers for library automation are discussed here.

Table 5.31. Software Being used for Automation of Libraries.

Sl. No.	Name of the Software	No. of Libraries	%age
1	SOUL	01	12.50
2	CDS/ ISIS	01	12.50
3	WINSIS	01	12.50
4	Alice for Windows	01	12.50
5	Local	02	25.00
6	Not Use Any Software	02	25.00
	Total	08	100.00

Table 5.31 shows that out of a total eight libraries using computers for automation, two libraries were using locally developed softwares, while another implemented SOUL for automation. A library has implemented CDS/ ISIS and other two were using WINSIS and Alice for Windows respectively. Two libraries had not used any library automation software but prepared databases of documents in 'Microsoft Word' and 'Microsoft Access' respectively. It was observed that majority of the libraries were using computer to perform housekeeping operations. All libraries were using computers to create databases of books. Five of these also created databases of journals, magazines and newspapers in addition to databases of books.

INTERNET

Majority of the libraries did not have the Internet connectivity, though the NCTE requires a library to have computer with the Internet facility for the use of faculty and student-teachers. Only six libraries were providing the Internet service to users.

ATTEMPTS TO PROMOTE USE OF LIBRARIES

Library staff of 17 libraries responded of making efforts to promote use of libraries, whereas in remaining two libraries no such attempts were being made. Both of these libraries did not have librarians and these were being run by restorers.

Library staff of 17 libraries responded of ascertaining information needs of users to improve the resources and services to promote use of libraries. Responses revealed that in three libraries, the library staff displayed the lists of recent arrivals and in six libraries they displayed the recent acquisitions to promote use of libraries. Librarians were further asked to indicate the methods used to ascertain information needs of users.

Table 5.32. Methods Used to Ascertain Information Needs of Users.

Sl. No.	Method to Ascertain Information Needs	No. of Libraries	% age
1	Discussion with Users	17	100.00
2	Maintain Suggestion	06	35.50
3	Record Queries	03	17.64
4	Conduct Survey	02	11.77
	Total	28	100.00

It is obvious from Table 5.32 that discussion with users was the most useful method to ascertain their information needs, as the staff of all 17 libraries ascertaining information needs of users was using this method. In addition, six libraries had maintained suggestion boxes. Two librarians reported about conducting user surveys to ascertain the information needs of their users and take necessary action wherever applicable. Three librarians responded of maintaining record of users' queries.

Inadequate staff was the major problem faced by librarians in promoting use of libraries. Nine librarians expressed the need to appoint more staff to serve users effectively. A librarian of a government aided college not having adequate supporting staff in library commented "I remain busy in locking and unlocking almirahs throughout the day and do not get time for this."

PROBLEMS FACED BY LIBRARIANS

Librarians were asked to express the problems being faced by them in managing libraries.

Inadequate Staff

Lack of adequate staff was the major obstacle in functioning of libraries, influencing their organization and administration. Nine librarians responded that they did not have adequate staff to serve the users. It has been found that three libraries were being run by restorers. Many GACE did not have the sanctioned posts of library restorers and library attendants. Librarians were overburdened with the non-professionals jobs due to lack of adequate staff.

Problem of Space

Some libraries including library of Government College of Education, Jalandhar were suffering from the problem of insufficient space. Only five libraries had separate reading room for users whereas, in remaining libraries chairs were arranged in stack area. A librarian complained of shortage of furniture.

Paucity of Funds

Funds are the nerve centre of an organization. Responses of the library staff of four colleges revealed that they were facing the problem of scarcity of funds for purchase of reading material. Purchase of documents largely depended upon the UGC grants. The administration of colleges contributed less towards libraries. A librarian shared that they did not have funds even to purchase catalogue cabinet and cards.

Status

Society has not recognized librarians equivalent to teachers. Three librarians complained that they were not given equal recognition with teaching staff. In spite of the higher academic and professional qualification they were thought as a part of clerical staff. One of the librarians went to the extent of saying that they were on a par with the teachers in terms of salary only but not in status.

SUGGESTIONS OF LIBRARY STAFF

Library staff was required to give suggestions to improve the services of libraries to make them more effective. Library staff of 10 libraries made suggestions for the provision of more staff in libraries to serve the users, as majority of the libraries did not have adequate staff. A restorer serving at a government aided college library, where post of librarian was vacant responded that college should appoint librarian to relieve her from the responsibility of managing library. Four librarians expressed the need for supporting staff to assist them in proper organization of libraries. Staff of five libraries suggested that libraries should be provided independent buildings to accommodate the growing collection and users.

A librarian demanded the provision of adequate furniture in library. Library staff of four colleges suggested for the provision of adequate funds for purchase of reading material, furniture and equipment to make library services more effective. A librarian responded that he has computer in library, but it was not being used for any purpose as the authorities had not sanctioned the requisite funds to purchase library automation software. Three librarians suggested for computerization of library operations for effective functioning.

FUTURE PLANS

Librarians of only five colleges expressed their future plans regarding libraries, whereas library staff of majority of the colleges had not responded to questions. Librarians of DAV College of Education, Hoshiarpur and Dev Samaj College of Education for Women, Ferozepur City had plans to develop local area network with in college campus. They also planned to introduce the Internet service in respective libraries. A librarian responded that he want to develop library as per the requirements of National Assessment and Accreditation Council (NAAC). Library of Khalsa College of Education, Amritsar had two computers to provide the Internet service. Its librarian was planning for automation of library operations using standard software. Similarly, two more librarians had plans to implement computers in libraries. One of them was interested in using SOUL software for library automation.

CONCLUSION

To conclude, libraries did not have adequate staff leaving librarians overburdened with the semi-professional and nonprofessional jobs. Six libraries did not have regular librarians, having its influence on the organization and administration of libraries. Moreover, the NCTE has not provided any detailed norms regarding library staff. It has been found that the functioning of library committees was restricted to acquisition and writing off missing books rather than the overall development of libraries. Student's involvement in committees was almost absent, as only one college library had students' representatives as members of library committee. By and large libraries did not have any collection development policy.

Analysis brought forward that teachers and principals were playing leading role in selection of documents, while librarians had little say in selection of subject related books. Availability of financial support influenced the collection size of libraries. Libraries of GCE had more volumes than libraries of GACE and UCE. Non-book material was almost absent in libraries. A few libraries had CD's that came free with books, though the NCTE prescribed for colleges to have 'electronic publications' in collection. Many libraries did not meet the NCTE norms regarding annual addition of books and minimum number of journals on subscription.

Only five libraries had separate reading rooms, while in remaining libraries chairs were arranged with in stack area. The NCTE norms about library buildings need to be revised, as it requires each college to have library-cum-reading room. It was observed that in a government aided college library books were arranged on shelves touching the ceiling. When users need books they express their demand to library staff and then library attendant take out books from shelves using ladder. Except UCE, none of the colleges had provision for library budget.

The UGC grants, library fee, library development fund and amalgamated fund constituted the regular source of finance. The NCTE remained silent about financial provision for libraries. Survey revealed the lack of standardization for technical processing of collection. In seven libraries, collection was partially classified, whereas in the library of a college established in 1942, collection has not yet been classified. Eleven libraries had partially catalogued collection. Eight libraries gave the privilege to the teachers to borrow as many books as they wish, while 10 libraries allowed them to keep books with themselves for as long as desired. Shockingly, two libraries were using demand box system and another was using slip system for lending books to B.Ed. students. Majority of the libraries were being opened for 6-7 hours a day, leaving users with little time to use libraries.

In addition to circulation, reference service was the only service provided by all libraries. Eleven librarians admitted of providing Current Awareness Service (CAS), but on the other hand only one student and a few teachers were aware about this service. Eight libraries were rendering photocopy service. Libraries did not provide any advance library services. Only eight libraries were using computer for automation of their operations. In addition, a library had two computers to provide the Internet service. Only six libraries had the Internet connectivity, though the NCTE prescribed that college library should have computer with the Internet connectivity. Library staff of 17 libraries responded of ascertaining information needs of users to improve resources and services to promote use of libraries.

Discussion with users was the most useful method to ascertain information needs of users. In addition, two librarians reported about conducting user surveys to find information needs of users. Lack of staff and paucity of the funds were the major problems faced by librarians. Another major problem is related with the status of library staff vis-à-vis. teachers, they feel that that they are not on a par with the teaching staff and this leads to frustration and apathetic mind set of library staff. It is in the hands of the library staff also to change this attitude and make a place for themselves in the college. It was good to find that many librarians were planning to implement computers and provide the Internet services in libraries.

6

Financial Resources

INTRODUCTION

In this chapter we first present the data compiled and discuss their validity. Then Trends over the eight-year period are established. Expenditure is then analysed 'per capita' - to normalise the results between large and small countries. Most CEE States show very low levels of resources in financial terms. The reason of this may be due to currency conversion problems, but much can be attributed to lower standards of living and of national resource in the economy of those states. To understand this better the main data are, finally, analysed as a proportion of Gross Domestic Product (GDP) devoted to library resources.

METHODOLOGY

The most comprehensive and reliable Expenditure data are provided for materials. It is unusual for library managers not to have a materials budget, so figures on materials expenditure are generally maintained and reported. The cost of rebinding and preservation activity is often not included with expenditure on new books. 'Servicing' operations - special physical labelling and reinforcement plus catalogue cards or records - is often done by the supplier and included here: but sometimes it is done by library staff and charged to a general account. Data on staff expenditure are usually available - although there can be comparability problems where payroll is managed by a parent sponsoring department rather than by the library itself. There are also different practices regarding the inclusion or exclusion of the costs of recruitment, staff training - though it is now generally accepted that indirect items - pensions, social security, etc. - need to be included. Figures for total revenue expenditure are less complete: many returns give expenditure on materials and on staff but not total expenditure. There are comparability problems with various overhead items - particularly premises, security, refurbishment, and computer systems. For these reasons comparisons between Materials and Staff figures are generally more reliable and these possible pitfalls must be kept in mind when making comparisons. However, there has been little change in accounting procedures and conventions during the period, so the percentage change calculations can be treated with confidence.

INFLATION

While in real terms expenditure has increased significantly - the precise percentage depends on the index of general price inflation selected for the calculation. This varies significantly between countries - as is shown in Table. However, between 1991 - 1997 general price inflation in most Western European states varied within the 15 - 20 per cent range. The composite EU Consumer Price Index published in the Eurostat Yearbook 1997 gives 18.7% between 1991 and 1997 - with the rate of inflation slowing markedly since 1995. For our purposes inflation between 1991-98 is taken as about 20 per cent. Inflation in the price of books can be taken as within the same range but periodical prices increased by a vastly greater percentage. So, in broad terms, reported overall increases of expenditure above 20 per cent can certainly be treated as genuine increases in real terms.

Trends

There has been greatly increased activity in Tertiary Libraries and lack of growth - overall - in the Public Library sector, with modest growth in National Libraries. The obvious expectation from this is that levels of expenditure have increased more in the Tertiary sector than in others. Here we look at the situation overall - and at the main trend results as given in Table 6.1.

Table 6.1. Main Trends in Financial Results.

		Expenditure	
	1991 € millions	**1998 € millions**	**%age change**
Staff	5,007	6,697	34
Materials	2,342	3,121	33
Electronic information	317	528	67
Total Revenue Expenditure	10,347	13,965	35
INCOME ITEMS	382	648	70
Fees and Charges			
Other' (i.e.special funds)	432	1,034	139
CAPITAL PAYMENTS	487	695	43

Since staffing costs represent the largest part of the budget, expenditure on staff has increased at a rate reflected by the charge in total expenditure. The total expenditure on conventional materials also shows an average increase, but this average conceals an estimated + 64% for Special Libraries, + 40% for Tertiary, + 27% for National, + 33% for Schools, and only + 1% for Public Libraries. As anticipated the data show a dramatic 67 per cent increase in expenditure on Electronic Materials.

This is heavily concentrated in the Tertiary and Special Libraries sectors - and Special Libraries are more fully represented in these statistics than ever before. It is significant, however, that the 1998 results show Electronic Information still at only 15 per cent of total materials expenditure - so confirming that conventional materials are still dominant. Capital payments are reported by only a minority of states and are affected by inconsistent accounting both within and between states. The increase reported in Capital Payments contains some impressive investment in National Libraries during the period. No separate figure is necessary for total income, as all library organisations balance their books – at least over a number of years. Perhaps the most surprising revelation in this set of statistics lies in the specifically identified 'Income Items'.

The magnitude of the increase in Fees and Charges - 70 per cent - is impressive, and the pattern is virtually universal across all countries. At this strength this is a new trend. It would be interesting to explore how far it relates to income from conventional services and how far it is associated with new electronic resources and networked provision of materials. The even larger increase in 'Other' income will relate to specific grants for development and modernisation as well as to diversified funding sources. Again it would be interesting and important to have more detailed information on this - now that these statistics establish the magnitude of this trend. The net result of these 'Income Items' is that they now cover 12 per cent of total library expenditure - the balance coming from regular institutional sources.

Countries and Sectors

We present here a number of 'Cross Sector Total' tables covering the main financial variables. Each table consists first of the 1998 data entered onto the database for each country. Three dots (...) shows that no satisfactory information was provided for that feature in that country. The next part contains the grossed up estimates for All States and for regions and geographical areas. The 'Response%' gives the proportion of the All States grossed up figure that is represented by actual data. Finally percentages are calculated to show, for this feature, the relative strength of each sector overall - which have already been presented in Table.

MATERIALS SPEND

Table 6.2 summarises the available data - uncorrected for population or for living standards. This gives a useful indication of the size of the library market for suppliers of print materials. The returns are particularly comprehensive for the Tertiary sector. The data in table take no account of country size.

Table 6.2. Materials Costs (€ 000s).

0	National 1	Tertiary 2	Public 3	Special 4	Other 5	School 6	1998 Total 7
Bulgaria	98	391	450	240	158	79	
Czech Republic	495	3,253	4,485	...	0	...	
Estonia	385	1,049	2,860	272	702	809	
Hungary	382	...	3,630	6,553	...	...	
Latvia	261	281	849	...	77	...	
Lithuania	232	436	960	340	264	3,942	
Poland	382	7,932	...	...	...	...	
Romania	190	...	798	...	0	...	
Slovak Republic	176	1,008	962	...	...	6	
Slovenia	...	3,844	6,116	...	0	5,566	
Austria	1,352	26,526	5,038	...	...	...	
Belgium	...	14,408	23,238	...	...	...	
Denmark	2,155	13,831	46,576	4,801	0	16,197	
Ireland	344	10,754	7,131	...	0	...	
Finland	735	14,259	32,928	1,497	...	...	
France	...	57,044	100,661	...	...	...	
Greece	...	...	...	...	...	...	
Iceland	...	...	1,492	...	0	...	
Italy	...	65,603	...	...	...	...	
Liecht-enstein	...	...	...	...	0	...	
Luxembourg	...	...	...	...	0	...	

(*Contd...*)

0	1	2	3	4	5	6	7
Netherlands	1,396	32,180	...	55,114	0	...	
Norway	424	16,468	15,505	6,385	0	...	
Portugal	336	7,600	2,310	3,685	22	...	
Spain	2,047	49,883	22,575	35,053	4,365	...	
Sweden	710	23,184	40,985	2,200	...	...	
Switzerland	733	...	...	...	0	...	
UK	19,675	175,985	179,920	327,452	0	76,161	
Germany	32,725	198,427	86,406	94,623	...	...	
All States	98,752	779,841	761,850	900,389	14,574	565,555	3,120,961
CEE	2,566	27,560	32,470	52,412	2,257	75,041	192,306
EU	94,999	708,594	686,870	831,036	12,317	480,480	2,814,296
EFTA	1,187	43,687	42,510	16,941	0	10,033	114,358
Northern Europe	4,052	68,738	137,486	15,269	466	38,356	264,367
Central Europe	72,538	542,317	456,069	662,916	5,198	304,879	2,043,917
Southern Europe	19,597	141,226	135,826	169,791	6,653	147,278	620,371
Baltic States	878	1,767	4,669	20,296	1,043	6,427	35,080
Eastern Europe	1,688	25,793	27,801	32,116	1,215	68,614	157,227
Response total	65,151	724,346	585,875	538,215	5,588	102,760	2,021,935
Response%	66	93	77	60	38	18	65
Sector proportions	3.2	25	24.4	28.8	0.5	18.1	100

In order to produce figures that are more comparable between countries, these data have been presented on a 'per capita' basis in Table 6.3. The base for this table is not the sector's 'Target Population to be served': while this can be satisfactorily calculated for Tertiary, School and Public library clientele, there are severe difficulties in arriving at meaningful figures for the National and Special Library sectors. So in the interests of comparability the base here is Total Population.

Table 6.3. Materials Spend Per 1,000 Population (€ 000s).

0	National 1	Tertiary 2	Public 3	Special 4	Other 5	School 6	1998 Total 7
Bulgaria	11	45	51	27	18	9	
Czech Republic	48	316	436	...	0	...	
Estonia	252	686	1,869	178	458	529	
Hungary	38	...	359	648	...	...	
Latvia	102	110	332	...	30	...	
Lithuania	63	118	259	92	71	1,065	
Poland	10	207	...	...	...	...	
Romania	8	...	35	...	0	...	
Slovak Republic	33	188	180	...	...	1	
Slovenia	...	1,976	3,144	...	0	2,861	
Austria	169	3,319	630	...	...	...	
Belgium	...	1,488	2,400	...	...	...	
Denmark	422	2,707	9,115	940	0	3,170	
Ireland	99	3,101	2,056	...	0	...	
Finland	146	2,836	6,549	298	...	...	
France	...	1,031	1,819	...	...	...	
Greece	...	...	...	...	...	...	
Iceland	...	...	5,587	...	0	...	
Italy	...	1,159	...	...	...	...	

(*Contd...*)

0	1	2	3	4	5	6	7
Liechte-nstein	...	...	...	...	0	...	
Luxembourg	...	...	...	...	0	...	
Netherlands	95	2,181	...	3,735	0	...	
Norway	97	3,765	3,545	1,460	0	...	
Portugal	33	748	227	363	2	...	
Spain	53	1,299	588	913	114	...	
Sweden	81	2,647	4,679	251	...	...	
Switzerland	107	...	...	...	0	...	
UK	345	3,085	3,154	5,740	0	1,335	
Germany	411	2,490	1,084	1,187	...	...	
All States	206	1,627	1,589	1,878	30	1,180	6,510
CEE	24	261	308	497	21	711	1,822
EU	262	1,956	1,896	2,294	34	1,326	7,768
EFTA Northern	103	3,788	3,686	1,469	0	870	9,916
Europe Central	172	2,920	5,841	649	20	1,629	11,231
Europe Southern	308	2,305	1,939	2,818	22	1,296	8,688
Europe	170	1,227	1,181	1,476	58	1,280	5,392
Baltic States	113	227	600	2,606	134	825	4,505
Eastern Europe	17	264	285	329	12	702	1,609
Response total	***	***	***	***	***	***	***
Response %	***	***	***	***	***	***	***
Sector proportions	3.2	25	24.4	28.8	0.5	18.1	100

So, in 1998, European libraries spent on conventional materials €3.121 billion - and this represented an average of €6.5 per capita. A number of conclusions can be drawn from table:

* With the exception of Estonia and Slovenia it appears that the level of expenditure is very much lower in CEE states than in EU states. How far this is due to lack of economic wealth in those states generally - and how far to low resources devoted to libraries.
* In the EU States there is a tendency for high spending countries to spend at high levels in all sectors. The lower spending countries, on this 'per capita' basis, appear to be Portugal, Spain and France - with Scandinavian countries spending most.
* Again in the EU States there is much more homogeneity in the Tertiary sector than in Public Libraries.

The very high expenditure figure for UK Special Libraries stands out as quite exceptional.

This could be the result of either:

* More comprehensive and innovative statistical analysis,
* Exaggeration in the statistical estimating and/or
* A more developed information economy in the UK - particularly with respect to libraries in industry and commerce.

Table 6.4. Staff Expenditure (€ 000s).

0	National 1	Tertiary 2	Public 3	Special 4	Other 5	School 6	1998 Total 7
Bulgaria	315	636	2,808	259	785	444	
Czech Republic	1,586	...	12,175	...	0	612	
Estonia	1,853	1,266	3,944	489	620	1,121	
Hungary	3,422	...	17,186	...	...	...	

(*Contd...*)

0	1	2	3	4	5	6	7
Latvia	697	451	3,265	...	295	...	
Lithuania	1,241	1,174	6,635	759	322	...	
Poland	3,081	12,703	...	...	...	...	
Romania	555	...	2,656	...	0	...	
Slovak Republic	1,005	...	3,904	...	...	...	
Slovenia	...	...	10,927	...	0	8,100	
Austria	13,125	...	...	...	...	...	
Belgium	...	24,698	124,273	...	...	...	
Denmark	12,313	34,062	183,781	10,516	0	20,841	
Ireland	2,011	22,250	28,183	...	0	...	
Finland	4,951	26,400	125,322	7,198	...	...	
France	...	126,698	530,943	...	...	...	
Greece	...	...	...	...	...	...	
Iceland	...	...	3,580	...	0	...	
Italy	...	104,480	...	...	...	...	
Liechte-nstein	...	...	...	...	0	...	
Luxem-bourg	...	...	...	...	0	...	
Nether-lands	...	...	...	...	0	...	
Norway	...	...	61,386	...	0	...	
Portugal	4,075	4,732	10,358	7,908	858	...	
Spain	10,407	82,664	87,790	52,444	25,460	...	
Sweden	10,047	54,680	157,034	10,899	...	...	
Switzerland	6,139	...	...	...	0	...	
UK	91,000	298,768	662,676	547,430	0	188,576	

(*Contd...*)

0	1	2	3	4	5	6	7
Germany	84,495	240,319	477,250	67,986	...	...	
All States	372,581	1,209,703	3,348,022	1,253,91	760,041	453,134	6,697,398
CEE	14,012	28,530	105,038	11,701	4,109	83,165	246,555
EU	332,297	1,131,053	3,080,070	1,215,475	55,932	356,853	6,171,680
EFTA	26,272	50,120	162,914	26,741	0	13,116	279,163
Northern Europe	47,368	135,134	531,102	39,279	7,403	120,809	881,095
Central Europe	259,889	825,443	2,085,673	951,791	14,807	214,303	4,351,906
Southern Europe	51,312	220,596	626,209	251,146	33,722	34,857	1,217,842
Baltic States	3,791	2,890	13,843	1,460	1,237	4,744	27,965
Eastern Europe	10,221	25,640	91,195	10,241	2,872	78,422	218,591
Response total	252,318	1,035,981	2,516,076	705,888	28,340	219,694	4,758,297
Response %	68	86	75	56	47	48	71
Sector proportions	5.6	18.1	50.0	18.7	0.9	6.8	100.1

Further study is called for - and the encouragement of more data collection in this area. Comparisons with the situation in large countries in the Western Hemisphere would also be pertinent.

Comparing Tertiary with Public library materials expenditure at the country level is enlightening. States can be broadly placed in three categories:

Public Double Tertiary	Public = Tretiary	Tertiary Double Public
Bulgaria, Czech Republic	Slovak Pepublic	Austria
Estonia, Latvia	Solvenia	Ireland
Lithuania, Belgium, Denmark,	Norway	Germany
Finland, Sweeden, France	UK	Spain

There are a number of possible explanations for this:

- Historical emphasis in developing one sector earlier than another;
- Unequal allocation of resources;
- Public libraries in some countries taking on a major role for students;
- In some countries the public using academic libraries for some Non Fiction and Reference material.

These point either to institutional differences in the scope of each sector or to abnormal resource allocation. It is important to establish which is the main feature. This is not the place to speculate on particular situations - but the contrasts are so unexpectedly large that the reasons for these differences deserve serious consideration by policy makers in the states concerned. The low Tertiary results suggest the possibility of intellectual deprivation through inadequate provision of scientific and technical journals in the academic libraries of smaller or poorer countries - though this may be made good where national library is a major academic library *e.g.* Slovenia, Slovak Republic and Estonia.

While the newly compiled data on Special Libraries is incomplete and more subject to errors of estimation than more established statistical series, the data from Hungary, the Netherlands, Spain and the UK suggest that the level of expenditure on Materials may be as high, or even higher, in the Special Libraries sector than in Public and Tertiary libraries. Data from the School Library sector is much more sparse - sufficient only to point to the need for more data in what is an important area. The estimates of 28.8% for Special Libraries and of 18.1% for School Libraries must be treated with considerable caution at this stage: but their size certainly alters the perspective in which these sectors have traditionally been regarded.

EXPENDITURE ON STAFF

The response here is not quite as complete as for Materials expenditure. Comparing the two heads a very much higher proportion is spent on staff in public libraries (50% of all staff expenditure) - and to a lesser extent in national libraries. This largely reflects the much higher prices required for materials in the Tertiary and Special Library sectors compared to Public and School Library sectors. A simple but interesting ratio can be derived by combining Expenditure on Staff with Staff Numbers to give the data contained in table Staff Expenditure per Member of Staff.

Table 6.5. Staff Expenditure Per Member of Staff (€ 000s).

	National	Tertiary	Public	Special	Other	School	1998
0	1	2	3	4	5	6	Total 7
Bulgaria	957	...	...	...	...	...	
Czech Republic	3,573	...	2,803	...	...	...	
Estonia	3,527	2,541	2,689	3,109	4,770	2,098	
Hungary	6,337	...	4,428	...	...	...	
Latvia	1,557	1,365	1,718	...	2,953	...	
Lithuania	2,009	1,817	1,612	1,745	2,119	...	
Poland	3,397	1,924	...	...	...	...	
Romania	1,580	...	530	...	...	...	
Slovak Republic	3,573	...	2,803	...	...	...	
Slovenia	...	...	14,100	...	...	10,384	
Austria	42,613	...	...	...	...	...	
Belgium	...	34,786	31,541	...	...	...	
Denmark	38,941	38,101	35,347	26,965	...	17,966	
Ireland	29,569	29,666	21,679	...	...	...	
Finland	27,519	23,943	29,888	28,791	...	...	
France	...	32,621	25,843	...	...	...	
Greece	...	...	...	...	...	...	

(*Contd...*)

0	1	2	3	4	5	6	7
Iceland	...	...	...	...	...	...	
Italy	...	...	...	...	...	...	
Liechtenstein	...	...	...	...	...	...	
Luxembourg	...	...	...	...	...	...	
Netherlands	...	...	...	...	...	...	
Norway	...	...	32,286	...	...	...	
Portugal	12,853	5,029	7,149	6,173	9,431	...	
Spain	20,013	17,970	15,962	16,544	17,320	...	
Sweden	34,525	34,895	30,037	33,230	...	...	
Switzerland	59,482	...	...	...	...	...	
UK	31,347	22,982	25,656	30,413	...	36,265	
Germany	38,582	25,936	25,251	10,665	...	...	
All States	24,456	19,559	19,791	20,009	7,996	7,822	99,632
CEE	3,049	1,895	2,341	1,129	981	1,792	11,187
EU	32,629	25,474	25,863	23,775	16,842	33,054	157,637
EFTA	57,665	20,982	31,250	22,694	...	18,171	150,762
Northern Europe	41,605	29,908	31,801	27,309	16,826	27,266	174,715
Central Europe	34,272	25,875	26,034	24,748	16,826	35,492	163,246
Southern Europe	26,753	21,272	22,780	20,247	16,852	33,229	141,134
Baltic States	2,383	1,960	1,850	1,856	3,239	1,650	12,938
Eastern Europe	3,402	1,888	2,440	1,069	755	1,801	11,354

(*Contd...*)

0	1	2	3	4	5	6	7
Response total	***	***	***	***	***	***	***
Response %	***	***	***	***	***	***	***
Sector proportions	24.5	19.6	19.9	20.1	8.0	7.9	100

It should be remembered that the data requested here are the average cost per member of staff and not staff salaries, *i.e.* they should include social security and other indirect costs incurred by the employing organisation. But, with these reservations, the table will point to variations in staff salary levels.

A number of observations can be made:

- First, one value of these ratios is their use to check and query data supplied - to reveal transposition or categorisation errors and to get wrong data corrected.
- Generally there is consistency within a country where the figures for the main sectors show relatively low variation.
- The fact that the Special Library ratios mostly correspond to the norm gives confidence to them.
- The low costs in the few Schools figures may reflect less qualified personnel employed in Schools libraries – or failure to apply the FTE formula to part time staff.
- The above average levels in National and Special Libraries are no surprise given the technically advanced work requirements there and lower proportions of unqualified staff employed.

Again, however, it is clear that most of the CEE States and Portugal are showing very low figures. How far are these to be explained by low salary levels for librarians and how far by the low standard of living in those countries' economies? One approach to answer this question lies in relating library salary levels to the countries' Gross Domestic Product (GDP).

The table 6.6 shows "Employee Expenditure per member of Staff" related to each country's Per capita GDP - adjusted for Purchasing Power Parity to take account of the lower cost of goods and services in some countries.

Table 6.6. Librarian Salary Levels Related to GDP 1998 €s.

	National	Public Libraries Economy		National Libraries	
1	GDP Per Capita 2	Employee Expenditure Per Member of Staff 3	As Proportion of GDP 4	Employee Expenditure Per Member of Staff 5	As Proportion of GDP 6
Bulgaria	4,352	...	...	957	0.22
Czech Republic	12,351	2,803	0.23	3,573	0.29
Estonia	6,391	2,689	0.42	3,527	0.55
Hungary	8,391	4,428	0.53	6,337	0.76
Latvia	4,656	1,718	0.37	1,557	0.33
Lithuania	5,006	1,612	0.32	2,009	0.40
Poland	7,879	...	...	3,397	0.43
Romania	4,955	530	0.11	1,580	0.32
Slovak Republic	9,536	2,026	0.21	2,879	0.30
Slovenia	13,867	14,100	1.02	...	...
Austria	25,342	...	...	42,613	1.68
Belgium	26,237	31,541	1.20	...	...
Denmark	27,643	35,347	1.28	38,941	1.41
Ireland	25,597	21,679	0.85	29,569	1.16
Finland	23,794	29,888	1.26	27,519	1.16

(Contd...)

1	2	3	4	5	6
France	25,369	25,843	1.02	...	...
Greece	14,452	...	...	...	...
Iceland	26,163	...	...	...	...
Italy	23,315	...	...	...	...
Liechtenstein	32,231	...	...	...	...
Luxembourg	35,767	...	...	...	...
Netherlands	24,505	...	...	...	...
Norway	28,706	32,286	1.12	...	...
Portugal	16,698	7,149	0.43	12,853	0.77
Spain	18,525	15,962	0.86	20,013	1.08
Sweden	22,827	30,037	1.32	34,525	1.51
Switzerland	28,706	...	...	59,482	2.07
UK	24,124	25,656	1.06	31,347	1.30
Germany	24,416	25,251	1.03	38,582	1.58
All States	20,089	19,791	0.99	24,456	1.22
CEE	7,464	2,341	0.31	3,049	0.41
EU	23,344	25,863	1.11	32,629	1.40
EFTA	28,657	31,250	1.09	57,665	2.01
Northern Europe	25,219	31,801	1.26	41,605	1.65
Central Europe	24,848	26,034	1.05	34,272	1.38
Southern Europe	20,354	22,780	1.12	26,753	1.31
Baltic States	5,158	1,850	0.36	2,383	0.46
Eastern Europe	7,644	2,440	0.32	3,402	0.45

Per capita GDP is taken here to indicate the relative cost of living and labour cost in each country. 'Salary levels' are given for Public Libraries and for National Libraries - those being the sectors with most complete responses on the database. As an example we find that, in Estonia, Public library staff cost 2,689-6,391 = 0.42 (or 42%) of average labour costs: National Library staff cost 3,527-6,391 = 0.55 (or 55%) of average labour costs. In the average for All States the cost of public library labour equates almost exactly to the European average but labour costs in National Libraries are 22% above the European average. When comparing CEE to EU and EFTA it is obvious from the individual country data that the CEE ratios are very much lower. The calculated averages are:

	Public	**National**
CEE	0.31	0.41
EU	1.11	1.40
EFTA Norway	1.12	
Switzerlant		2.01

So these statistics show:

* That library salaries are much below country averages in CEE states,
* That they are somewhat above country averages in EU states, and
* That in both sectors they are higher in national libraries than in public libraries.

Thus, not only are the CEE states less wealthy economies, but the cost of library staff is below average within those countries. In layman's terms librarians earn less than half the average salary in CEE States, but they are paid slightly above average in EU States - and will above average in Northern Europe. An important corollary of this state of affairs is that there is less incentive in economic terms to introduce labour saving automation in the CEE states - since labour costs are relatively low already.

TOTAL REVENUE EXPENDITURE

Comparisons between EU and CEE financial statistics are greatly complicated by the different economic conditions pertaining. To a lesser extent this also applies to comparisons between Mediterranean states and Northern Europe. This is the reason why, for most purposes, it is more valid to concentrate on the operational, non financial. However, for completeness, the data on Total Revenue Expenditure is presented in another 'Cross Sector Total' table and the 'per capita' results (per 1000 total population).

Table 6.7. Total Revenue Expenditure (€ 000s).

0	National 1	Tertiary 2	Public 3	Special 4	Other 5	School 6	1998 Total 7
Bulgaria	488	1,342	3,481	550	1,389	527	
Czech Republic	4,951	...	29,536	...	0	...	
Estonia	3,416	2,539	8,757	1,041	1,753	2,026	
Hungary	...	...	29,914	...	...	...	
Latvia	1,844	938	6,528	...	591	...	
Lithuania	3,312	2,004	11,284	1,284	820	...	
Poland	8,962	26,331	...	...	...	...	
Romania	955	...	4,864	...	0	...	
Slovak Republic	2,987	...	7,656	...	...	316	
Slovenia	...	9,697	23,493	...	0	14,290	
Austria	16,977	...	33,955	...	...	...	
Belgium	6,162	45,864	...	...	...	...	
Denmark	19,104	57,694	304,652	17,625	0	37,892	
Ireland	3,318	37,083	47,393	...	0	...	
Finland	11,502	57,202	218,681	11,618	...	...	
France	...	235,364	...	...	...	...	
Greece	...	...	...	...	...	...	
Iceland	...	...	7,459	...	0	666	
Italy	6,841	242,976	...	...	...	...	

(*Contd...*)

1	2	3	4	5	6	7	
Liechtenstein	...	...	...	...	0	...	
Luxembourg	...	...	...	...	0	...	
Netherlands	...	...	...	...	0	...	
Norway	16,884	48,069	99,953	15,544	0	...	
Portugal	6,875	13,194	14,787	12,623	1,079	...	
Spain	17,061	142,524	125,414	93,746	36,372	...	
Sweden	17,378	99,945	327,907	15,581	...	...	
Switzerland	11,149	...	...	...	0	...	
UK	205,583	588,822	1,211,735	1,205,000*	287,902		
Germany	139,868	...	787,475	...	...	...	
All States	757,230	2,780,005	6,279,359	2,969,001	105,469	1,073,461	13,964,525
CEE	39,925	84,437	246,126	77,460	9,745	169,693	627,386
EU	665,332	2,496,377	5,763,733	2,812,544	95,724	879,605	12,713,315
EFTA	51,973	199,191	269,500	78,997	0	24,163	623,824
Northern Europe	91,057	318,330	1,060,630	79,579	10,941	168,640	1,729,177
Central Europe	531,802	1,875,606	3,829,170	2,224,444	28,194	547,006	9,036,222
Southern Europe	94,446	501,631	1,143,433	587,518	56,589	188,122	2,571,739
Baltic States	8,581	5,757	28,923	26,347	3,229	11,778	84,615
Eastern Europe	31,344	78,681	217,204	51,113	6,516	157,915	542,773
Response total	505,617	1,611,588	3,304,924	1,374,612*	42,004	343,619	5,977,364
Response %	67	58	53	6	40	32	43
Sector proportions	5.4	19.9	45.0	21.3	0.8	7.7	100.1

Notes:

* Calculated by adding the average 38% to {Materials + Staff Expenditure}

There is little in the results for individual countries that has not already been noted in the analysis of Materials and Staff expenditure.

Table 6.8. Total Revenue Expenditure Per 1,00 Population €s.

0	National 1	Tertiary 2	Public 3	Special 4	Other 5	School 6	1998 Total 7
Bulgaria	56	153	397	63	158	60	
Czech Republic	481	...	2,869	...	0	...	
Estonia	2,232	1,659	5,722	680	1,146	1,324	
Hungary	...	...	2,957	...	...	...	
Latvia	721	367	2,553	...	231	...	
Lithuania	895	542	3,050	347	222	...	
Poland	233	686	...	...	...	...	
Romania	42	...	213	...	0	...	
Slovak Republic	558	...	1,430	...	...	59	
Slovenia	...	4,984	12,074	...	0	7,345	
Austria	2,124	...	4,249	...	...	...	
Belgium	636	4,736	...	...	...	...	
Denmark	3,738	11,290	59,619	3,449	0	7,415	
Ireland	957	10,693	13,666	...	0	...	
Finland	2,288	11,377	43,493	2,311	...	...	
France	...	4,253	...	...	...	...	
Greece	...	...	...	...	...	...	
Iceland	...	...	27,937	...	0	2,494	
Italy	121	4,293	...	...	...	...	

(Contd...)

1	2	3	4	5	6	7	
Liechtenstein	...	...	...	...	0	...	
Luxembourg	...	...	...	...	0	...	
Netherlands	...	...	...	...	0	...	
Norway	3,860	10,990	22,852	3,554	0	...	
Portugal	677	1,298	1,455	1,242	106	...	
Spain	444	3,713	3,267	2,442	948	...	
Sweden	1,984	11,409	37,432	1,779	...	...	
Switzerland	1,625	...	...	...	0	...	
UK	3,604	10,321	21,240	21,222	0	5,047	
Germany	1,755	...	9,882	...	...	...	
All States CEE	1,580 378	5,800 800	13,100 2,333	6,194 734	220 92	2,240 1,609	29,134 5,946
EU	1,836	6,890	15,909	7,763	264	2,428	35,090
EFTA	4,507	17,273	23,370	6,850	0	2,095	54,095
Northern Europe	3,868	13,524	45,058	3,381	465	7,164	73,460
Central Europe	2,261	7,973	16,278	9,456	120	2,325	38,413
Southern Europe	821	4,360	9,938	5,106	492	1,635	22,352
Baltic States	1,102	739	3,714	3,383	415	1,512	10,865
Eastern Europe	321	805	2,223	523	67	1,616	5,555
Response total	***	***	***	***	***	***	***
Response %	***	***	***	***	***	***	***
Sector proportions	5.4	19.9	45.0	21.3	0.8	7.7	100.1

Here it is the grossed up totals that are particularly important - as they provide the best estimate available of the magnitude of library services in Europe overall. The grand total estimate is that, on average, €29.1 are spent per head of population on library services. Of this €6.5 go on traditional Materials and €14.0 on Staff. Compared to an EU estimated average of €35 per head of population the estimates for Eastern Europe are €5.6 and for the Baltic States €10.9. There is again a wide spread between countries. Of the four countries that replied for all sectors the lowest was €0.9 per head and the highest €86. These overall estimates are of limited value since there are such wide differences between each sector, and because the statistical validity of the data is much better for some sectors than for others, and because of exchange rate complexities. Analysis at the sector level is therefore more valid and of more interest - and it is that on which most of this report concentrates. Within the EU States we see the same pattern of low spending and high spending countries with a wide gap between the Nordic highs and the Mediterranean lows. There is also a very wide range within the CEE group of countries - which would be even lower but for the relatively high and complete results reported from Slovenia and Estonia. There are two further hypotheses suggested by these results - which can only be established after further study.

* There is a correlation between countries with the most complete statistics and those with the most developed services.
* Small countries have to devote relatively more resources to libraries since they do not benefit from economies of scale to the same extent as large countries.

Both these hypotheses deserve further investigation: but it is particularly recommended that more complete statistical reporting is given a high priority by agencies funding library and information service development.

LIBRARY RESOURCES AS PROPORTION OF GDP

This leads into the next stage of analysis - to explore what proportion of the economic wealth of Europe is devoted to libraries - how far variation is due to lack of economic wealth in individual states generally - and how far to a low proportion of that wealth is devoted to libraries. Table shows Total Revenue Expenditure as a proportion of GDP adjusted for Purchasing Power Parity.

Table 6.9. Total Revenue Expenditure as Proportion of GDP and PP €s Spent Per Million GDP.

0	National 1	Tertiary 2	Public 3	Special 4	Other 5	School 6	1998 Total 7
Bulgaria	13	50	132	22	49	14	
Czech Republic	42	...	291	...	...	...	
Estonia	349	271	970	106	179	208	
Hungary	...	...	469	...	...	...	
Latvia	156	88	615	...	55	...	
Lithuania	179	111	654	69	44	...	
Poland	30	87	...	...	...	...	
Romania	8	...	43	...	...	...	
Slovak Republic	59	...	150	...	...	10	
Slovenia	...	485	1,049	...	...	536	
Austria	91	...	388	...	...	...	
Belgium	31	181	...	...	...	...	
Denmark	148	476	2,530	135	...	268	
Ireland	37	496	548	...	...	...	
Finland	96	503	2,154	97	...	...	
France	...	196	...	...	...	...	
Greece	...	...	...	...	...	...	
Iceland	...	...	1,069	...	...	167	

(*Contd...*)

1	2	3	4	5	6	7	
Italy	32	190	...	...	...	...	
Liechtenstein	...	...	...	...	...	...	
Luxembourg	...	...	...	...	...	...	
Netherlands	...	...	...	...	...	...	
Norway	306	597	797	237	0	...	
Portugal	48	90	97	96	7	...	
Spain	29	242	211	180	59	...	
Sweden	96	557	1,691	87	...	...	
Switzerland	62	...	...	...	0	...	
UK	152	428	880	...	...	209	
Germany	85	...	488	...	...	...	
All States	79	289	652	308	11	111	1,450
CEE	51	107	313	98	12	216	797
EU	79	295	681	333	11	104	1,503
EFTA	157	603	816	239	0	73	1,888
Northern Europe	153	536	1,787	134	18	284	2,913
Central Europe	91	321	655	381	5	94	1,546
Southern Europe	40	214	488	251	24	80	1,098
Baltic States	214	143	720	656	80	293	2,107
Eastern Europe	42	105	291	68	9	211	727
Response total	***	***	***	***	***	***	***
Response %	***	***	***	***	***	***	***
Sector proportions	5.4	19.9	45.0	21.3	0.8	7.7	100.1

On average 0.145 per cent of GDP was spent on libraries. Only four countries provided data for all six sectors, and they ranged from a low of 0.03 per cent to a high of 0.36 per cent. As elsewhere it is best to concentrate on those sectors that are comprehensively reported - National, Tertiary and Public; the EFTA totals should be disregarded as only one EFTA state provided data. While the CEE average of 0.08% is well below the 'All States' 0.145%, when we look at the Baltic States separately we find that their proportion of GDP devoted to libraries is actually above average (0.21 per cent). It is Eastern Europe (0.0727 per cent) and Southern Europe (.1098 per cent) where library spending - proportionate to GDP - is significantly below average. Policy makers in every country, and those interested in a particular sector, should benefit from studying this table - in addition to the ratios per head of population. Relating sector expenditure to the 'All States' average per sector may be even more valuable than focus on the overall average.

7

Human Resources

INTRODUCTION

"Human Resource" is regarded as the most important resource for the advancement of the nation. If it is not properly developed, it cannot be put to proper use. Human force is the basic raw material for the development of an advanced nation. Peter Drucker "The most valuable asset of a 21st century institution will be its knowledge workers and their productivity. In an organization staff development and staff training are parts of the bigger concept of human resource development (HRD). The HRD encompasses the broad set of activities that improve the performance of the individual and teams of an organization. The HRD is considered as the most vital link of the library. The HRD involves both management and operative functions. Operative functions include procurement, development, compensation, integration and maintenance of personnel.

It is the most powerful tool for any organization's success and the training of employees is regarded as one of the most important functions of effective resource management. In order to obtain a competitive edge in providing the best services to the customer, training which will develop a well-trained workforce is vital to render efficient and effective services in modern library and Information centers. Further, libraries require appointing staff, which possess IT skills so that they are in a position to perform a wide range of functions. This particular chapter has been brought out to get a view of human factor, which is one of the most complicated aspects of any system. Yet, it's the one that gets the least attention, is least discussed, the least researched, and perhaps the least understood.

METHODOLOGY

Questionnaire method and on the spot interview was conducted for collecting the data. The target group comprises almost all the staff of each and every library. Altogether a total of 160 questionnaires were distributed among the three types of libraries of which 118 were collected. The Age group of the respondent was divided into three categories *viz.*, 31-40, 41-50, 51-58 and 58 and above respectively. It was found that the majority of the staff was in the age group of 41-50 followed by those in 51-60, 31-40 and 60 above. Sexwise, the ratio of male and female was found to be 66.94 male to 33.05 female.

TRAINING PROGRAMME FOR STAFF

Effective training programme for the library staff is a must to acquire authentic meaning of a library. There are different methods of training, which can be adopted by an organization.

Some are:

* Sending staff for relevant courses and seminars.
* Library professionals must regularly read literature not only in their field of specialization but also allied fields especially on IT.
* Job learning training can be carried out at work place itself.
* Information literacy programme within the libraries.
* Network literacy programme.
* Computer literacy programme.
* UGC sponsored programme.
* Staff must be trained to install software and tackle simple technical problems.

* Training must be given to familiarize with some Operating Systems (OS) such as MS DOS, MS WORD, MS EXCEL, MS POWERPOINT, etc.
* Knowledge of e-mail technology must be given.
* Training in data organization, structuring and presentation of contents must be given to library professionals.

STATUS OF AUTOMATION

Sl. No.	Category	No. of Libraries not Automated at All	No. of Libraries Partially Automated	No. of Libraries Fully Automated	Total
1	Public		2	-	2
2	Special	5	4	-	9
3	Academic	12	6	-	18
	Total	17	12	–	29

From the data collected, it was brought to light that most of the libraries were partially automated doing minimal of jobs or sometimes just for namesake. Not even a single library was found to be fully automated. Out of 29 libraries, 12 were partially automated and the rest was far from the idea of automation for the next 5-10 years.

TRAINING RECEIVED BY STAFF REGARDING APPLICATION OF IT

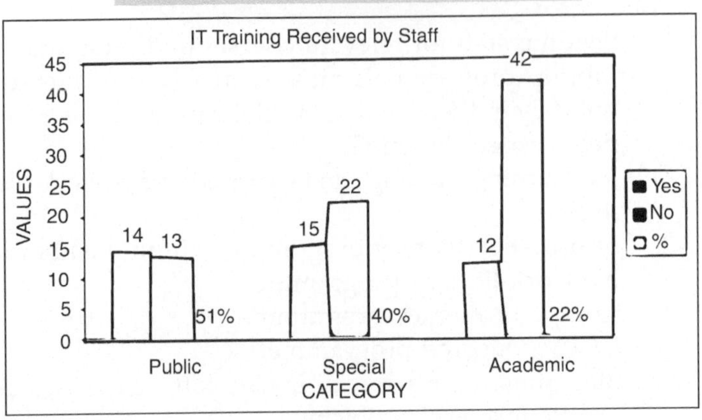

Fig. 7.1.

Since, we found that the status of automation in libraries was very poor. Hence, the training received by library personnel was also naturally very few. It is clear that only 34.74% received training in one way or the other through orientation, conferences, seminars held in the state as well as in other parts of country outside Manipur. This reflects the sad picture of the functioning of all the Government institute libraries of Manipur. A strong library Movement is the need of the hour to propagate the importance of library to the society by those person who is in these fields.

NECESSITY OF IT TRAINING

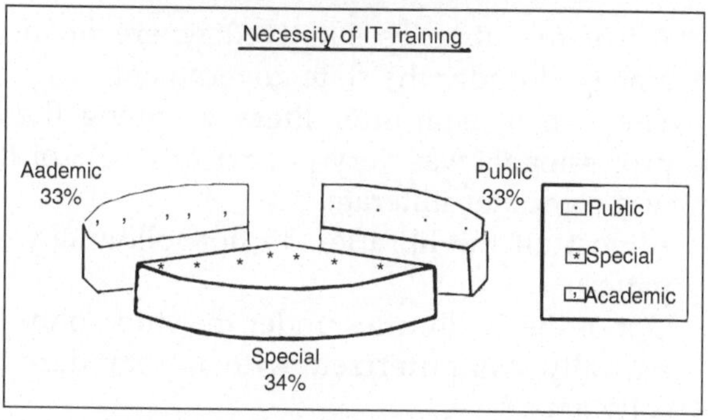

Fig. 7.2.

Regarding the advancement in Information Technology and its application in libraries, majority of the respondent accounting for 90.67% agreed to the necessity of training in application of IT in their libraries. A mere 9% or so did not respond to it for they were just office bearers, helpers etc. Not only majority of the respondent agreed to the importance of IT training, but they all voice the same opinion of automating their libraries at the earliest possible time to provide efficient and effective services to the readers.

The table reveals that maximum respondents were of the opinion that the main factor which affects application of IT of the libraries is equipments to a great extent, followed by finance, training of library professionals, motivation and support from the authority.

Table 7.1 Factors which Effects the IT Application in Libraries.

Sl. No.	Reasons	Great Extent	Small Extent	Not at all	Total
1	Equipments	111	7	-	118
2	Finance	97	21	-	118
3	Motivation	20	40	58	118
4	Support from Authority	18	19	81	118
5	Training	110	8	–	118

FINDINGS

The finding of the data analysis can be summarized as follows:

* All of the libraries surveyed where financed and managed under the state government.
* The rate of computer literacy among the library professionals was very poor nearly 65% of the staff was computer illiterate.
* Almost all the libraries do not follow any staffing pattern.
* Out of the 29 libraries under the study only 12 were partially computerized with no standard library softwares.
* The scope of continuing education, training of the professionals was very limited.

Problems of IT Application in the Libraries

The step motherly treatment by the colleges authority as well as the government towards the development of libraries is one of the main problems plaguing the state.

* Lack of funds.
* Lack of innovation and professional ethics amongst the Library professionals.
* Lack of qualified staff.
* High cost of IT infrastructures.
* Library professionals lack knowledge and training in IT application.

SUGGESTIONS

* The professionals should be provided with required motivators such as monetary gain, working conditions, authority in decision-making, personal growth and development, self-esteem etc. to upgrade their skills in the ever-changing digital environment.
* Selection and recruitment of library professionals should be more stringent and the skill and qualification required should be consistent with the nature of the jobs to be performed.
* The main hurdle from the study towards digitization of the libraries was the finance. Here as a suggestion we would like INFLIBNET or any such organization/ agencies to provide financial assistance or minimum hardware and software which at present are being provided to Universities all over India.
* Professionals should be encouraged to participate in training programmes, seminars, conference etc to keep abreast of the latest trends in the field of their studies.
* The professionals should also try to develop their skills and competencies in a changing library situation.

CONCLUSION

The Indian system of Higher education during the last 30 years or so has been expanding primarily for social and political reasons rather than on economic and manpower considerations. Nearly one-third of the total outlay on education in India is spent on higher education. Unfortunately, our colleges resemble the inherited imperial pattern of pre-independence India and suffer from the worst effect. Development of human resources lies at the core of the knowledge productive organizations, like libraries. The survival and success of organizations will increasingly depend on their ability to ensure that they are "smart" at all levels rather than only at the top.

In this fast changing environment the library and information workers are required to possess enhanced managerial, professional and technical skills, adequate knowledge and right kind of experience. So, training the existing manpower or recruiting new professionals will become essential. They must possess flexibility of attitude, imagination and scientific bend of mind. Further, the libraries need to be upgraded along with the changing environment from its traditional to a digital environment.

Even though the introduction and use of Information technology in the said libraries is in the initial stage in Manipur. Steps may be taken up to develop the libraries with IT rather than being just a custodian of documents. In the near future, if the conditions of the libraries doesn't change within 5-10 years than there is a chance that the libraries may be replaced by Internet café, knowledge kiosks etc. making way for other IT professionals. As a final word we would like to remind that immediate steps should be taken up for Human Resource Development keeping into view the changing digital environment.

8

Standards for Public Library

USING THE YOUNG ADULT STANDARDS

These standards have been developed for use by:

* Young Adult Librarians to support requests to Library Directors and Boards for increased resources.
* Library Administration to advance young adult services with local and state governments and Boards of Trustees.
* Trustees to increase awareness of and support for young adult services.
* Regional Administrators and Regional Youth Services Consultants and Coordinators to strengthen existing services and create new ones.
* The Massachusetts Board of Library Commissioners to develop an action plan for implementation on a state level and to consider when formulating funding policy for Massachusetts libraries.
* The Massachusetts Library Association to advocate for young adult services in the professional community at large.
* Library School Faculty to strengthen the professional education of young adult librarians.
* Citizens to increase awareness of young adult library needs in their communities.

* Government and Local Officials to increase knowledge of the importance of library services to teens and the need for funding these services.
* Teens and Teen Advisory Boards to help develop a vision for services in their libraries and communities.

YOUNG ADULTS AS LIBRARY USERS

The Young Adult Library Services Association (YALSA), the term "young adults" refers to young people ages 12 to 18 who no longer see themselves as children but are not recognized by society as adults. The terms "YA," "teens," "teenagers," "adolescents," "youth," and "students" also identify young adults and will be used interchangeably throughout this document. As teens struggle to find their place in the family and society, they must work out new relationships with parents, peers and others. They experience rapid physical, emotional and social changes while developing their intellectual capabilities and personal values, understanding and accepting their sexuality, and identifying their educational and occupational options.

Young adult library users deserve to be taken seriously and to have their requests treated equitably and their confidentiality preserved. Direct, respectful communication with them is the most effective means of engaging their interest in library services. A cornerstone of young adult library services is the principle that young adults must be actively involved in decisions regarding collections, services and programmes intended for them. Their active participation ensures that the needs and ever changing interests of teens are being addressed. Young adults become lifelong library users and supporters when they are enthusiastically engaged in planning and decision-making.

They play a key role in attracting their peers to the library. Public libraries must provide more than token services to young adults. Since adolescents are not generally advocates on their own behalf, it is important that the library director, staff, and trustees understand their responsibility to give equal consideration to the needs of young adults in planning and implementing library and information services. Youth advocacy begins with the policies, procedures, space, collections and services within the library. It also extends to the networks and coalitions library staff develop with schools and other libraries and community agencies.

These standards are constructed in the belief that "by fully supporting library service to young adults, the library community is much more likely to retain members of this age group as library users who will, as adults, become lifelong learners and library supporters."1 The standards are based on the philosophy and definitions of library services established in three basic documents of the Young Adult Library Services Association: Directions for Library Service to Young Adults, New Directions for Library Service to Young Adults, and Young Adults Deserve the Best: Competencies for Librarians Serving Youth. The Search Institute's Forty Developmental Assets as well as the Intellectual Freedom documents of the American Library Association (ALA), particularly the Library Bill of Rights, are also fundamental to quality service to young adults.

SERVICE

Quality library service to young adults is provided by staff who understand and respect their unique informational, educational and recreational needs. In accordance with the principles expressed in the Library Bill of Rights and Free Access to Libraries for Minors teenagers must have access on an equal basis with adults to all the services and materials the library provides. Cooperation among public, school and other libraries in the community is essential to serving young adults well.

Principles

Services to young adults in each public library must be based on a written policy outlining philosophy, goals and objectives consistent with established roles as stated in the library's long-range plan. The Young Adult Services staff and the library director should review both this essential document and its corresponding action plan on a regular basis to determine its effectiveness in serving the needs and interests of young adults in the community.

The policy should be based on the following principles:

* Young adults need and are entitled to free and equal access to all library services and resources, including programmes, information services, technology, reserves and interlibrary loan, virtual and remote services.
* Young adult department service hours will be no less than those of adult services, and staff will be available to serve young adults all the hours that the library is open.
* Young adults have the right to privacy and confidentiality in accordance with the principles expressed in the American Library Association's Statement of Professional Ethics and Massachusetts State Laws regarding confidentiality.
* Public library services for young adults complement but do not take the place of school libraries in the community.
* Each public library has the responsibility to make access to electronic resources, such as online databases and unfiltered Internet access, equally available to people of all ages.

Practices

To ensure that young adults are provided with the materials and information they need for school assignments, personal pleasure, and responsible decision-making each library must:

* Develop procedures for involving young adults in planning space, collections, services and programmes.
* Establish a physical space for young adult collections, which creates an environment that invites teen use.
* Employ at least one qualified librarian who is responsible for planning and supervising services to young adults.

* Develop and maintain a collection of diverse and current materials in various formats.
* Develop and provide reference services, including homework assistance, personal, career and college information. This reference service also extends to telephone and electronic information and referral.
* Plan and implement a variety of programmes that promote library use.
* Provide reader's advisory assistance.
* Provide library orientation and skills instruction.
* Develop meaningful volunteer opportunities for young adults within the library.
* Publicize the resources and services offered to young adults.
* Collaborate and cooperate with schools and other community agencies serving teenagers.
* Create and maintain a web presence specifically geared towards the needs of youth.
* Participate in resource sharing among networks and regions.
* Allocate sufficient funding to accomplish a complete service package including programming, collections, staffing, and facilities.

STAFF

The library acknowledges the distinct needs and characteristics of young adults by designating a staff member who will have professional expertise and responsibility in planning and supervising services for them. The library director and young adult librarian will work together to provide leadership that assures good library service to young adults, seeking additional expertise from the Regional Youth Services Consultant as needed. It is also essential that all staff members convey a service commitment to young adults since they are expected to use the full range of public library services. The goal of each library will be to employ a young adult librarian who has earned a master's degree from an ALA accredited programme with course work related to young adult materials and services.

Competencies

In order to be an advocate for young adults and an effective provider of library services, the librarian serving this age group must possess a wide variety of competencies and personal qualities.

As a person who is expected to attract young adults to the library, the librarian must have:

* Genuine respect for teenagers and an ability to establish rapport with them.
* Communication skills to involve young adults in planning and implementing services intended for their benefit.
* The ability to elicit the input of young adults on library programmes and services and to present their ideas to the library administration and staff.
* Interest in and ability to learn new technologies and adapt them for use in young adult services.
* Interest in seeking out new trends in services to young adults.

As a professional librarian who is expected to develop services appropriate to this age group, the librarian must have:

* A broad and current knowledge of young adult literature, audio and visual materials, electronic resources, and emerging technologies.
* A broad knowledge of the intellectual, emotional, psychological, and physical development of adolescents.

As part of the management team of the library in which young adult services are valued, the librarian must have:

* A knowledge and understanding of the library's mission, goals, objectives, and policies.
* The ability to plan and implement programmes and to participate in the overall management and evaluation of library activities.

As an effective advocate for young adults, the librarian must have:

* The ability to communicate the needs of teenagers to library staff and administration.

* An awareness of current issues affecting adolescents in that community and society.
* The ability to communicate and collaborate with school personnel and other community agencies serving young adults.

Responsibilities of the Young Adult Librarian

The young adult librarian must assume a wide variety of responsibilities in the areas of management, service, community outreach and professional development.

As a manager the young adult librarian will:

* Plan and implement activities to achieve short and long term goals and objectives for young adult services as part of the overall library planning process.
* Assess budgetary needs of the young adult department and work with other library personnel to plan and implement the budget.
* Advocate for young adults in library discussions of policy-making and implementation of budget priorities.
* Work with library administration to seek supplementary funding to enhance library services.
* Train, supervise, and evaluate staff and volunteers.
* Identify, collect and interpret statistics as needed.

As a service provider the young adult librarian will:

* Select, evaluate, maintain, and discard young adult materials based on the preferences of young adults and the use of a variety of review sources.
* Provide reference, reader's advisory, and library orientation services to young adults.
* Promote information literacy skills by providing instruction in and access to electronic databases, the Internet, and other emerging technologies, and using those technologies to communicate with teens virtually.
* Involve young adults in planning and implementing services and selecting materials for their age group.
* Recognize diverse groups of young adults and develop programmes and acquire materials appropriate to their needs.b

As coordinator of outreach services the young adult librarian will:

* Establish contacts and collaborate with schools and other agencies to serve young adults.
* Promote, publicize, and represent young adult services and the library to the community and local agencies in cooperation with other library departments.

As a professional, the young adult librarian will:

* Participate actively in professional associations, take advantage of continuing education opportunities, and read professional literature related to libraries, youth services, and adolescent development.
* Identify current trends and issues affecting young adults and incorporate these findings into overall services to this age group.

Responsibilities of the Administration

The library administration will ensure quality services to young adults by supporting the young adult librarian in the provision of these services and working with the young adult librarian in maintaining contacts with other community agencies serving youth.

In addition, the administration will:

* Provide written job descriptions, which are regularly reviewed, for all staff responsible for young adult services.
* Assure regular performance evaluations are conducted using the job descriptions along with the goals and objectives set by each staff member.
* Designate a professional position in the library that will include responsibility for young adult services in the event the young adult librarian's position cannot be full-time.
* Develop a specific budget for young adult materials, programmes and services, with the young adult librarian's input.

* Assure scheduled time in the designated librarian's workweek that allows the librarian to serve young adults effectively.
* Allocate time for community outreach to schools and other agencies, for development of appropriate networks for serving young adult information needs, and for job-related professional activities.
* Compensate the young adult librarian with a salary commensurate with the formal qualifications mandated by the library and equivalent to that of other staff within the library who have similar levels of responsibility. The Massachusetts Library Association provides minimum salary recommendations.

Responsibilities of the Regional Library Systems

Each regional library system, in its plan of service, must include:

* A consultant with expertise in young adult services who provides advisory services to staff in local public libraries.
* A programme of service to those working with young adults.
* Continuing education programmes on young adult services.
* Opportunities for regular meetings between local young adult services staff and regional consultants.

JOB DESCRIPTION

Definition

Professional, administrative and supervisory work in planning and managing the activities of young adult services in the library and all other related work as required.

Supervision

* Works under the general direction of the Library Director or Coordinator of Youth or Adult Services.

* Performs responsible functions requiring considerable judgment and initiative in planning and overseeing services to young adults both within the library and the community.
* Supervises two part-time employees and an active volunteer programme.

Job Environment

* Performs work under typical library conditions; library hours may require evening and weekend work.
* Makes frequent contacts with the public, schools, other libraries, social service agencies, civic organizations and other professional organizations.
* Uses computers, peripherals, current technologies and other standard office equipment.

Essential Functions

* Plans, organizes, implements, supervises and evaluates services to young adults.
* Participates as part of the management team in developing goals, policies and procedures as relating to young adults.
* Advocates for young adults and young adult services with other community agencies.
* Initiates, plans and conducts a variety of programmes and activities to encourage the use of the library by young adults between the ages of 12 to 18.
* Involves young adults in planning and implementing services for their age group.
* Selects, evaluates, maintains and discards young adult materials based on professional judgment, preferences of young adults and acknowledged review sources.
* Provides reference and readers' advisory services, and library orientation to young adults.
* Collaborates with schools and other agencies to serve young adults.

* Promotes, publicizes and represents young adult services and the library to the community and local agencies in cooperation with other library departments.
* Works with library administration to seek supplementary funding to enhance library services, including state and federal grants.
* Trains, supervises and evaluates staff and volunteers.
* Identifies, collects and interprets statistics as needed.

RECOMMENDED MINIMUM QUALIFICATIONS

Education and Experience

Master's Degree in Library Science from an ALA accredited school; two years of professional experience, including supervisory and administrative experience, experience with young adults is preferred.

Knowledge, Ability and Skills

* Broad and current knowledge of young adult literature, digital and multimedia materials, and electronic resources, including communication tools such as e mail and instant messaging.
* A broad knowledge of the intellectual, emotional, psychological and physical development of adolescents is essential.
* Genuine respect for young adults and an ability to establish rapport with them.
* Ability to administer and direct the work of staff and volunteers.
* Ability to express oneself orally and in writing.
* Flexibility, initiative, energy, patience and tact to deal effectively with the public.
* Excellent people and reference skills.
* Planning and organizational skills needed.
* Has access to a limited amount of confidential information.

* Errors could result in lower standards of library service, waste of public funds and poor public relations.
* Familiarity with online circulation systems and online searching is required.

Physical Requirements

* Light physical effort required in carrying and shelving books, and in performing other typical library functions.
* Frequent standing, walking, bending, reaching and climbing.
* Ability to operate a keyboard at an efficient speed.
* Frequently required to sit and talk or hear, use hands to operate objects, tools or controls, and reach with hands and arms.
* The employee must regularly lift and/or move materials weighing up to 40 pounds.
* Vision and hearing at or correctable to "normal ranges."

COLLECTIONS

The young adult collection represents the unique needs and interests of adolescents in the community. Resources selected for teenagers should contribute to their intellectual and emotional growth as well as appeal to their popular, current and recreational interests. Both the public library and the school library collections are necessary for meeting the educational needs of young adults.

This collection is the bridge for adolescents making the transition from juvenile collections and services to adult collections and services. It should contain materials appropriate for a wide range of abilities and maturity levels. Therefore, the collection may include items commonly found in either the adult or children's collections. In accordance with the Library Bill of Rights and its interpretations, young adults must have access to all areas of the library's collections.

Policy

Every public library's collection development policy, endorsed by the library's governing board, must define the purpose of the young adult collection by stating the following:

* Responsibility and criteria for selection and evaluation.
* General and specific populations and interests to be served.
* Level of curriculum and homework support.
* Roles of young adults in collection development.
* Relationship between the young adult collection and other collections in the library.

Content

Personal interest materials reflecting the needs and interests of teenagers are the primary focus of the young adult collection. Materials should be available in a variety of formats and subject areas, and the collection should meet the needs of teens of various ages and levels of maturity as well as reading abilities. No limit should be made on the availability of any material to all patrons. Paperbacks, graphic novels, magazines and popular music recordings are included in any collection for this age group. Other media such as DVD's, web sites, computer/video games and recorded books are also popular. The young adult collection must reflect the cultural and socio-economic diversity of the community and acknowledge the emotional and informational needs of teens of all sexual orientations. It should serve the needs of the visually and hearing impaired, learning disabled, and non-English speaking populations. Collection development also encompasses the full range of electronic resources available through the library website.

Budget

A portion of the library budget must be designated for young adult materials. Evaluation of the usage patterns of the library's entire collection, as well as a variety of statistics and output measures supplied by the young adult librarian, should determine budget allocations. The young adult librarian should have full responsibility for expending the young adult materials budget. When the public library also serves as the school library, arrangements must be made for reimbursements from the school department budget.

Selection

The young adult librarian will:

* Select materials intended primarily for young adults, consulting a variety of professional selection and evaluation aids.
* Involve young adults in the selection process.
* Communicate with other library departments selecting materials used by young adults to determine the best location for these materials.
* Ensure prompt processing and full cataloging of young adult materials.
* Evaluate the strengths and weaknesses of the collection on a regular basis.
* Discard worn and outdated materials.

Promotion

To promote the collection effectively, the young adult librarian will:

* Identify the needs of the community, its teens, and its young adult service providers.
* Be familiar with materials in the collection in order to provide expert guidance to young adult and adult users.
* Encourage the independent use of the collection by using marketing strategies and reader's advisory tools such as booklists, displays, signage, and an active web presence to help youth locate materials they will find enjoyable and suited to their developmental needs.
* Work with schools and community groups to keep teens and adults abreast of materials in the collection.
* Maintain and update a web page devoted to the

library's young adult services which publicizes materials to teens both inside and outside the library and encourages use of online databases.

Responsibilities of the Regional Library Systems

The regional library systems are responsible for assisting member libraries in collection development by providing:

* Patron access to online databases that meet the informational needs of young adults.
* Access to a collection of professional resources.
* Continuing education programmes.
* On-site consultations.
* Supplementary collections/deposits of young adult materials for public libraries under 25,000 population may be available.

CORE COLLECTION CHECKLIST

Though school assignments motivate teenagers to visit the library, a dynamic young adult collection focusing on popular, high interest materials will keep them coming back. Teen input is essential in developing a collection that reflects the interests and needs of a community's young people, and affords young adults the opportunity to become involved in library decision-making.

Your YA collection should include:

* Series books.
* *Fiction:*
  - Horror.
  - Realistic teen novels.
  - Mystery/suspense.
  - Romance.
  - Science fiction.
  - Fantasy.
  - Sports.
  - Adventure/survival.
  - Historical fiction.
  - Short stories.
  - Classics in paperback editions.
  - Multicultural fiction.

* Comics and graphic novels.
* Media tie-ins.
* Magazines.
* *Non-fiction:*
  - Recreational, *e.g.* rock and rap music, skateboarding.
  - Informational, *e.g.* health and sex education.
  - Educational, *e.g.* careers and college.
  - Reference, *e.g.* encyclopedias, student dictionaries, atlases.
* *Non-print:*
  - Musical media.
  - DVD and video.
  - Computer/video games
  - Learning tools.
  - Audio books.
* Pathfinders, both print and web-based.
* Website/collection of links.

FACILITIES

Every public library must have a clearly defined, separate area designated for young adults. This young adult area should be accessible to all adolescents, easily visible, functional and flexible in design. An environment that is comfortable and arranged to accommodate noise and movement will make young adults feel welcome. The design and graphics should make it evident that the area is for teens. Young adult involvement is essential in establishing an effective, dynamic young adult area.

Space

The young adult space should be established in a location that is easily supervised without making young adults feel intimidated. Because young adults need access to reference materials and assistance, proximity to reference services is important. The space should not be adjacent to the children's service area. If the young adult area is unable to house programmes and activities, teens should have equal access to other programme facilities within the library. The space itself should be in compliance with the Americans with Disabilities Act.

The area should accommodate:

* Leisure reading, socializing, and snacking.
* Individual and group study.
* A public service area and workspace for the young adult librarian.
* Sufficient shelving for a diverse collection.
* Displays and exhibits.
* Computer access proportional to teen population.

Furnishings

Furnishings should be flexible so that as needs and activities change the area can be adapted accordingly.

The young adult area will include:

* Shelving for materials in various formats.
* Comfortable and durable seating and tables.
* Directional and informational signs.

The young adult area should include or be in proximity to:

* A public service desk, clock and telephone.
* Listening and viewing equipment.
* Computers and peripherals.
* Display equipment such as bulletin boards, display cases and slat-wall shelving.

Infrastructure

Services for young adults must take advantage of new methods to deliver the most effective access to information, learning and leisure pursuits. The library's infrastructure should support changing technology and ensure adequate lighting, ventilation, temperature controls, and acoustics.

Items to consider in the young adult area include:

* Electrical outlets in a variety of locations.
* Adequate wiring, including wireless capability, with flexibility to reposition and upgrade.
* Connections for in-house and external tele-communication resources.

* Soundproofing as required.
* Telephone jacks with convenient access.
* Trash receptacles.

Web Presence

Just as libraries set aside physical spaces in their buildings for young adults, so should they set aside web spaces by creating and maintaining a page or pages specific to the interests and developmental needs of young adults. An attractive and functional page should be designed with young adult input, evaluated regularly by young adults, and have interactive features.

The page may include but is not limited to:

* General contact information for library and specific contact information for the young adult librarian.
* A collection development policy for website content and links that includes a procedure for addressing challenges to controversial websites.
* Library programmes and activities for young adults.
* Annotated booklists and book reviews, or links to young adult literature sites that provide reader's advisory services.
* Promotion of young adult collections and resources.
* Informational and recreational links.
* Opportunities for teens to post reviews of materials.
* Interactive content that helps teens learn how to use library resources.
* Opportunities for teens to connect with each other.
* Opportunities for teens to connect with librarians who can assist them with research needs.
* Opportunities for taking part in programmes virtually.

PROGRAMMES

Successful library programmes support teens by meeting their developmental needs. They foster a sense of ownership and provide a structure for meaningful participation. Programming should be as varied as the needs and interests of young adults themselves and encourage use of the library. It is crucial that programmes presented for this age group include teenagers in planning and implementation. Teens who are involved in the programming process are essential advocates and promoters of a library's young adult services.

Principles

Programmes can range from informal activities to formally planned events and are intended to connect teens and libraries.

The following principles govern the development, organization and management of library programmes for young adults:

* The philosophy, goals and objectives for young adult programming should be included in the library's written programme policy and long-range plan, and should be revised as necessary.
* All programmes should be created and developed with youth input, since the most successful programmes are the ones in which the young adults themselves participate in planning and executing.
* A specific proportional budget should be designated for planning, publicizing, and presenting young adult programmes.
* The young adult librarian must be provided with time and opportunities to establish relationships with teen users and to plan, prepare for, and carry out young adult programming.
* Ongoing communication and collaboration with schools and other community agencies serving young adults is essential in developing successful programming.

Practices

The young adult librarian, with the support of the administration and other staff members, will assume the responsibility of implementing the library's young adult programmes.

To ensure success, the following practices are necessary:

* Scheduling informational, cultural and recreational programmes for young adults, parents, and community members who work with teens on a regular basis.
* Developing personal contacts with young adults and encouraging promotion among teens themselves in order to publicize programmes.
* Utilizing high-quality print media, e mail notification or "blasts", and website publicity to create visibility in the community.
* Evaluating programmes and maintaining statistics unique to the young adult department to ensure continued improvement of and support for programming.
* Providing refreshments is an essential part of programming for teens.

Programme Content

Programming for young adults can be a rewarding and stimulating part of library service to adolescents. Library programmes can attract new teen users to the library and increase awareness of resources and services provided by the library for young adults. As teens strive for competence, programmes that allow them to showcase skills are important.

Youth participation programmes give teens opportunities to become involved in library decision-making and should address a genuine need of both adolescents and the library. If the library discusses the creation of responsible roles and tasks for young adults and solicits their opinions, then the administration must be sincere in its efforts to implement reasonable recommendations. Examples of youth participation programmes include young adult advisory councils, teen trustees, teen Friends groups, young adult book review groups and literary magazines. Teens should also be active participants in the creation and maintenance of the library's web pages for teens.

The following is a list of different types of youth participation programmes with examples of each:

* Educational programmes offer support for formal education and curriculum needs. Examples include SAT workshops, school booktalking programmes, college application workshops and library skills orientation/tours.
* Cultural programmes excite and involve teenagers in literature and the arts. Examples include art shows, photography exhibits, theater productions, poetry coffeehouses or "slams," book discussion groups and writers' workshops.
* Informational programmes provide needed knowledge on a variety of subjects and may fill a void in the community. They also provide opportunities to form partnerships with other youth agencies. Examples may include substance abuse programmes, career programmes, babysitting workshops, craft classes, modeling seminars and forums on minors' legal rights.
* Recreational programmes are purely entertainment-oriented. Examples include role-playing or computer/video game tournaments, "battle of the bands" concerts, talent shows or "open-mic" nights.
* Intergenerational programmes feature projects in which teenagers interact with and gain appreciation for younger and older members of the community. Examples include theater groups, a senior/teen book discussion group, community gardens and storytelling for young children.
* Volunteer programmes in libraries foster self-confidence, self-esteem and dignity in young adults. Opportunities for volunteerism should include work that matters, not simply "busywork. Examples include summer reading programme volunteers and computer instruction for younger and older patrons.

Responsibilities of the Regional Library Systems

Regional library systems are responsible for assisting member libraries in programme development by providing:

* Continuing education programmes for librarians on effective young adult programming.
* Consultations, including on-site visits, to address specific needs.
* Professional resources to assist the young adult librarian in programming efforts.

PROGRAMME PLANNING WORKSHEET

LIBRARY: ______________________ LIBRARIAN: ______________

PROGRAMME TITLE: ______________________________________

Brief Description of Programme

PURPOSE OF PROGRAMME: ______________________________________

DATE: _____ DAY: _______ START TIME: ______ END TIME: _______

Date Checked on Library Calendar
Date Checked on School Calendar
Date Checked on community Calendar

LOCATION FOR PROGRAM:
Library Meeting Room YA Area Other

TARGET AUDIENCE:
Children YA Adult All

EXPECTED ATTENDANE:
Children YA Adult

Budget

* Estmated Cost:
  - Speaker's cost
  - Supplies and equipment
  - Staff time
  - Public relations
  - Other costs
* Funding Source:
  - Budget line- general revenue
  - Grant funds
  - Friends of the Library
  - Corporate sponsorship

- Outside donations
- Other

* Programme Approved:
- Preliminary planning should be approved at this point before proceeding any further.
- Approved by supervisor
- Approved by director
- Off desk planning time approved

* Equipment Needed: (make arrangements to rent, if necessary)

* Speaker Confirmation:
- Contract sent
- Contract returned and executed
- Follow-up call(s)

* Room Set-up: (preliminary plan)

* Publicity and Promotion:
- All library staff informed
- Programme information posted to library website
- Fliers distributed to schools, community groups, businesses and other libraries
- Media releases to local newspapers, school newspapers, radio, TV, Friends of the Library
- Newsletter, etc.
- Visits to schools planned and approved
- Book displays
- E mail or direct mailings to YAs, school and community liaisons

* Programme Details:
- Room set-up
- Equipment and supplies
- Refreshments
- Speaker's introduction
- Speaker's check
- Evaluation form and pencils
- Fliers for next programme
- Room clean up
- Other

SAMPLE VOLUNTEER POLICY

The library often has uses for volunteers. These volunteers can fulfill permanent or temporary needs.

Volunteers and their supervisors must adhere to the following when performing duties:

* Anyone wishing to learn, have a direct impact on the library, and become more involved in the community is encouraged to volunteer at the library.
* Any teenager who is legally old enough to work may volunteer at the library. This includes anyone over the age of 14. Any volunteer under the age of 16 must comply with Massachusetts Child Labour Laws4. This includes, but is not limited to, not working after 7 pm on a school night5, more than three hours on a school day6, and more than eighteen hours a week during the school year7.
* Volunteers can be asked to perform a variety of duties at the discretion of the volunteer supervisor. Temporary duties include working at programmes, or helping with a planning process. Teenaged volunteers are especially encouraged to become involved in writing any policies related to their needs and services.
* Volunteers will not be asked to perform duties also performed by paid staff. This includes working at public service desks. Adolescent volunteers should not be required to do identical work as high school pages.
* Those who are volunteering on a temporary basis, such as during a programme, a Friends of the Library event, or on a planning committee are not expected to perform duties not related to that event.
* Volunteers who will be helping on a more permanent basis will set up a regular schedule with the volunteer supervisor. Volunteers are welcome to terminate the arrangement at any time. Volunteers are free to take vacations or days off, although they are asked to please give notice to the volunteer supervisor.

CONFIDENTIALITY LAW

G.L.c. 78, Section 7. Establishment by Cities and Towns; records

Section 7. A town may establish and maintain public libraries for its inhabitants under regulations prescribed by the city council or by the town, and may receive, hold and manage any gift, bequest or devise therefor. The city council of a city or the selectmen of a town may place in such library the books, reports and laws which may be received from the commonwealth. That part of the records of a public library which reveals the identity and intellectual pursuits of a person using such library shall not be a public record as deemed by clause Twenty-six of section seven of chapter four. Library authorities may disclose or exchange information relating to library users for the purposes of interlibrary cooperation and coordination, including but not limited to, the purposes of facilitating the sharing of resources among library jurisdictions as authorized by clause (1) of section nineteen E or enforcing the provisions of sections ninety-nine and one hundred of chapter two hundred and sixty-six.

Library Bill of Rights

The American Library Association affirms that all libraries are forums for information and ideas, and that the following basic policies should guide their services.

* Books and other library resources should be provided for the interest, information, and enlightenment of all people of the community the library serves. Materials should not be excluded because of the origin, background, or views of those contributing to their creation.
* Libraries should provide materials and information presenting all points of view on current and historical issues. Materials should not be proscribed or removed because of partisan or doctrinal disapproval.
* Libraries should challenge censorship in the fulfillment of their responsibility to provide information and enlightenment.

* Libraries should cooperate with all persons and groups concerned with resisting abridgment of free expression and free access to ideas.
* A person's right to use a library should not be denied or abridged because of origin, age, background, or views.
* Libraries which make exhibit spaces and meeting rooms available to the public they serve should make such facilities available on an equitable basis, regardless of the beliefs or affiliations of individuals or groups requesting their use.

Madras Public Libraries Act

The Madras Public Libraries Act, subsequently renamed as the Tamil Nadu Public Libraries Act, was enacted in Madras State, India, in 1948. The act was the first of its kind to be enacted in India after independence. The Connemara Public Library became the first library to come under the purview of this act, as a "State central library". Subsequently, nine district libraries were added during the Five year plan from 1951. The act was enacted based on research and activity by S. R. Ranganathan and the Madras Library Association. Other states have enacted public library acts modelled on the Madras Public Libraries Act.

Background

R. K. Bhatt has highlighted how free-to-access public library systems are a necessary adjunct to a developing society, with growing industrialisation and improving rates of literacy, and argues that legislation "is an essential need in any country because it puts the structure, management and finance of library systems on proper legal footing". Ranganathan recognised this. He had spent time training as a librarian in London around 1923 and was impressed by the system of public library legislation which existed there. Upon returning to India he began to campaign for something similar to exist in his own country.

The situation was complicated by the existence of various types of government, including provinces which were administered by the British Raj and various States under the control of princes. The fruits of his research and consultations were presented at the First All India Educational Conference in 1930. This report included a proposed Model Library Act. Although some areas, such as Baroda, had established public library systems prior to 1945, it was then that the first Act was passed, being the Kolhapur Public Libraries Act.

This was followed in 1948 by the Madras Public Libraries Act, which became the first such Act to be passed in the newly independent republic of India. Acts for other areas, such as Kerala and Haryana, followed and generally improved on the earlier legislation. Prior to the Act, the principal library of Madras was the Connemara Public Library, which had opened in 1860 and became a public library in 1896. A small refundable deposit was required to use it but it was essentially free. It became the State Central Library in 1948 and, in 1981, a depository library.

Provisions

The Madras Public Libraries Act provides for overall governance by a State Library Committee, presided over by the incumbent Education Minister for the State. The committee comprises members from various walks of life, including representatives from universities and from the State Library Association, as well as a Secretary whose primary function is as assistant to the Director of Public Libraries (DPL). The latter role is assumed by the incumbent Director of Public Instruction. Revenue is obtained via a cess, a tax which is collected by local administrative bodies such as the Nagar Palikas and Panchayats.

Those bodies remit the tax to their Local Library Association (LLA), which operates as an umbrella organisation at the mid-tier District administrative level. The rate of taxation is fixed in law but the LLA can request a higher rate if the State government agrees to it. The State government matches the funds generated by the cess. The LLA determines the conditions of entry to the libraries under its control. Cities with a population in excess of 50,000 must have a central library of their own and provisions exist for expansion to include branch libraries and other means of devolved access if demand should require such. In addition to libraries that are administered by the LLA, the Act provides for a register of other libraries.

This is maintained by the DPL, who has the power to issue grants from State resources to those institutions listed. With the exception of the city of Madras, these grants cannot be less than the cess collected elsewhere. Further resources are obtained by a modification caused by the Act. The Press and Registration of Books Act of 1857 is amended such that a situation somewhat akin to copyright libraries exists. All publishers within the State are required to provide five copies of their output to the State government, which in turn passes on four of those copies to the State Central Library. Until various reorganisations of States, the Act applied to parts of what are now Andhra Pradesh and Kerala.

Evolution

Several perceived failings in the Madras Public Libraries Act have been addressed in subsequent Acts elsewhere. For example, the Hyderabad legislation, which later became the Andhra Pradesh Public Libraries Act, states that there should be a completely separate department of government to administer the libraries; that the head of the State Library Committee should be elected rather than defaulting to the portfolio of the current Education Minister; and that all local administrative areas should have their own library authority. Furthermore, the amount and extent of the cess collected was improved by extending the range of taxes upon which the surcharge was levied; and the government, through the State Library Council, has a duty to train the librarians.

A key strategy which was embodied in the Act was the formulation of a hierarchical system whereby the local libraries were connected to the District libraries and they, in turn, were connected to the State Central Library and the National Library. Centralised acquisition and resource sharing was envisaged. This strategy had formed a part of the Second Five Year Plan but it appears not to have been enforced with any haste; Brahmanda Barua wrote in 1992 that throughout India

"The network principle has nowhere been applied in organising the libraries."

Bhatt believes that the Karnataka Public Libraries Act is the most adequate and best functioning in the evolution of such Acts, and notes that the lack of provision for a cess in the later Acts for Maharashtra and West Bengal are a significant failing. In the case of Karnataka, there is a State Library Authority which is presided over by the Minister for Education, and also a fully-fledged Department of Public Libraries and local administrative bodies. The cess applies to a wide range of taxes, including those on property and vehicles, and there is further funding in non-city areas as a consequence of the stipulation that the State government must give to the local bodies 3% of all revenues received from land taxes in their area. The financing of the State Library Authority is determined by the lower authorities and private libraries can request grants but are not automatically entitled to them.

Recent Situation Nationally

By 2002 there had been a total of 12 public library acts in place, although two of those - for Hyderabad and Kolhapur - had been superseded due to changes in the administrative structure of those areas, and two others had not been enforced. Narasimha Raju considered that these Acts had proved to be "by and large ineffective", due to a combination of poor financing, poor administrative structure and, in some States, the "lethargy and negative attitude" of their governments. Raju also identified problems with the rapidly changing face of technology and noted that most of the libraries were unable to adapt to developments in television, radio and video recording. The Indian Library Association had taken on the campaign to improve matters, principally by promoting new legislation to replace that which already existed and Raju noted that many believed legislation should exist for the entire country rather than being a piecemeal system.

Despite only eight Acts being in force, all 25 States and seven Union Territories had a central library and 75% of the Districts, which are the next tier of administration, had a similar facility. While legislated areas such as Maharashtra relied on volunteers and development of free libraries from the core of an existing subscription library system, Tamil Nadu, Karnataka and Andhra Pradesh were thought by T. Malleshappa to be the most developed when quantified by density of libraries and percentage of the population who had free access. D. B. Eswara Reddy, writing in the same publication, bemoaned the poor provision below District level, with 90% of the rural population not having access even to a reading room or circulating library, let alone modern multimedia and computing technology. Despite legislation and theoretical targets, library facilities remained the preserve of the urban elite and, for example, in Andhra Pradesh most children in rural areas were first-generation literates.

FREE ACCESS TO LIBRARIES FOR MINORS

An Interpretation of the Library Bill of Rights

Library policies and procedures that effectively deny minors equal and equitable access to all library resources available to other users violate the Library Bill of Rights. The American Library Association opposes all attempts to restrict access to library services, materials, and facilities based on the age of library users. Article V of the Library Bill of Rights states, "A person's right to use a library should not be denied or abridged because of origin, age, background, or views." The "right to use a library" includes free access to, and unrestricted use of, all the services, materials, and facilities the library has to offer. Every restriction on access to, and use of, library resources, based solely on the chronological age, educational level, literacy skills, or legal emancipation of users violates Article V. Libraries are charged with the mission of developing resources to meet the diverse information needs and interests of the communities they serve. Services, materials, and facilities that fulfill the needs and interests of library users at different stages in their personal development are a necessary part of library resources.

The needs and interests of each library user, and resources appropriate to meet those needs and interests, must be determined on an individual basis. Librarians cannot predict what resources will best fulfill the needs and interests of any individual user based on a single criterion such as chronological age, educational level, literacy skills, or legal emancipation. Libraries should not limit the selection and development of library resources simply because minors will have access to them. Institutional self-censorship diminishes the credibility of the library in the community, and restricts access for all library users. Children and young adults unquestionably possess First Amendment rights, including the right to receive information in the library. Constitutionally protected speech cannot be suppressed solely to protect children or young adults from ideas or images a legislative body believes to be unsuitable for them. Librarians and library governing bodies should not resort to age restrictions in an effort to avoid actual or anticipated objections, because only a court of law can determine whether material is not constitutionally protected.

The mission, goals, and objectives of libraries cannot authorize librarians or library governing bodies to assume, abrogate, or overrule the rights and responsibilities of parents. As "Libraries: An American Value" states, "We affirm the responsibility and the right of all parents and guardians to guide their own children's use of the library and its resources and services." Librarians and governing bodies should maintain that parents – and only parents – have the right and the responsibility to restrict the access of their children – and only their children – to library resources. Parents who do not want their children to have access to certain library services, materials, or facilities should so advise their children. Librarians and library governing bodies cannot assume the role of parents or the functions of parental authority in the private relationship between parent and child. Lack of access to information can be harmful to minors. Librarians and library governing bodies have a public and professional obligation to ensure that all members of the community they serve have free, equal, and equitable access to the entire range of library resources regardless of content, approach, format, or amount of detail.

This principle of library service applies equally to all users, minors as well as adults. Librarians and library governing bodies must uphold this principle in order to provide adequate and effective service to minors.

The Freedom to Read Statement

The freedom to read is essential to our democracy. It is continuously under attack. Private groups and public authorities in various parts of the country are working to remove or limit access to reading materials, to censor content in schools, to label "controversial" views, to distribute lists of "objectionable" books or authors, and to purge libraries. These actions apparently rise from a view that our national tradition of free expression is no longer valid; that censorship and suppression are needed to counter threats to safety or national security, as well as to avoid the subversion of politics and the corruption of morals.

We, as individuals devoted to reading and as librarians and publishers responsible for disseminating ideas, wish to assert the public interest in the preservation of the freedom to read. Most attempts at suppression rest on a denial of the fundamental premise of democracy: that the ordinary individual, by exercising critical judgment, will select the good and reject the bad. We trust Americans to recognize propaganda and misinformation, and to make their own decisions about what they read and believe. We do not believe they are prepared to sacrifice their heritage of a free press in order to be "protected" against what others think may be bad for them. We believe they still favour free enterprise in ideas and expression.

These efforts at suppression are related to a larger pattern of pressures being brought against education, the press, art and images, films, broadcast media, and the Internet. The problem is not only one of actual censorship. The shadow of fear cast by these pressures leads, we suspect, to an even larger voluntary curtailment of expression by those who seek to avoid controversy or unwelcome scrutiny by government officials. Such pressure towards conformity is perhaps natural to a time of accelerated change. And yet suppression is never more dangerous than in such a time of social tension. Freedom has given the United States the elasticity to endure strain. Freedom keeps open the path of novel and creative solutions, and enables change to come by choice. Every silencing of a heresy, every enforcement of an orthodoxy, diminishes the toughness and resilience of our society and leaves it the less able to deal with controversy and difference. Now as always in our history, reading is among our greatest freedoms.

The freedom to read and write is almost the only means for making generally available ideas or manners of expression that can initially command only a small audience. The written word is the natural medium for the new idea and the untried voice from which come the original contributions to social growth. It is essential to the extended discussion that serious thought requires, and to the accumulation of knowledge and ideas into organized collections. We believe that free communication is essential to the preservation of a free society and a creative culture.

We believe that these pressures towards conformity present the danger of limiting the range and variety of enquiry and expression on which our democracy and our culture depend. We believe that every American community must jealously guard the freedom to publish and to circulate, in order to preserve its own freedom to read. We believe that publishers and librarians have a profound responsibility to give validity to that freedom to read by making it possible for the readers to choose freely from a variety of offerings. The freedom to read is guaranteed by the Constitution. Those with faith in free people will stand firm on these constitutional guarantees of essential rights and will exercise the responsibilities that accompany these rights.

We therefore affirm these propositions:

* It is in the public interest for publishers and librarians to make available the widest diversity of views and expressions, including those that are unorthodox, unpopular, or considered dangerous by the majority

- Creative thought is by definition new, and what is new is different. The bearer of every new thought is a rebel until that idea is refined and tested. Totalitarian systems attempt to maintain themselves in power by the ruthless suppression of any concept that challenges the established orthodoxy. The power of a democratic system to adapt to change is vastly strengthened by the freedom of its citizens to choose widely from among conflicting opinions offered freely to them. To stifle every nonconformist idea at birth would mark the end of the democratic process. Furthermore, only through the constant activity of weighing and selecting can the democratic mind attain the strength demanded by times like these. We need to know not only what we believe but why we believe it.

* Publishers, librarians, and booksellers do not need to endorse every idea or presentation they make available. It would conflict with the public interest for them to establish their own political, moral, or aesthetic views as a standard for determining what should be published or circulated.
  - Publishers and librarians serve the educational process by helping to make available knowledge and ideas required for the growth of the mind and the increase of learning. They do not foster education by imposing as mentors the patterns of their own thought. The people should have the freedom to read and consider a broader range of ideas than those that may be held by any single librarian or publisher or government or church. It is wrong that what one can read should be.
* It is contrary to the public interest for publishers or librarians to bar access to writings on the basis of the personal history or political affiliations of the author.
  - No art or literature can flourish if it is to be measured by the political views or private lives of its creators. No society of free people can

flourish that draws up lists of writers to whom it will not listen, whatever they may have to say.

* There is no place in our society for efforts to coerce the taste of others, to confine adults to the reading matter deemed suitable for adolescents, or to inhibit the efforts of writers to achieve artistic expression.
  - To some, much of modern expression is shocking. But is not much of life itself shocking? We cut off literature at the source if we prevent writers from dealing with the stuff of life. Parents and teachers have a responsibility to prepare the young to meet the diversity of experiences in life to which they will be exposed, as they have a responsibility to help them learn to think critically for themselves. These are affirmative responsibilities, not to be discharged simply by preventing them from reading works for which they are not yet prepared. In these matters values differ, and values cannot be legislated; nor can machinery be devised that will suit the demands of one group without limiting the freedom of others.
* It is not in the public interest to force a reader to accept the prejudgment of a label characterizing any expression or its author as subversive or dangerous.
  - The ideal of labeling presupposes the existence of individuals or groups with wisdom to determine by authority what is good or bad for others. It presupposes that individuals must be directed in making up their minds about the ideas they examine. But Americans do not need others to do their thinking for them.
* It is the responsibility of publishers and librarians, as guardians of the people's freedom to read, to contest encroachments upon that freedom by individuals or groups seeking to impose their own standards or tastes upon the community at large; and by the government whenever it seeks to reduce or deny public access to public information.

- It is inevitable in the give and take of the democratic process that the political, the moral, or the aesthetic concepts of an individual or group will occasionally collide with those of another individual or group. In a free society individuals are free to determine for themselves what they wish to read, and each group is free to determine what it will recommend to its freely associated members. But no group has the right to take the law into its own hands, and to impose its own concept of politics or morality upon other members of a democratic society. Freedom is no freedom if it is accorded only to the accepted and the inoffensive. Further, democratic societies are more safe, free, and creative when the free flow of public information is not restricted by governmental prerogative or self-censorship.

* It is the responsibility of publishers and librarians to give full meaning to the freedom to read by providing books that enrich the quality and diversity of thought and expression. By the exercise of this affirmative responsibility, they can demonstrate that the answer to a "bad" book is a good one, the answer to a "bad" idea is a good one.
  - The freedom to read is of little consequence when the reader cannot obtain matter fit for that reader's purpose. What is needed is not only the absence of restraint, but the positive provision of opportunity for the people to read the best that has been thought and said. Books are the major channel by which the intellectual inheritance is handed down, and the principal means of its testing and growth. The defence of the freedom to read requires of all publishers and librarians the utmost of their faculties, and deserves of all Americans the fullest of their support.

We state these propositions neither lightly nor as easy generalizations. We here stake out a lofty claim for the value of the written word. We do so because we believe that it is possessed of enormous variety and usefulness, worthy of cherishing and keeping free. We realise that the application of these propositions may mean the dissemination of ideas and manners of expression that are repugnant to many persons. We do not state these propositions in the comfortable belief that what people read is unimportant. We believe rather that what people read is deeply important; that ideas can be dangerous; but that the suppression of ideas is fatal to a democratic society. Freedom itself is a dangerous way of life, but it is ours.

STATEMENT ON LABELLING

An Interpretation of the Library Bill of Rights

Labeling is the practice of describing or designating materials by affixing a prejudicial label and/or segregating them by a prejudicial system.

The American Library Association opposes these means of predisposing people's attitudes towards library materials for the following reasons:

* Labeling is an attempt to prejudice attitudes and as such, it is a censor's tool.
* Some find it easy and even proper, according to their ethics, to establish criteria for judging publications as objectionable. However, injustice and ignorance rather than justice and enlightenment result from such practices, and the American Library Association opposes the establishment of such criteria.
* Libraries do not advocate the ideas found in their collections. The presence of books and other resources in a library does not indicate endorsement of their contents by the library.

A variety of private organizations promulgate rating systems and/or review materials as a means of advising either their members or the general public concerning their opinions of the contents and suitability or appropriate age for use of certain books, films, recordings, or other materials. For the library to adopt or enforce any of these private systems, to attach such ratings to library materials, to include them in bibliographic records, library catalogs, or other finding aids, or otherwise to endorse them would violate the Library Bill of Rights. While some attempts have been made to adopt these systems into law, the constitutionality of such measures is extremely questionable. If such legislation is passed which applies within a library's jurisdiction, the library should seek competent legal advice concerning its applicability to library operations. Publishers, industry groups, and distributors sometimes add ratings to material or include them as part of their packaging. Librarians should not endorse such practices. However, removing or obliterating such ratings—if placed there by or with permission of the copyright holder—could constitute expurgation, which is also unacceptable. The American Library Association opposes efforts which aim at closing any path to knowledge. This statement, however, does not exclude the adoption of organizational schemes designed as directional aids or to facilitate access to materials.

9

Succession Planning in Public Libraries

AN OVERVIEW

Imagine this: You come to work one day to find out that your library director has accepted another job, decided to retire, or become ill or had an accident. In any event, you have a top position open. What will happen? The procedure in academic libraries is very familiar. A search committee will be appointed, and a position description will be written and advertised. Occasionally it will be decided to limit the search to current staff members, an in-house search. This will speed up the process.

However, if a national search is conducted, the hiring process will take months. Contrast this scenario with one at a major corporation such as McDonald's Corp. Jim Cantalupo, chair and CEO suddenly died. Within days the corporation was announcing a new chair. Before the stockholders reading the financial page had time to respond, McDonald's was back to business as usual. How can they respond so fast? What planning and preparation make this possible? The answer is called succession planning. Organizations such as Dow Chemical, Eli Lilly, Sonoco, and Dell Computer are anticipating changes in leadership, assessing the skills and knowledge of their employees, identifying those that possess the potential to be effective leaders, and providing training, mentoring, and experience so that when the moment happens the plan is in place. Companies are not just doing this for the top executive; they are pushing this planning down the ladder. Succession planning is becoming workplace planning. William J. Rothwell, author of the major book on succession planning, defined it as anticipating changes in management, creating a strategic plan to identify potential staff members, determining the gaps in their knowledge, and providing training and coaching, special assignments, and experiences so that they are ready to step up when the time comes.

REVIEW OF THE LIBRARY LITERATURE

Are some libraries following the lead of these corporations and adopting succession planning? A review of the literature turned up only one article about succession planning in academic or public libraries in the United States, "Your Library's Future," a 2004 article published in Library Journal. This stage discusses how one library, the Multnomah County Library in Portland, Oregon, developed a programme to prepare and train younger staff members for the anticipated upperlevel positions. This plan included making staff aware of the future needs, encouraging them to make their interest known, and then providing peer reviews, mentors, and a training programme.

A side bar called "Succession Planning Tool Kit" gives an excellent but brief outline of the steps to take to set up a programme. Besides this object, there is one book on succession planning in libraries, Staff Planning in a Time of Demographic Change, which is based on a series of conferences held in Ontario, Canada, in 2002 and 2003. Libraries in the United Kingdom, Canada, and Australia have more seriously discussed succession planning, and this book provides a thorough discussion of the issues, many which apply to U.S. library situations. With the exception of the Library Journal object and a small set of objects centering on special libraries, there is almost nothing in journal literature about libraries in the United States using succession planning. The lack of objects about U.S. libraries is a red flag. Should libraries use succession planning? Why are U.S. libraries not using such plans? Are libraries just behind the times and missing a technique that could be useful? The primary reason that the business world uses succession planning is the shortage of capable people in the management ranks to fill the senior executive positions. In other words, major corporations cannot hire the leaders they need, so they are growing their own. Are libraries facing the same problem? Is there a shortage of leaders in the library field?

IS SUCCESSION PLANNING SOMETHING LIBRARIANS SHOULD CONSIDER?

A Look at the Leadership Supply in the Library Profession as a Whole

Within the next few years, many librarians, especially those holding the top-level positions, such as directors, deans, associate directors, and heads of libraries, will be retiring. The Bureau of Labour Statistics said that more than three in five librarians are age 45 years or older and will become eligible for retirement in the next 10 years. Mary Jo Lynch, director of American Library Association's Office for Research and Statistics, confirmed that in the near future a surge of retirements will take place peaking between 2015 and 2019. "In total, the decade beginning in 2010 will see 45% of today's librarians reach age 65, representing the early wave of baby-boom librarians reaching the traditional retirement age". Earlier statistics similarly outlined the coming librarian shortage and predicted that 83,366 librarians will be age 65 years by the year 2010.

The general conclusion of many objects on the future of the profession is that the cause of the projected shortage is the expected retirements. Not satisfied with this general conclusion Larry Hardesty took a more analytical look at the recruitment and hiring statistics in his object in portal: Libraries and the Academy. He identified and investigated the possible causes: closing library schools, more attractive positions for MLS graduates in information science fields, or low salaries. He concluded, "The most plausible explanation for the current situation is the increased number of retirements". The problem is even more pronounced in Canada, which may explain why the Canadian libraries have been paying more attention to this phenomenon than U.S. libraries.

The Canadian Library Association conducted a questionnaire survey sent to 386 members that focused on retirement trends from 2002–2010 and looked for strategies and the level of preparedness to deal with the future shortage of librarians. The survey found that between 30%–50% of the Canadian librarians will retire by 2010 and most libraries (74%) feel that they are not prepared or only somewhat prepared. Further data indicates that there is a decrease in the number of librarians in the 25–34 age range; the figure is 12% in Canadian Association of Research Libraries (ARL) libraries. These numbers are far from the ideal figures of 20% at the senior level and 20% at the newcomer level. The full report on the Canadian situation has just been released in a publication by the 8Rs Research Team.

Despite statistics that indicate a shortage of librarians and lack of middle-level librarians trained in the competencies of leadership, only 9% of the libraries surveyed have a succession plan in place. Although this is a dismal figure, ARL libraries in the United States are probably even less prepared. In the past the profession has solved similar shortages by promoting mid-career librarians and filling their positions with new graduates. However, there is now a shortage of mid-career librarians and new MLS graduates. The situation is complicated by the fact that the 1990s were lean times in libraries, and the number of new hires during this time was limited.

Many of the jobs went to boomers who changed careers and became librarians later in life. The result is that many librarians in middle management positions are the same age as the directors and associate directors, and they will be retiring along a similar time table. To further complicate the labour situation, over the past 15 to 20 years, there has also been a shortage of new MLS graduates to fill the ranks vacated by promotions of middle-level librarians. This shortage is predicted to extend into the peak baby boomer retirement years, 2015– 2019. "Estimated retirements outpace graduations in the United States, even accounting for reduced growth in professional-level library staffing in public and academic libraries".

The library professional associations have made valiant efforts to address this problem by recruiting more people into the profession, but the prediction is that there is still a shortage of new MLS graduates. The retirement of the boomers coupled with the shortage of new librarians will complicate the already tight recruiting market, but there is yet another phenomenon occurring that is blackening the outlook even more. That is poor retention of new librarians, or "the five year itch." Many new librarians are leaving the profession dissatisfied and restless within their first five years as librarians. In survey research reported by Markgren and her research colleagues, one half of the 464 new librarians who answered their survey said they are thinking of leaving the profession and list some of the top reasons as "limited or no opportunities," and "position or role is not challenging enough."

They feel there are no growth opportunities, that they cannot move up the ladder, and that to advance they need to change jobs. Many are leaving librarianship as a career. So while library managers are despairing because they cannot find qualified staff especially for middle and upper-level positions, the new recruits feel there is no job advancement possible.

There seems to be a serious communication gap between the generations. My own personal experience with gen Xers parallels what is written about them. They are described as self focused and impatient but also very motivated and success oriented; they want to learn and take on responsibility including management and supervision. The time is ripe for formal succession planning programmes that open up the discussion of opportunities for leadership and set up educational and training programmes to prepare new librarians to step up.

IS THE SHORTAGE OF LIBRARIANS TRUE FOR BUSINESS LIBRARIANS AND BUSINESS LIBRARY MANAGERS?

Statistics on Business Librarians and the Job Market for Business Librarians

The focus of this journal is business librarianship, and there is data on this niche of the library world. Two objects published since 2000 shed some light.Researchers did a thorough statistical study of business librarians and found that in the United States the average business library manager was a 51-year-old white and as likely to be female as male. As a group business librarians were well educated with 68% of the 25 managers in the survey holding multiple post-undergraduate degrees and about one third of them having a MBA.

They averaged 22 years of experience as a librarian and nearly 17 years as business librarians. Amajor finding of this research was that 50% of the managers indicated that they did not anticipate being an academic business librarian longer than five years. So research indicates that we should be in the midst of a major shift in the managers/directors/heads in business libraries right now. However, a quick review of the Academic Business Library Directors (ABLD), the same group Pagell and Lusk surveyed, indicates little change in the demographics of this group in the last seven years.

The average age now is 55 years; their education level is approximately the same with 67% holding multiple higher education degrees; 37% hold a second master's degree other than an MBA, and 30% hold an MBA; and 55% are female So in seven years the group has aged respectively, but the education level has not altered. New directors were more likely female as the ratio of male to female has altered. However, many business library directors are not retiring yet, as Pagell and Lusk's survey expected. To ascertain when the retirement exodus will begin, I asked when each ABLD member plans to retire. Sixteen of the 27 in the group (or 60%) plan to retire by 2014; but only three of these 16 plan to retire within the next two years.

As just as the Census Bureau predicts, the retirement blitz will occur between 2010 and 2015. Are the upcoming business librarians being prepared for these positions? The major way (36%) was by personal contact, followed by internal postings (28%). It is the internal posting statistic that is of interest to this object. If in the 2000 survey over one fourth of the business library directors came to their jobs by internal promotions, then some rudimentary "succession planning" techniques were happening in their library, even if it was not called that.

I found this so surprising that I asked a few related follow-up questions of the ABLD group in August 2007. Sixty per cent stated that they were internal candidates. Twenty-two per cent were internal promotions without any search, in-house or external. Another 11% were promotions after an in-house search, and 26% were internal candidates in an external search. These statistics clearly show that libraries are "growing their own" business library directors. Business librarians in the ranks are being prepared to manage the library and being promoted from within the same library.

Do mid-career, non-managing business librarians feel they are ready and willing to be promoted to leadership positions when the business managers retire? Again some of Pagell and Lusk's survey results give us some clues as they asked skill related questions. Interestingly, non-managing business librarians' self ratings for information skills did not deviate from managers' skills; however, there was a significant gap in management skills in two areas: human resource responsibilities and conflict resolution. There was a wide variation especially in conflict resolution; about 60% of the managers rated themselves high in this area, whereas only 30% of the non-managers felt they were able to handle this. So business librarians in the ranks know their subject but feel they lack management skills, and they feel they particularly lack human resources skills such as conflict resolution skills. The Pagell and Lusk object did not attempt to determine if there will be enough business librarians to fill the upcoming management positions.

However, another object by did address this question. Their research, based on a survey to libraries that had advertised for a business librarian between March 1, 2000 and March 31, 2001, emphasized that at that time there was a lack of available business librarians. The major conclusion was that 70% of the employers were not satisfied with the applicant pool, with the quantity of candidates being the major problem. "Low supply of business information professionals" and "too much competition" for librarians were the major reasons listed by libraries that experienced difficulties in hiring. A huge 40% of the searches were reopened at least once. Researchers concluded that "a good business librarian is hard to find" and "recruiting internally and providing extensive professional development and training may also be a cost-effective alternative" to searching for an outside business librarian.

Their recommendations have the sound of succession planning. Like major corporations, perhaps libraries need to grow their own. All the statistics indicate that there will be a major shortage of librarians, starting in 2010 and peaking at 2015, caused by retirements and shortages of young people choosing librarianship as a career. This shortage will affect business libraries. Succession planning seems like a logical approach. So why are U.S. libraries not readily using it? One reason is that in most libraries "the bench is too narrow." In other words, libraries do not have enough staff members to mentor and train new leaders. Major corporations have thousands of employees and hundreds of top-level managers. Identifying a handful of them that have the potential and interest to lead is possible. In a library with a few dozen librarians, this may not work. Another reason is that higher education institutions are actively working on increasing diversity; every opening is an opportunity. And the institutions have stated goals to increase the diversity of the faculty and staff; internal promotions do not met this goal.

The whole diversity problem is a topic for another object, but American Library Association's Office for Research and Statistics is following these statistics closely. They concluded that the "persistent lag in diversity in our LIS schools, the number of librarians and library assistants leaving the profession prematurely, the aging of racial and ethnic minority library workers, and the continued under representation of workers with disabilities, suggest a proportionally less diverse library workforce on the horizon". Furthermore, they suggested strategically planning around human resource development and succession planning. A third reason is the "grass is greener" perception. Libraries always want to hire the best candidate, and somehow librarians are not inclined to believe the best is on the staff right now.

The last reason is the "new broom theory"; libraries have a strong desire for a change in management. Unlike the business world that is dependent on stockholders' desire for consistency, libraries use upper-level staff openings as an opportunity to bring in new ideas and people that can implement creative strategic changes. Verbalizing and then discussing these reasons can help a library assess whether succession planning or some strategies of succession planning might be useful. Even if a fully developed succession planning programme is not the choice, there is much to be learned and borrowed from succession planning.

HOW TO START A SUCCESSION PLANNING PROGRAMME

The business literature on the topic is clear on two essentials: succession planning only works if the top-level administrators are 100% behind it; and the programme needs to be an open process. It cannot be done by the human resource department alone or by middle managers mentoring and grooming staff members reporting to them. The administration has to be deeply involved; likewise staff members need to be involved, with feedback going to the employees that have been identified as possessing the potential for leadership.

The basic steps of succession planning are:

* Analyse the demographics of your key positions
* Identify potential employees for lead positions
* Assess candidates strengths and weaknesses
* Develop a training programme to build competencies.

Analyse Your Demographics

In a large academic or public library this would mean figuring out the age of your current directors, assistant or associate directors, department heads, and any other key positions, such as the main computer technician or business manager. In a smaller library system or a business library within a larger library system this might be a short list including only the managing librarian and possibly the assistant or associate managers. This step is easy to do; the main obstacle, because birth dates may not be readily available, is ascertaining ages.

However a fairly close estimate can be obtained by assuming each librarian was age 22 years when the undergraduate degree was earned. This analysis does give some insights. Using the Purdue Faculty Directory I did this exercise for Purdue libraries just to see what our demographics are. The average age of librarians in management positions has dropped over the past five years as younger people have been hired. One surprise was the number of internal promotions and in-house hires; over one half of the changes were internal promotions. We are not officially using succession planning, but these internal promotions indicate that we are preparing our mid-career librarians for upper-level positions.

Identify Potential Employees

This step is much more involved. Following the philosophy that top level administrators need to be involved in the process does not mean that other people in the library system are not included. Even in business setting, identifying potential employees involves many people; in some instances it is done by committee. For each position the qualifications and competencies need to be agreed upon. These might include such additional skills as ability to speak influentially to a large group, or ability to handle multiple projects at the same time, or ability to influence staff.

These skills and competencies need to grow from the libraries' strategic plan and emphasize future needs. One way of developing this list of skills is to interview the staff currently in these positions. This is also a good opportunity to ask for their nominations for a successor, recommendations for a training programme, and their willingness to mentor candidates for succession. This step is similar to writing job descriptions. Next potential employees are nominated and staff are asked to self identify listing their personal goals. The openness of the process is critical. Doing this step behind closed doors is generally not successful as it leads to staff distrust and accusations of unfair opportunities.

Assess Candidates' Strengths and Weaknesses

Once a list of potential candidates is developed, interview each of these employees to identify his or her interest, experience, and potential skills in librarianship and management. For example, does the candidate have extensive reference skills but lacks supervisory skills? Pay particular attention to management and leadership skills and gaps, and then prioritize the gaps. This needs to be a frank discussion, and help from mentors and supervisors will be critical for the success.

At this point it is important to have an agreement with the incumbents about their skill gaps and willingness to address these gaps and build the competencies needed. Is he or she willing to be mentored and willing to outline a self-development programme? Is the candidate willing to travel to attend association pre-conferences and workshops, to take courses at the university that provide needed skills such as financial management or personnel management skills? Likewise the library administration needs to make a commitment to the incumbents. This would include funds for training and travel, release time from current responsibilities, and such things as supporting mentors. One of the major challenges of succession planning in libraries is "bench strength." In a small library there might not be anyone in the ranks who has the potential or interest in managing or leading the library. If this is the conclusion then the library needs to look closely at new hires in the future and to search for beginning librarians with career objectives of leadership and management.

Develop a Training Programme to Build Competencies

There are many choices for meeting skill gaps. Many libraries already have extensive training programmes in place, and libraries connected with universities have university employee training programmes as well as formal courses available. The major library associations offer many opportunities to learn leadership and management skills. In addition there are leadership institutes available at the University of California–Los Angeles, Harvard and Emory. The Association of Research Libraries also has programmes on leadership. Besides these formal training programmes, other options are job rotation, job shadowing, or interim positions. Managing a library while the head is on an extended vacation or sabbatical can help fill the management experience gap. Budget planning; staff selection, training, and evaluation; crisis management; and donor relations are all areas that mid-career librarians need training to be ready to step up to director-level positions.

The major one is William J. Rothwell's Effective Succession Planning. A second useful title is Growing Your Company's Leaders. The third recent book is the Whitmell's Staff Planning in a Time of Demographic Change. It is the only book available specifically on succession planning in libraries. It is a collection papers from a conferences held in Ontario, Canada, and covers mentoring, training, and demographic statistics and information from the business literature. Like many of the objects on succession planning, this book focuses on Canadian, Australian, and U.K. libraries. Whitmell is executive director of the Legislative Library for the Legislative Assembly of Ontario.

CONCLUSION

Although the literature indicates that few U.S. libraries are utilizing succession planning techniques, statistics on the demographics of librarians, and business librarians in particular, indicate that there is and will continue to be shortage of qualified middle-level librarians available for the projected management positions. This shortage will peak between 2010 and 2015. The business world has successfully used succession planning to identify, train, and prepare employees to be ready to step up the executive positions. This idea of "grow your own" leaders could help to accomplish the following goals for libraries: increasing career advancement opportunities for interested staff that will lead to the retention of young librarians looking for a more challenges and career development, encouragement of targeted diversity candidates who have leadership potential, as well as being ensured of leadership at a critical moment when the boomers retire.

10

Library Rules

DEFINITIONS

* *Board of Governors:* The Board of Governors of the National Academy of Higher Education/ University Grants Commission.
* *Competent Authorty:* Any authority of the University Grants Commission/National Academy of Higher Education having full financial and administrative powers or part thereof.
* *Director General:* The Director General of National Academy of Higher Education.
* *Employees:* The employees of the National Academy of Higher Education, University Grants Commission and University Grants Commission's Regional Offices.
* *Inter-Library Loan:* Giving or taking of books and other reading material on loan to and from other libraries or agencies.
* *Librarian:* The Librarian of the National Academy of Higher Education's library.
* *Library:* The Library of the National Academy of Higher Education.
* *Members:* Registered members of the National

Academy of Higher Education Library as laid down in rules 3and4.

- * *Officers:* The employees declared by the Government as officer *i.e.* all employees of BP&-16 and above of the National Academy of Higher Education and the University Grants Commission.
- * *Officials:* All employees BP&-l to BP&-15 of the University Grants Commission and the National Academy of Higher Education.
- * *Pre-Service/In-Service Training Participatnts:* Participants attending training Programmes in the National Academy of Higher Education.
- * *University:* Any University in Pakistan recognized by the Government.
- * *University Librarian:* Librarian/ Incharge Librarian/ Acting Librarian/Chief Librarian of any of the Pakistani Universities.
- * *University Departmenta Librarian:* Librarian of a departmental library of any of the Pakistani Universities.

LIBRARY RULES

Working Hours

1 The library shall remain open for service during the working hours observed by the National Academy of Higher Education/University Grants Commission.

2 The" library hours may be changed from time to time according to the service of the National Academy of Higher Education/University Grants Commission.

Loan Privileges

3. The following categories of persons will be allowed to make use of the library resources:

   3.1. Employees of the University Grants Commission/National Academy of Higher Education.

   3.2. In-service and Pre-Service training participants.

3.3. Teachers/resources persons etc. deputed by UGC/NAHE for teaching.

3.4. Members of the Board of Governors of UGC/NAHE.

3.5. Other persons allowed in writing by Director General/Librarian.

3.6. University/University Department Librarians.

4. Persons desirous of using the library must apply for membership on a form obtainable from t he library.

4.1. A borrower's card will be issued to each member on presentation of which reading material will be issued (except rule 3.6 for which the Librarian will maintain a proper record). The same procedure will be followed when the books are returned. This card will not be transferable and should be surrendered at the time of obtaining a clearance certificate.

4.2. A borrowers card will be valid up- to the date mentioned on it. A borrower should get the card renewed before it expires, if he so desires.

4.3. Members should not mark or write on their borrower cards in any way Defaulters may be dealt with as per rule 30.

5. A Member, who loses his card shall at once inform the Librarian. A duplicate card will be. issued. Any member sub- lending reading material from the library on his card to any other person shall do so at his own responsibility.

Loan Period

6. The following categories of members shall observe the loan schedule mentioned against each.

1. Members of the Board of Governors	4 books for 15 days
2. Employees of UGC/ NAHE`	1 book for 15 days
i. Officials	2 book for 15 days
ii. Officers	2 book for 15 days
3. In service/pre-service trainees (during their training period - at the NAHE/UGC)	2 books for 7 days

(Contd...)

4. Teachers/resource persons their stay	5 books for the period of
5. Other persons allowed in writing by Director General/Librarian	3 books for 15 days
6. University/ University Department Librarian.	2 books for 1 month

Relaxation of loan schedule will be at the discretion of the Librarian:

7. Books borrowed once may be issued provided these are not required by other members. Books will not be reissued more than twice. Books will have to be presented for re-issue. However, in case of need the Librarian may relax the condition.
8. Reading material of the following nature shall not be issued but can be consulted in.the library (except in special cases *e.g.* classroom use of a teacher for a short period/photocopying purposes)
   8.1 Reference material (*i.e.* Encyclopedias, dictionaries, atlases and the material marked 'R')
   8.2 Theses, reports, pamphlets, syllabi, acts etc.
   8.3 Microfilms, slides, cassettes, tape recorders and other allied material.
   8.5 All unprocessed material.
   8.6 Current periodicals.
   8.7 Other material assigned by the Librarian.

Damage and Loss of Books

9. Book(s) lost, dam ed, or mutilated in any way by a member shall have to be replaced or paid for. The cost of such book(s) shall be double the prevailing cost plus an additional 25% departmental charges. The price of rare book(s) shall be decided by the Librarian.
10. If books and other materials borrowed from the library are not returned notices will be issued. In case the books are not returned even after the second notice, Rule 9 will be applied.

11. The amount realised from a member as cost of lost or damaged book(s) or material(s) or for not returning the books after due notices shall be credited to NAHE Library's head 'Books and Journals'.
12. Book.,(s) or other material lost or found to be lost on stock-taking shall be reported to the competent authority for write-off.
13. If a member leaves his organization without returning books borrowed from this library, the price of the book(s) will be adjusted against his dues with the organization. (In case there is no outstanding balance in his name, the price will be paid by his guarantor).

Weeding

14. On receipt of a written request from the Librarian, the Director General shall depute one or two members other than the library staff for weeding out outdated worn-out and/ or seriously damaged or mutilated books and other materials. He/ She/ they shall submit their recommendations in writing to the competent authority for approval.

Write-off Losses

15. The Librarian shall report all books/ non- print material damaged, and/or worn-out through fair wear and tear to the competent authority for write off action.
16. Losses to the extent of 3% per annum of the available stock in an open access library shall be written off by the competent authority.
17. Losses to the extent of 2% per annum of the available collection of a close access or partially open access library shall be written off by the competent authority.
18. Losses written off by the competent authority shall be struck off from the stock and the records of the

library, including public catalogues, and transferred to the with-drawl register indicating the authority under which the losses were written off.

19. The permanent irrecoverable loans of mutilated, damaged and worn-out books found to be beyond repairs during the physical verification of the library shall also be reported to the competent authority for write-off.

Mail Loan

20. The library shall offer postal loan service to the Librarian(s) of the out station Universities provided Rule 4.2 is followed. University Librarian/Department Librarian will be responsible for Safe return.
21. In view of the insecurity of mail, inconveniences of the postal-loan service and other discrepancies of non-receipt of materials expected to arise by this/ these facility (ies) loss of book(s) and other materials shall be safeguarded by adopting the Registered Parcel procedure of dispatch to avoid loss in transit.
22. In case there is a loss in transit, it shall be recorded by the Librarian and reported to the competent authority for write-off action.

Inter-Library Loans

23. With a view to extending and/or utilizing book and non-book resources of other institutions of higher education in the country, the Librarian shall enter into, and maintain any mutually agreed upon interlibrary loan system with Academic, Research, Special, Public and Government Departmental Libraries.

General Rules

24. Members shall not mutilate, or damage by writing or marking on pages, any book or publication, nor shall they trace or perform mechanical reproduction of any material belonging to the library without

formal permission of the Librarian. Violation of this rule shall require replacement of the damaged volume or payment of its price as specified under rule 9.

25. If one volume of a set/series is damaged and it is not available separately, the whole set shall have to be replaced or paid for by the member as specified under rule 9.
26. Following Rules 24 and 25 paying the cost the member may, if he/she so desires, retain the damaged book(s) or volumes for which the price has been recovered from him/her.
27. Members are advised to inspect books or other material at the time of issue. They must direct the attention of the staff at the Charging Desk to defects, if any.
28. The Library Reading Room shall remain open during stock-taking but the borrowing privileges will remain suspended for the same period. All books on loan 'with the members must irrespective of the date-due, be returned to. the library before the date of stock-taking. Two week advance notice will be given.
29. All members must without fail intimate, the librarian of any change of address.
30. The Librarian is authorized to withdraw library facilities from any member who is found misusing the library material or facilities.
31. Members of the library shall deposit their personal belongings at the counter near the entrance.
32. In case any personal reading material has to be taken in-side the library, permission must be sought from the Librarian. All reading material issued to them shall be shown to the attendant at the exit before leaving.
33. Eating, sleeping, smoking and audible conversation within the library premises is prohibited.
34. Members shall make their own arrangement for carrying book(s) etc. from and to the library.

Bibliography

Aghatise, E.: *Libraries, Community and Technology*, Maharashtra: Pune Publications, 2004.

Agrawal, A.: *Public Library Service in India,* New Delhi: Long Life Publication, 2003.

Anderson, B.: *The Basics of Librarianship*, Toronto: Thomson Nelson, 2008.

Bandyopadhyay, N.: *History and Development of Libraries in India,* Hyderabad: Economic and Political Weekly Press, 2005.

Baruah, N.: *Public Libraries: An Introduction*, New Delhi: Long Life Publication, 2003.

Bertozzi, S.: *The Academic Library,* Maharashtra: Pune Publication, 2006.

Chattopadhyay, A.: *An Introduction to Library Science,* Hyderabad: Economic and Political Weekly Press, 2005.

Cockburn, A.: *Current Tools and Techniques in Library Science,* New Delhi: Long Life Publication, 2006.

D'Cunha, J.: *Public Libraries System,* Toronto: Thomson Nelson, 2008.

Doezema, J.: *Library and Information Science: Emerging Trends,* Maharashtra: Pune Publication, 2000.

Evans, C.: *The Public Library Start-Up Guide,* New Delhi: Long Life Publication, 2003.

Gajic-Veljanoski, O.: *Public Library in the Development of Mizo Society,* Toronto: Thomson Nelson, 2007.

George, A.: *The Public Library Service,* Hyderabad: Self Publication, 2000.

Jana, S.: *Public Library System and Services,* New Delhi: Long Life Publications, 2003.

Jeffreys, S.: *National Policy on Library and Information System,* Toronto: Thomson Nelson, 2006.

Kapur, R.: *Library Public Relations,* Maharashtra: Pune Publications, 2001.

Kempadoo, K.: *50 Years Library and Information Services in India,* Hyderabad: Self Publications, 2000.

Madhusudana, B.: *Guidelines for Public Library Services and Systems,* Hyderabad: Economic and Political Weekly Press, 2002.

Misra, G.: *Librarianship: Philosophy, Laws and Ethics.,* Hyderabad: Self Publications, 2000.

Nag, M.: *Encyclopedia of Library and Information Science,* Hyderabad: Economic and Political Weekly Press, 2006.

Nair, P.M.: *Library Development in India,* Toronto: Thomson Nelson, 2010.

Parker, Michael: *Public Library Acts in India,* New Delhi: Long Life Publications, 2003.

Index